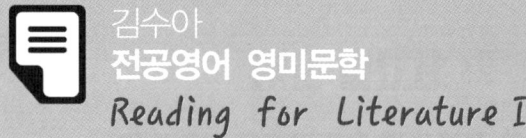

김수아
전공영어 영미문학
Reading for Literature I

PREFACE

MY DEVOTION

If I Can . . .

If I can stop one heart from breaking,

I shall live in joy;

If I can ease one life the uncertainty,

Or cool one pain,

Or help one fainting mind

Unto her position again,

I shall live in joy for life.

* Edited from Sua's favorite poem
"If I Can Stop One Heart from Breaking" by Emily Dickinson

INFORMATION

김수아 영미문학 학습 가이드

임용시험의 특성에 맞게 학습 내용·범위·방향·전략 설정
→ 자신의 학습 스타일에 맞는 학습 방법·계획 설정
→ 출제 경향 파악 → 문제 풀이 전략과 스킬 연습
"단단한 마음가짐으로 꾸준히 학습하기!"

1. 임용시험의 특성 알기

- **시험에서 요구되는 학습 수준을 파악해야합니다.**
  영미문학은 영역이 특정화되지 않으므로 시험에 맞는 영역과 난이도, 지문의 분량 등 학습 대상을 최대한 좁혀서 시작하지 않으면 아주 방대한 양으로 다가와 학습 방향을 잃고 포기하거나 일반영어 실력에만 의존하는 학습이 되기 쉽습니다.

- **문제를 효과적·효율적으로 풀 수 있는 전략과 스킬을 길러야 합니다.**
  시험을 위한 학습이므로 철저하게 문제를 파악하고 답을 도출해서 쓰는 응용 전략이 연계되는 학습이어야 합니다. 열심히 내용을 공부하다보면 문제도 잘 풀 것이라는 생각으로는 빠른 시간 안에 점수를 올릴 수가 없습니다.

2. 김수아 영미문학 수업 특징

임용 시험에서 영미문학 문제는 문제마다 평가하고자 하는 문학 개념이 있습니다. 또한 지문을 읽을 때는 장르적 특성에 맞게 읽어야 빠른 독해가 가능합니다. 이를 위해, 핵심 **문학 개념 이해**와 장르적 특성에 맞는 전략적 작품 읽기 (focused-reading)를 먼저 학습하도록 안내합니다.

- **영미문학 기본학습 Ⅰ : Reading For Literature Ⅰ (Poetry) (1~2월)**
  - 영문으로 된 기본서를 읽으면서 문학 이해에 필요한 주요 **개념**과 **키워드**를 학습합니다.
  - 임용시험에서 자주 다루는 **주제 중심**으로 작품을 보면서 **내용 스키마**를 형성합니다.
  - 시는 **분석**을 스스로 할 수 있도록 **분석표**(Poetry Analysis Worksheet)로 연습합니다.

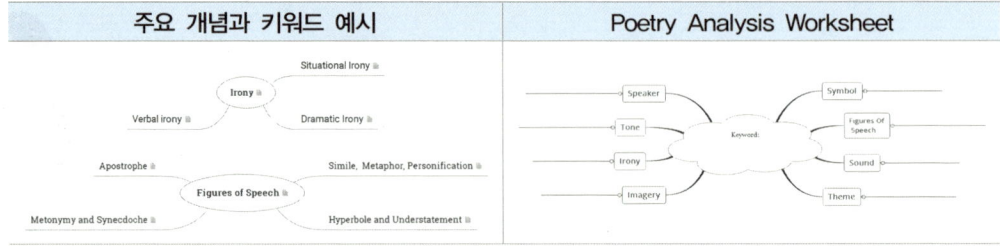

- 영미문학 기본학습 II : Reading For Literature II (Novels & Dramas) (3~4월)
  - 영문으로 된 기본서를 읽으면서 소설과 드라마 장르적 특성 이해해 필요한 주요 개념과 키워드를 학습합니다.

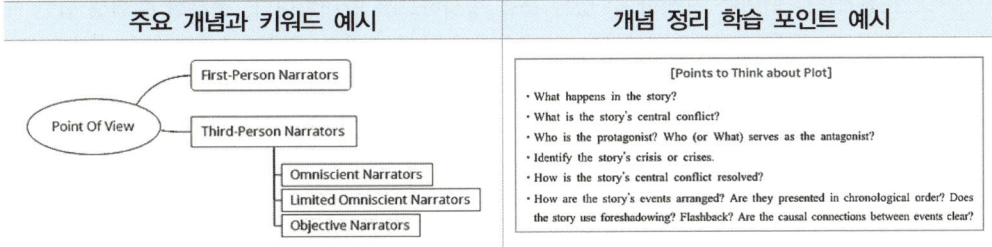

- 기출 메타 분석 및 TOKS 학습 (5~6월)
  - 기출 문제를 과제(Task) 유형으로 분류하고 각 과제의 특징과 평가 요소를 확인하여 향후 문제풀이 학습의 범위와 방향을 제시합니다.
  - 기출 작품에서 빈번하게 다루는 주제를 파악하여 내용 스키마를 형성합니다.
  - 기출문항의 과제(Task) 유형과 각 유형에 따른 답안 구조(Organization)를 확인하여, 임용시험에서 요구하는 독해와 쓰기 수준을 확인하고 효과적인 문제풀이 전략을 도출합니다.

- TOKS 문제풀이 (7~11월)
  - 기출 문제와 유사한 문항 과제(Task)에 따른 답안 구성구조(Organization)와 필요한 키워드(Keyword), 대체 단어(Synonym)를 준비하는 연습으로 효율적이고 효과적인 문제풀이 전략을 내재화해 나갑니다.

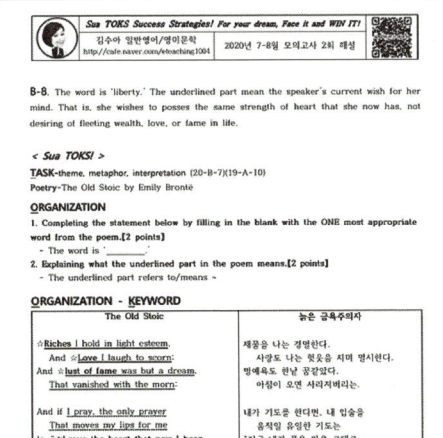
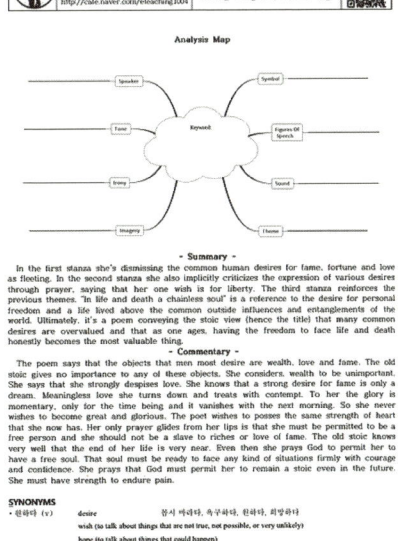

INFORMATION

- **첨삭 및 Writing Seminar**
  - 답안 첨삭을 통해 공통된 오류 유형을 분석해 수업을 통해 수정 방법을 제시합니다.
  - 효율적으로 답안을 작성할 수 있는 틀을 형성하도록 안내합니다. 풍부한 수험생 답안 예시를 통해 각 개인의 수준에 적합하고 수월한 답안 작성 방법을 개발할 수 있는 방안을 제시합니다.

3. 김수아 수업 내 것 만들기

- **기본개념부터, 기출문제, 응용문제까지 학습합니다.**

  교재에는 해당 장르에 대한 충분한 학습을 할 수 있도록 순차적으로 기본 개념학습, 형성평가, 기출문제 및 모의고사 문제 순으로 구성하였습니다. 예습, 강의, 복습, 문제 연습까지 종합적인 학습 계획을 가지고 학습하시기 바랍니다.

- **영미문학 학습 과정은 작품을 이해하는 방법론을 배우는 것입니다.**
  - 수업에서 배운 내용을 직접 적용하는 **과제를 성실히** 해야 자기 것으로 확실히 습득할 수 있습니다.
  - **상반기 첨삭 과제에는** 자신의 상태를 정확하게 처방받고 학습할 수 있도록 **적극적으로 참여**하시기 바랍니다. 내 실력을 드러내고 처방받아 고쳐보는 것이, 필요한 쓰기 수준에 도달할 수 있는 가장 빠른 방법입니다.
  - **하반기에는 복습과제**를 활용하여 작품과 지문을 새롭게 보면서 강의에서 학습한 내용을 이해하고 다시 한 번 문제를 풀어봅니다. 복습은 학습의 정확성을 담보해줍니다.

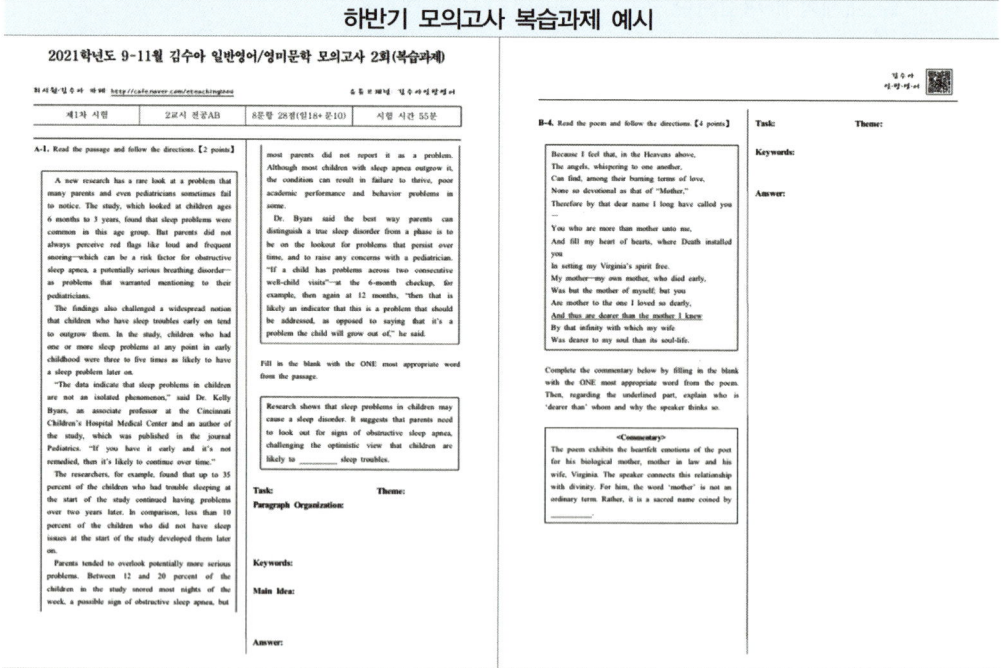

하반기 모의고사 복습과제 예시

김수아
전공영어 영미문학
Reading for Literature I

CONTENTS

PART 01 Reading for Basics

Chapter 01 General Understanding — 14
1. What is Literature? — 14
2. Types of Literature: The Genres — 15
3. Reading Literature — 16
4. Writing about Literature — 22

PART 02 Reading for Poetry

Chapter 01 Poetry Analysis — 24
1. What is Poetry? — 24
2. Voice — 27
3. Word Choice, Word Order — 30
4. Imagery — 33
5. Figures of Speech — 36
6. Sound — 46
7. Form — 55
8. Symbol, Allegory, Allusion — 60
9. Themes — 65

Chapter 02 Poems To Read — 68
1. Summary of Poems To Read — 68
2. Poems To Read — 71
3. Analysis of Poems To Read — 147
4. Translated Poems to Read — 159

PART 03 Reading for Practice

Chapter 01 Poems in the Text ———————————————— 214
Chapter 02 Poems in the Exam ———————————————— 235
Chapter 03 Poems in the Mock-Exam by Task ———————— 249

PART 04 Literary Terms

Chapter 01 Literary Terms ————————————————————— 334

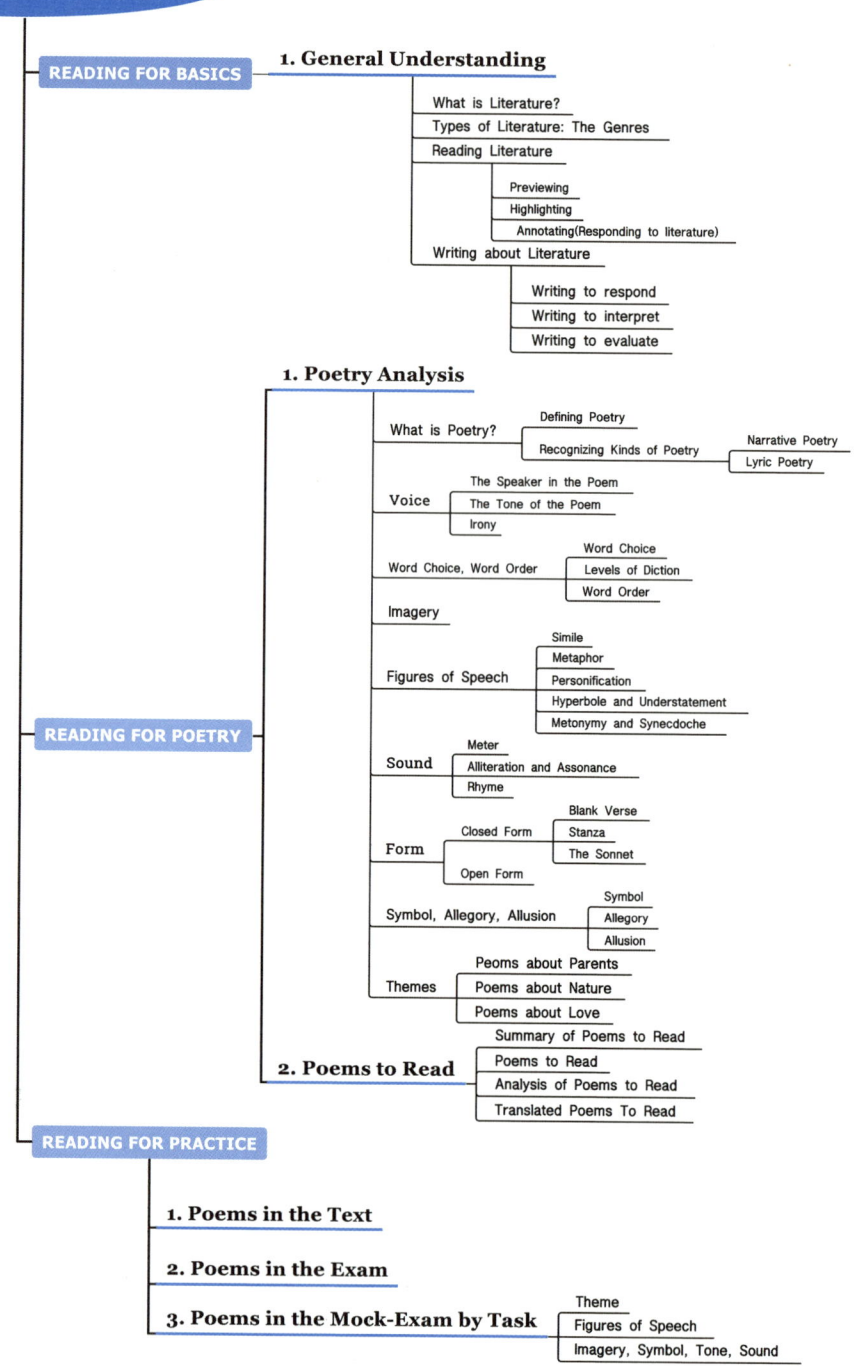

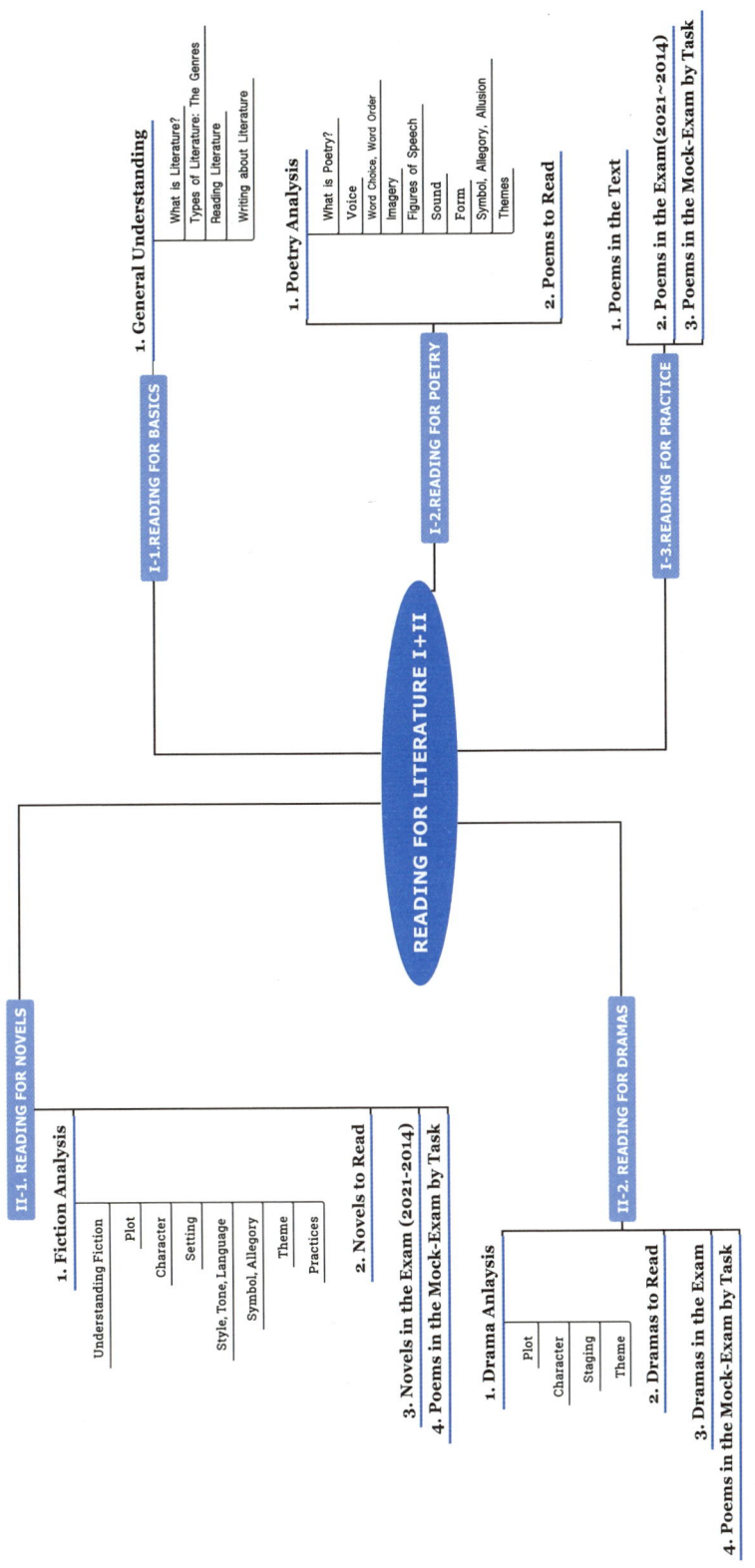

김수아
전공영어 영미문학
Reading for Literature I

PART 01

Reading for Basics

Chapter 01 General Understanding

Chapter 01 General Understanding

general understanding
- What is Literature?
- Types of Literature: The Genres
- Reading Literature
- Writing about Literature

1. What is Literature?

Although the word **literature** broadly includes just about everything that is written, we use it more specifically to mean written compositions that tell stories, dramatize situations, express emotions, and analyze and advocate ideas. Most literary works during recorded history were designed only for the printed page, and we read them silently. Works composed before history began, however, were originally oral, and, fortunately, many of these have been preserved and now exist as printed texts. Also a great deal of literature is designed to be read aloud (many poems), and much is designed to be spoken and acted out by live actors (plays).

Whatever the form, literature has many things to offer, almost as many things as there are people. In fact, people often cannot explain why they enjoy reading, for goals and ideals are not easily articulated. There are, however, areas of general agreement about some of the things that the systematic and extensive reading of literature can do.

Literature helps us grow, both personally and intellectually; it provides an objective base for knowledge and understanding; it links us with part; it enables us to recognize human dreams and struggles in different places and times that we would never otherwise know; it helps us develop mature sensibility and compassion for the condition of all living things — human, animal, and vegetable; it gives us the knowledge and perception to appreciate the beauty of order and arrangement, just as a well-structured song or a beautifully painted canvas can; it provides the comparative basis from which we can see worthiness in the aims of all people, and it therefore helps us see beauty in the world around us; it exercises our emotions through interest, concern, tension, excitement, hope, fear, regret, laughter, and sympathy. Through cumulative experience in reading, literature shapes goals and values by clarifying our own identities, both positively, through acceptance of the admirable in human beings, and negatively, through rejection of the sinister. It helps us shape our judgements through the comparison of the good and the bad. Both in our everyday activities and in the decisions we make as individuals and as citizens, it enables us to develop a perspective on events occurring locally and globally, and thereby it gives us understanding and control. It encourages us to assist creative, talented people who need recognition and support. It is one of the shaping influences of life. It makes us human.

2. Types of Literature: The Genres

Literature may be classified into four categories or *genres*; (1) prose fiction, (2) poetry, (3) drama, and (4) nonfiction prose. While all are art forms, each with its own requirements of structure and style, usually the first three are classed as **imaginative literature.**

The genres of imaginative literature have much in common, but they also have distinguishing characteristics. **Prose fiction**, or **narrative fiction**, includes **novels, short stories, myths, parables, romances,** and **epics.** *Fiction* originally meant anything made up, crafted, or shaped, but as we understand the word today, it means a prose story based in the imagination of the author. While fiction, like all imaginative literature, may introduce true historical details, it is not real story, for its purpose is primarily to interest, divert, stimulate, and instruct. The essence of fiction is **narration**, the relating or recounting of a sequence of events or actions. Works of fiction usually focus on one or a few major characters and deal with problems. **Poetry** is more economical than prose fiction in the use of words, and it relies heavily on imagery, figurative language, and sound. **Drama** is literature designed to be performed by actors. Like fiction, drama may focus on a single character or a small number of characters, and it presents fictional events as if they were happening in the present, to be witnessed by an audience. Although most modern plays present dialogue in prose, on the ground that dramatic speech is to be as lifelike as possible, many plays from the past, like those of ancient Greece and Renaissance England, are in poetic form.

Imaginative literature differs from **nonfiction prose**, the fourth genre, which consists of news reports, feature articles, themes, editorials, textbooks, historical and biographical works, and the like, all of which describe or interpret facts and present judgements and opinions. A major goal of nonfiction prose is truth in reporting and logic in reasoning. It bears repeating that the truth in imaginative literature, unlike that in nonfiction prose, is truth to life and human nature, not to the factual world of news, science, and history.

3. Reading Literature

Do not expect a cursory reading to produce full understanding. After a quick reading of a work, it may be embarrassingly difficult to answer pointed questions or to say anything intelligent about it at all. A more careful, active reading gives us the understanding to make well-considered answers. Obviously, we must first follow the work and understand its details, but more importantly we must respond to the words, get at the ideas, and understand the implications of what is happening. We must apply our own experiences to verify the accuracy and truth of the situation and incidents, and we must articulate our own emotional responses to the characters and their problems.

Most of the time, readers are passive; they expect the text to give them everything they need, and they do not expect to contribute much to the reading process. In contrast, active reading means participating in the reading process;

thinking about what you read, asking questions, and challenging ideas. Active reading is excellent preparation for the discussion and writing.

Three strategies in particular—*previewing, highlighting,* and *annotating*—will help you to become a more effective reader. Keep in mind, though, that reading and responding to what you read is not an orderly process—or even a sequential one. You will most likely find yourself doing more than one thing at a time—annotating at the same time you highlight, for example.

(1) Previewing

You begin active reading by **previewing** a work to get a general idea of what to look for later, when you read it more carefully.

Start your prewriting with the work's most obvious physical characteristics. How long is a short story? How many acts and scenes does a play have? Is a poem divided into stanzas? The answers to these and similar questions will help you begin to notice more subtle aspects of the work's form. For example, previewing may reveal that a contemporary short story is presented entirely in a question-and-answer format, that it is organized as diary entries, or that it is divided into sections by headings. Previewing may identify poems that seem to lack formal structure; poems written in traditional forms (such as **sonnets**) or in experimental forms; or visual poetry. Your awareness of these and other distinctive features at this point may help you gain insight into a work later on.

Previewing can enable you to see some of the more obvious stylistic and structural features of a work—the point of view used in a story, how many characters a play has and where it is set, or the repetition of certain words or lines in a poem, for example. Such features may or may not be important; at this stage, our goal is to observe, not to analyze or evaluate.

Previewing is a useful strategy not because it provides answers but because it suggests questions to ask later, as you read more closely.

(2) Highlighting

When you read a work closely, you will notice additional, more subtle, elements that you may want to examine further. At this point, you should begin highlighting—physically marking the text to identify key details and to note relationships among ideas.

What should you highlight? As you read, ask yourself whether repeated words or phrases form a pattern. Because the word that appears so frequently appears at key points in the story, it helps to reinforce a key theme of the story. Repeated words and phrases are particularly important in poetry. In Dylan Tomas's "Do not go gentle into that good night[53]", for example, the repetition of two of the poem's nineteen lines four times each enhances the poem's rhythmic, almost monotonous, cadence. As you read, highlight your text to identify such repeated words and phrases. Later, you can consider why these elements are repeated.

During the highlighting stage, also pay particular attention to **images** that occur repeatedly, keeping in mind that such repeated images may form patterns that can help you to interpret the work. When you reread, you can begin to determine what pattern the images form and perhaps decide how this pattern enhances the work's ideas.

Checklist: Using Highlighting Symbols

1. Underline important ideas.
2. Box or circle words, phrases, or images that you want to think more about.
3. Put question marks beside confusing passages, unfamiliar references, or words that need to be defined.
4. Circle related words, ideas, or images and draw lines or arrows to connect them.
5. Number incidents that occur in sequence.
6. Set off a key portion of the text with a vertical line in the margin.
7. Place stars beside particularly important ideas.

My Arkansas by Maya Angelou(1928~2014)[1]

There is a deep brooding
In Arkansas.
Old crimes like moss pend
From poplar trees.

> The sullen earth
> Is too much
> Red for comfort.
>
> Sunrise seems to hesitate
> And in that second
> Lose its
> Incandescent aim, and
> Dusk no more shadows
> Than the noon.
> The past is brighter yet
>
> Old hates and
> Ante-bellum lace, are rent
> But not discarded
> Today is yet to come
> In Arkansas.
> It writhes. It writhes in awful
> Waves of brooding

(3) Annotating(Responding to literature)

At the same time you highlight a text, you also **annotate** it, recording your reactions as marginal notes. In these notes, you may define new words, identify allusions and patterns of language or imagery, summarize plot relationships, list a work's possible themes, suggest a character's motivation, examine the possible significance of particular images or symbols, or record questions that occur to you as you read. Ideally, your annotations will help you find ideas to write about.

The following paragraph is from John Updike's 1961 short story "A&P". Highlight and annotate to answer the question "Why does Sammy really quit his job?"

Part of "A&P"

Lengel sighs and begins to look very patient and old and gray. He's been a friend of my parents for years. "Sammy, you don't want to do this to your Mom and Dad," he tells me. It's true, I don't. But it seems to me that once you begin a gesture it's fatal not to go through with it. I fold the apron, "Sammy" stitched in red on the pocket, and put it on the counter, and drop the bow tie on top of it. The bow tie is theirs, if you've ever wondered. "You'll feel this for the rest of your life," Lengel says, and I know that's true, too, but remembering how he made that pretty girl blush makes me so scrunchy inside I punch the No Sale tab and the machine whirs "pee-pul" and the drawer splats out. One advantage to this scene taking place in summer, I can follow this up with a clean exit, there's no fumbling around getting your coat and galoshes, I just saunter into the electric eye in my white shirt that my mother ironed the night before, and the door heaves itself open, and outside the sunshine is skating around on the asphalt.

Lengel은 한숨을 쉬었고 이 상황을 인내하는 듯 보였지만 늙고 창백했다. 그는 몇 년 전부터 나의 부모님의 친구였다. "Sammy, 너희 부모님은 그만두는 짓 따윈 원치 않으실 텐데" 그가 나에게 말했다. 그래 사실이다. 그렇게 하질 원치 않으실 것이다. 그러나 나에게 있어 일단 행동을 시작한 이상은 겪어봐야 되지, 그렇지 않는다면 그것이 더 치명적인 일이었다. 나는 주머니가 있고 빨간색으로 된 앞치마를 접었다. 그리고는 카운터 위에 놓았다. 그리고 나비넥타이를 그 위에다 놓았다. 당신이 궁금할 수도 있는데, 나비넥타이는 그들의 것이었다. "너는 이제 남은 인생에서 이 사건이 얼마나 큰 타격을 주는 것인지 절실히 느낄 거다." Lengel이 말했다. 나는 그것이 또한 사실임을 안다. 그러나 그가 그 귀여운 소녀들을 어떻게 붉히게 만들었는지를 생각하면 아직도 내 안에서 분노가 끓어오른다. 나는 "No Sale" 탭을 두드렸고 기계는 "Pee-Pul" 소리를 내었고 서랍은 철썩 튀어 나왔다. 이 일들이 여름에 일어났다는 사실에 대해 참 다행인 것은 코트와 덧신을 찾을 필요 없이 곧장 출구로 그들을 쫓아갈 수 있었다는 데에 있다. 나는 어제 밤에 어머니가 다려준 하얀 셔츠를 입고 자동문 센서를 향해 뛰어갔다. 문이 열려졌고 바깥에는 햇볕이 아스팔트 위를 스케이트 타는 듯 미끄러지며 비추고 있었다.

Sample Annotation

Action isn't the result of thought.

Lengel sighs and begins to look very patient and old and gray. He's been a friend of my parents for years. "Sammy, you don't want to do this to your Mom and Dad," he tells me. It's true, I don't. But it seems to me that once you begin a gesture it's fatal not to go through with it. I fold the apron, "Sammy" stitched in red on the pocket, and put it on the counter, and drop the bow tie on top of it. The bow tie is theirs, if you've ever wondered. "You'll feel this

Sammy reacts to the girl's embarrassment.

for the rest of your life," Lengel says, and I know that's true, too, but remembering how he made the pretty girl blush makes me so scrunchy inside I punch the No Sale tab and the machine whirs "pee-pul" and the drawer splats out. One advantage to this scene taking place in summer, I can follow this up with a clean exit, there's no fumbling around getting your coat and galoshes, I just saunter into the electric eye in my white shirt that my mother ironed the night before, and the door heaves itself open, and outside the sunshine is skating around on the asphalt.

Need for a clean exit— romantic idea.

Romantic cowboy, but his mother irons his shirt (irony).

4. Writing about Literature

Writing about literature — or about anything else — is an idiosyncratic process during which many activities occur at once: as you write, you think of ideas; as you think of ideas, you clarify the focus of your essay; and as you clarify your focus, you reshape your paragraphs and sentences and refine your word choice.

Sometimes you write with a single **purpose** in mind. At other times, you may have more than one purpose. In general terms, you may write for any of the following three reasons:

(1) Writing to respond

When you write to **respond**, your goal is to discover and express your reactions to a work. To record your responses, you engage in relatively informal activities, such as brainstorming, listing, and journal writing. As you write, you explore your own ideas, forming and re-forming your impressions of the work.

(2) Writing to interpret

When you write to **interpret**, your aim is to explain a work's possible meanings. To do so, you may summarize, give examples, or compare and contrast the work to other works or to your own experiences. Then, you may go on to analyze the work: studying each of its elements in turn, putting complex statements into your own words, defining difficult concepts, and placing ideas in context.

(3) Writing to evaluate

When you write to evaluate, your purpose is to assess a work's literary merits. You may consider not only its aesthetic appeal, but also its ability to retain that appeal over time and across national or cultural boundaries. As you write, you use your own critical sense and the opinions of experts to help you make judgements about the work.

PART 02

Reading for Poetry

- **Chapter 01** Poetry Analysis
- **Chapter 02** Poems To Read

Chapter 01 Poetry Analysis

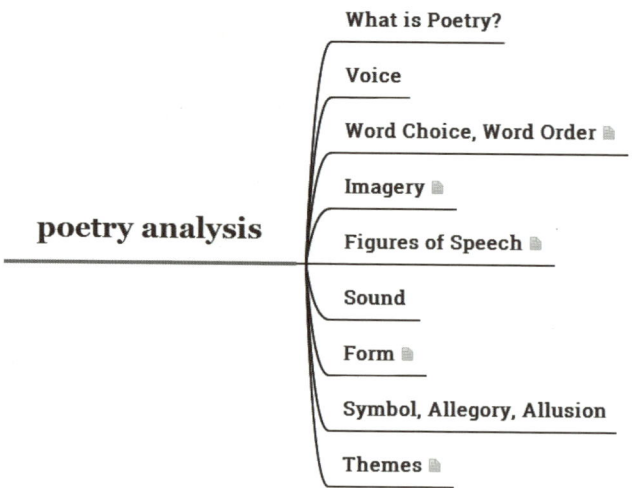

1. What is Poetry?

(1) Defining Poetry

One way of defining poetry is to examine how it is different from other forms of literature, such as fiction or drama. The first and most important element of poetry that distinguishes it from other genres is its **form**. Unlike prose, which is written from margin to margin, poetry is made up of individual **lines**. A poetic line begins and ends where the poet chooses: it can start at the left margin or halfway across the page, and it can end at the right margin or after only a word or two. A poet chooses when to stop, or break, the line according to his or her sense of rhythm and cadence.

Poets also use the **sound** of the words themselves, alone and in conjunction with the other words of the poem, to create a sense of rhythm and melody. **Alliteration** (the repetition of consonant sounds in consecutive or neighboring words), **assonance** (the repetition of vowel sounds at the ends of words), and **consonance** (the repetition of consonant sounds at the ends of words) are three devices commonly used by poets to help create the music of a poem. Poets can also use **rhyme** (either at the ends of lines or within the lines themselves), which contributes to the pattern of sounds in a poem.

In addition, poets are more likely than writers of other kinds of literature to rely on **imagery**, words or phrases that describe the sense. These vivid descriptions or details help the reader to connect with the poet's ideas in a tangible way. Poets also make extensive use of **figurative language**, including metaphors and similes, to convey their ideas and to help their readers access these ideas.

(2) Recognizing Kinds of Poetry

Most poems are either **narrative** poems, which recount a story, or **lyric** poems, which communicate a speaker's mood, feelings, or state of mind.

Narrative Poetry

Although any brief poem that tells a story, such as Edwin Arlington Robinson's "Richard Cory[2]", may be considered a narrative poem, the two most familiar forms of narrative poetry are the *epic* and the *ballad*.

Epics are narrative poems that recount the accomplishments of heroic figures, typically including expansive settings, superhuman feats, and gods and supernatural beings. The language of epic poems tends to be formal, even elevated, and often quite elaborate. In ancient times, epics were handed down orally; more recently, poets have written literary epics, such as John Milton's *Paradise Lost* (1667) and Nobel Prize-winning poet Derek Walcott's *Omeros* (1990), that follow many of the same conventions.

The **ballad** is another type of narrative poetry with roots in an oral tradition. Originally intended to be sung, a ballad uses repeated words and phrases, including a refrain, to advance its story. Some—but not all—ballads use the **ballad stanza**. "Ballad of Birmingham[3]" is an example of a contemporary ballad.

Lyric Poetry

Like narrative poems, lyric poems take various forms.

An **elegy** is a poem in which a poet mourns the death of a specific person, as in A.E. Houseman's "To an Athlete Dying Young[4]".

An **ode** is a long lyric poem, formal and serious in style, tone, and subject matter. An **ode** typically has a fairly complex stanzaic pattern, such as the **terza rima** used by Percy Bysshe Shelly in "Ode to the West Wind[5]".

An **aubade** is a poem about morning, usually celebrating the coming of dawn. An example is Philip Larkin's 1977 poem "Aubade.[6]"

An **occasional poem** is written to celebrate a particular event or occasion. An example is Billy Collins's poem "The Names[7]," read before a joint session of Congress to commemorate the first anniversary of the terrorist attacks on the World Trade Center.

A **meditation** is a lyric poem that focuses on a physical object, using this object as a vehicle for considering larger issues. Edmund Waller's seventeenth-century poem "Go, lovely rose[8]" is a meditation.

A **pastoral** — for example, Christopher Marlowe's "The Passionate Shepherd to His Love[9]" — is a lyric poem that celebrates the simple, idyllic pleasures of country life.

A **dramatic monologue** is a poem whose speaker addresses one or more silent listeners, often revealing much more than he or she intends. Robert Browning's "My Last Duchess[10]" and Alfred, Lord Tennyson's "Ulysses[11]" are dramatic monologues.

2. Voice

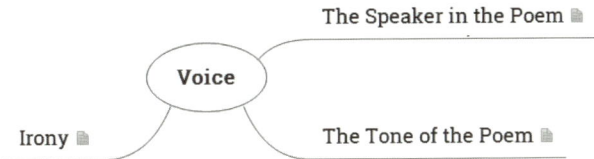

(1) The Speaker in the Poem

When they read fiction, readers form an impression of work's narrator and decide whether he or she is sophisticated or unsophisticated, trustworthy or untrustworthy, innocent or experienced. Just as fiction depends on narrator, poetry depends on a speaker who describes events, feelings, and ideas to readers. Finding out as much as possible about this speaker can help readers to interpret a poem. For example the speaker in Emily Dickinson's "I'm nobody! Who are you?[12]" seems at first to be playful, even flirtatious. In fact, she appears to be entering into a conspiracy with readers.

One question readers might ask about Emily Dickinson's "I'm nobody! Who are you?[12]" is how close the speaker's voice is to the poet's. Readers who conclude that the poem is about the conflict between a poet's public and private selves may be tempted to see the speaker and the poet as one. But this is not necessarily the case. Like the narrator of a short story, the speaker of a poem is a **persona**, or mask, that the poet puts on. Granted, in some poems little distance exists between the poet and the speaker. Without hard evidence to support a link between speaker and poet, however, readers should not simply assume they are one and the same.

In many cases, the speaker is quite different from the poet, even when the speaker's voice conveys the attitude of the poet either directly or indirectly. In his 1758 poem "The Chimney Sweeper[13]," for example, William Blake assumes the voice of a child to criticize the system of child labor that existed in eighteenth-century England.

Sometimes the poem's speaker is **anonymous**. In such cases—as in William Carlos William's "Red Wheelbarrow[14]", for instance—the first-person voice is absent and the speaker remains outside the poem. At other times, the speaker has **a set identity**—a king a beggar, a highwayman, a sheriff, a husband, a wife, a rich man, a murderer, an child, a mystical figure, an explorer, a teacher, a faithless lover, a saint—or even a flower, an animal, or a clod of earth. Whatever the case, the speaker is not the poet but rather a creation that the poet uses to convey his or her ideas.

Direct statements by speakers can help to characterize them. For example, in the poem "Negro[15]" by Langston Hughes, the first line of each stanza establishes the identity of the speaker—and defines his perspective.

(2) The Tone of the Poem

The tone of a poem conveys the speaker's attitude toward his or her subject or audience. In speech, this attitude can be conveyed easily: stressing a word in a sentence can modify or color a statement, drastically affect the meaning of the sentence. For poets, conveying a particular tone to readers poses a challenge because readers rarely hear poets' spoken voices. Instead, poets indicate tone by using techniques such as rhyme, meter, word choice, sentence structure, figures of speech, and imagery.

The range of possible tone is wide. For example, a poem's speaker may be joyful, sad, playful, serious, comic, intimate, formal, relaxed, condescending, or ironic.

In Robert Frost's "Fire and Ice[16]", notice how the tone conveys the speaker's attitude toward his subject.

Sometimes shifts in tone reveal changes in the speaker's attitude. In the poem "The Man He Killed[17]" by Thomas Hardy, subtle shifts in tone reveal a change in the speaker's attitude toward war.

(3) Irony

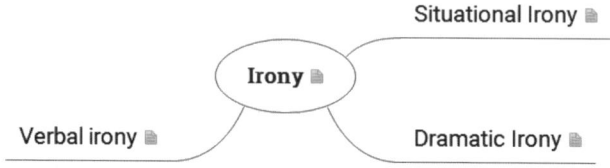

Just as in fiction and drama, irony occurs in poetry when a discrepancy exists between two levels of meaning or experience. Consider the tone of the following lines by Stephen Crane's "War is Kind[20]":

> Do not weep, maiden, for war is kind.
>
> Because your lover threw wild hands toward the sky
>
> And the affrightened steed ran on alone,
>
> Do not weep,
>
> War is kind.

How can war be "kind"? Isn't war exactly the opposite of "kind"? Surely the speaker does not intend his words to be taken literally. By making this ironic statement, the speaker actually conveys the opposite idea: war is a cruel, mindless exercise of violence.

Skillfully used, irony enables a poet to make a pointed comment about a situation or to manipulate a reader's emotions. Implicit in irony is the writer's assumption that readers will not be misled by the literal meaning of a statement. In order for irony to work, readers must recognize the disparity between what is said and what is meant, or between what a speaker thinks is occurring and what readers know to be occurring.

Situational Irony

One kind of irony is situational irony, which occurs when the situation itself contradicts readers' expectations. For example, in "Porphyria's Lover[18]" the meeting of two lovers ironically results not in joy and passion but in murder. Also, in Percy Bysshe Shelley's "Ozymandias[19]", the situation creates irony.

Dramatic Irony

Another kind of irony that appears in poetry is dramatic irony, which occurs when a speaker believes one thing and readers realize something else. In the poem "Porphyria's Lover[18]" by Robert Browning uses a deranged speaker to tell a story that is filled with irony. This poem is a dramatic monologue, a poem that includes an implied listener as well as a speaker. The speaker recounts his story in a straightforward manner, seemingly unaware of the horror of his story. In fact, much of the effect of this poem comes from the speaker's telling his tale of murder in a flat unemotional tone — and from readers' gradual realization that the speaker is mad.

Verbal irony

Perhaps the most common kind of irony found in poetry is verbal irony, which is created when words say one thing but mean another, often exactly the opposite. When verbal irony is particularly biting, it is called **sarcasm** — for example, Stephen Crane's use of the word *kind* in his antiwar poem "War Is Kind[20]." In speech, verbal irony is easy to detect through the speaker's change in tone or emphasis. In writing, when these signals are absent, verbal irony becomes more difficult to convey. Poets must depend on the context of a remark or on the contrast between a word and other images in the poem to create irony.

3. Word Choice, Word Order

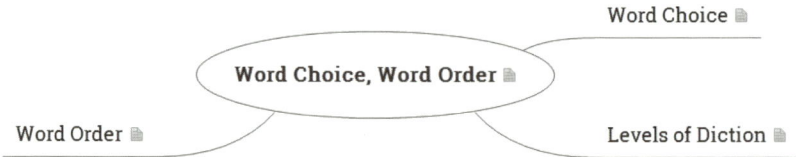

Words identify and name, characterize and distinguish, compare and contrast. Words describe, limit, and embellish; words locate and measure. Even though words may be elusive and uncertain and changeable, "tossed around as if / denied location by the wind" and "can change sooner than seasons," they still can "stalk our lives like policemen." In poetry, as in love and in politics, words matter.

Beyond the quantitative — how many words, how many letters and syllables — is a much more important consideration: the *quality* of words. Which words are chosen, and why? Why are certain words placed next to others? What does a word suggest in a particular context? How are the words arranged? What exactly constitutes the right word?

(1) Word Choice

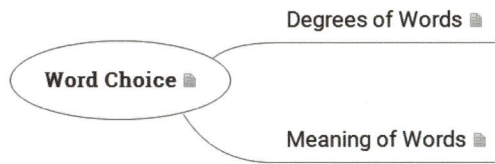

In general, poets (like prose writers) select words because they communicate their ideas. However, poets may also choose words for their sound. For instance, a word may echo another word's sound, and such repetition may place emphasis on both words; it may rhyme with another word and therefore be needed to preserve the poem's rhyme scheme; or it may have a certain combination of stressed and unstressed syllables needed to maintain the poem's metrical pattern Occasionally, a poet may even choose a word because of how it looks on the page.

Degrees of Words

At the same time, poets may choose words for their degree of concreteness or abstraction, specificity or generality. A concrete word refers to an item that is a perceivable, tangible entity—for example, a kiss or a flag. An abstract word refers to an intangible idea, condition, or quality, something that cannot be perceived by the senses—love or patriotism, for instance. Specific words refer to particular items; general words refer to entire classes or groups of items. As the following example illustrates, whether a word is specific or general is relative; its degree of specificity or generality depends on its relationship to other words.

Poem > closed form poem > sonnet > seventeenth-century sonnet > Elizabethan sonnet > sonnet by Shakespeare > "My mistress' eyes are nothing like the sun"

Sometimes a poet wants a precise word, on that is both specific and concrete. At other times, a poet might prefer general or abstract language, which may allow for more subtlety—or even for intentional ambiguity.

Meaning of Words

Finally, a word may be chosen for its **connotation**—what it suggests. Every word has one or more **denotations**—what it signifies without emotional associations, judgments, or opinions. The word *family*, for example, denotes "a group of related things or people." Connotation is a more complex matter; after all, a single word may have many different associations. In general terms, a word may have a connotation that is positive, neutral, or negative. Thus *family* may have a positive connotation when it describes a group of loving relatives, a neutral connotation when it describes a biological category, and an ironically negative connotation when it describes an organized crime family. Beyond this distinction, *family*, like any other word, may have a variety of emotional and social associations, suggesting loyalty, warmth, home, security, or duty. In fact, many words, then, they must consider what a particular word may suggest to readers as well as what it denotes. In Walt Whitman's "When I Heard the Learn'd Astronomer[21]", the poet chooses words for their sounds and for their relationships to other words as well as for their connotations.

(2) Levels of Diction

Like other writers, poets use various levels of diction to convey their ideas. The diction of a poem may be formal or informal or fall anywhere in between, depending on the identity of the speaker and on the speaker's attitude toward the reader and toward his or her subject. At one extreme, very formal poems can be far removed in style and vocabulary from everyday speech. At the other extreme, highly informal poems can be full of jargon, regionalisms, and slang. Many poems, of course, use language that falls somewhere between formal and informal diction.

Formal diction is characterized by a learned vocabulary and grammatically correct forms. In general, formal diction does not include colloquialisms, such as contractions and shortened word forms (*phone* for *telephone*). Margaret Atwood's "The City Planners[22]" illustrates that a speaker who uses formal diction can sound aloof and impersonal.

Informal diction is the language closest to everyday conversation. It includes colloquialisms—contractions, shortened word forms, and the like—and may also include slang, regional expressions, and even nonstandard words. For example, in the poem "Baca Grande," the speaker uses informal diction to highlight the contrast between James Baca, a law student speaking to the graduating class of his old high school, and the graduating seniors.

(3) Word Order

The order in which words are arranged in a poem is as important as the choice of words. Because English sentences nearly always have a subject-verb-object sequence, with adjectives preceding the nouns they modify, a departure from this order calls attention to itself. Thus, poets can use readers' expectations about word order to their advantage.

For example, poets often manipulate word order to place emphasis on a word. Sometimes they achieve this emphasis by using a very unconventional sequence; sometimes they simply place the word first or last in a line or place it in a stressed position in the line. Poets may also choose a particular word order to make two related — or startlingly unrelated — words fall in adjacent or parallel positions, calling attention to the similarity (or the difference) between them. In other cases, poets may manipulate syntax to preserve a poem's rhyme or meter or to highlight sound correspondences that might otherwise not be noticeable. Finally, irregular syntax may be used throughout a poem to reveal a speaker's mood — for example, to give a playful quality to a poem or to suggest a speaker's disoriented state. In Edmund Spenser's "One day I wrote her name upon the strand[23]", word order frequently departs from conventional English syntax.

4. Imagery

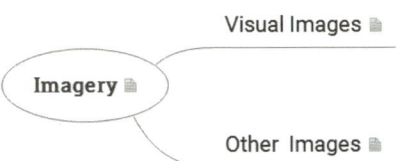

Because the purpose of poetry — and, for that matter, of all literature — is to expand the perception of readers, poets appeal to the senses. To call up images in the minds of an audience, a poet uses **imagery,** language that evokes a physical sensation produced by one or more of the five senses — sight, hearing, taste, touch, smell.

Although the effect can be quite complex, the way images work is simple: when you read the word *red*, your memory of the various red things that you have seen determines how you picture the image. In addition, the word *red* may have **connotations**—emotional associations that define your response. A red sunset, for example, can have a positive connotation or a negative one, depending on whether it is associated with the end of a perfect day or with air pollution. By choosing images carefully, poets not only create pictures in a reader's mind but also create a great number of imaginative associations. These associations help poets to establish the **atmosphere or mood** of the poem. For example, the image of softly falling snow in Robert Frost's "Stopping by Woods on a Snowy Evening[24]" creates a quiet, mystical mood. By conveying what the poet sees and imagines, images open readers' minds and enrich their reading with perceptions and associations different from—and possibly more original and complex than—their own.

(1) Visual Images

One advantage of imagery is its extreme **economy**. A few carefully chosen words enable poets to evoke a range of emotions and reactions. In William Carlos Williams's "Red Wheelbarrow[14]", simple visual images create a rich and compelling picture.

Images enable poets to present ideas that would be difficult to convey in any other way. One look at a dictionary will illustrate that concepts such as *beauty* and *mystery* are so abstract that they are difficult to define, let alone to discuss in specific terms. However, by choosing an image or a series of images to embody these ideas, poets can effectively make their feelings known, as Ezra Pound does in the brief poem that follows.

> ### In a Station of the Metro (1916)[25]
> The apparition of these faces in the crowd;
> Petals on a wet, black bough.

This poem is almost impossible to paraphrase because the information it communicates is less important that the feelings associated with this information.

The poem's title indicate that the first line is mean to suggest a group of people standing in a station of the Paris subway. The scene, however, is presented not as a clear picture but as an "apparition," suggesting that it is unexpected or even dreamlike. In contrast with the image of the subway platform is the image of the people's faces as flower petals on the dark branch of a tree. Thus, the subway platform — dark, cold, wet, subterranean (associated with baseness, death, and hell) — is juxtaposed with flower petals — delicate, pale, radiant, lovely (associated with the ideal, life, and heaven). These contrasting images, presented without comment, bear the entire weight of the poem.

(2) Other Images

Although images can be strikingly visual, they can also appeal to the senses of hearing, smell, taste, and touch. Gary Snyder's "Some Good Things to Be Said for the Iron Age[26]" uses images of sound and taste as well as sight.

Some Good Things to Be Said for the Iron Age (1970)[26]

A ringing tire iron
dropped on the pavement
Whang of a saw
brusht on limbs
the taste
of rust

Here Snyder presents two commonplace **aural** images: the ringing of a tire iron and the sound of a saw. These somewhat ordinary image gain power, however, through their visual isolation on separate lines in the poem. Together they produce a harsh and jarring chord that in turn creates a sense of uneasiness in the reader. This poem does more than present sensory images, though. It also conveys the speaker's interpretations of these images. The last two lines imply not only that the time in which we live (the Iron Age) is based and mundane, but also that it is declining, decaying into an age of rust. This idea is reinforced by the repeated consonant sounds in *taste* and *rust,* which encourage readers to hold the final image of the poem on their tongues.

5. Figures of Speech

Although writers experiment with language in all kinds of literary works, poets in particular recognize the power of a figure of speech to take readers beyond the literal meaning of a word. For this reason, **figures of speech** — expressions that use words to achieve effects beyond the power of ordinary language — are more prominent in poetry than in other kinds of writing. For example, Shakespeare's sonnet "Shall I compare thee to a summer's day[27]?" compares a loved one to a summer's day in order to make the point that, unlike the fleeting summer, the loved one will — within the poem — remain forever young. But this sonnet goes beyond the obvious equation (loved one = summer's day): the speaker's assertion that his loved one will live forever in his poem actually says more about his confidence in his own talent and reputation (and about the power of language) than about the loved one's beauty.

Shall I compare thee to a summer's day (1609)[27]

Shall I compare thee to a summer's day?
Thou art more lovely and more temperate.
Rough winds do shake the darling buds of May,
And summer's lease hath all too short a date.
Sometime too hot the eye of heaven shines,
And often is his gold complexion dimm'd;
And every fair from fair sometime declines,
By chance or nature's changing course untrimm'd;
But thy eternal summer shall not fade
Nor lose possession of that fair thou ow'st;
Nor shall Death brag thou wander'st in his shade,
When in eternal lines to time thou grow'st:

> So long as men can breathe or eyes can see,
> So long lives this, and this gives life to thee.

(1) Simile, Metaphor, Personification

A **simile** is a comparison between two unlike items that uses *like* or *as*. When an imaginative comparison between two unlike items does not use *like* or *as* — that is, when it says "a *is* b" rather than "a is *like* b" — it is a **metaphor**.

For example, when William Wordsworth opens a poem with "I wandered lonely as a cloud[28]", he conveys a good deal more than he would if he simply began, "I wandered, lonely."

I wandered lonely as a cloud (1807)[28]

I wandered lonely as a cloud
That floats on high o'er vales and hills,
When all at once I saw a crowd,
A host, of golden daffodils;
Beside the lake, beneath the trees,
Fluttering and dancing in the breeze.

Continuous as the stars that shine
And twinkle on the milky way,
They stretched in never-ending line
Along the margin of a bay:
Ten thousand saw I at a glance,
Tossing their heads in sprightly dance.

The waves beside them danced; but they
Out-did the sparkling waves in glee:
A poet could not but be gay,
In such a jocund company:
I gazed- and gazed- but little thought
What wealth the show to me had brought:

> For oft, when on my couch I lie
> In vacant or in pensive mood,
> They flash upon that inward eye
> Which is the bliss of solitude;
> And then my heart with pleasure fills,
> And dances with the daffodils.

By comparing himself in this loneliness to a cloud, the speaker suggests that like the cloud he is a part of nature and that he too is drifting, passive, blown by winds, and lacking will or substance. Thus, by using a figure of speech, the poet can suggest a wide variety of feelings and associations in very few words. (The phrase "I wandered lonely as a cloud" is a **simile**.)

Sometimes, as in Wordsworth's "I wandered lonely as a cloud", a single brief simile or metaphor can be appreciated for what it communicates on its own. At other times, however, a simile or metaphor may be one of several related figures of speech that work together to convey a poem's meaning. For example, Langston Hughes's "Harlem[29]" presents a series of related similes. Together, they suggest the depth of the problem the poem explores in a manner that each individual simile could not do on its own.

Harlem (1951)[29]

> What happens to a dream deferred?
>
> Does it dry up
> like a raisin in the sun?
> Or fester like a sore—
> And then run?
> Does it stink like rotten meat?
> Or crust and sugar over—
> like a syrupy sweet?

> Maybe it just sags
> like a heavy load.
> Or does it explode?

Sometimes a single **extended simile** or **extended metaphor** is developed throughout a poem. The following poem develops an extended simile, comparing a poet to an acrobat. In his extended comparison of a poet and an acrobat, Ferlinghetti characterizes the poet as a circus performer, at once swinging recklessly on a trapeze and balancing carefully on a tightrope.

Constantly Risking Absurdity (1958)[30]

Constantly risking absurdity
and death
whenever he performs
above the heads
of his audience
the poet like an acrobat
climbs on rime
to a high wire of his own making
and balancing on eyebeams
above a sea of faces
paces his way
to the other side of the day
performing entrechats
and sleight-of-foot tricks
and other high theatrics
and all without mistaking
any thing
for what it may not be
For he's the super realist
who must perforce perceive

> taut truth
>
> before the taking of each stance or step
>
> in his supposed advance
>
> toward that still higher perch
>
> where Beauty stands and waits
>
> with gravity
>
> to start her death-defying leap
>
> And he
>
> a little charleychaplin man
>
> who may or may not catch
>
> her fair eternal form
>
> spreadeagled in the empty air
>
> of existence

When Audre Lorde says "Rooming houses are old women[31]" in the poem, she uses a **metaphor**, equating two elements to stress their common associations with emptiness, transience, and hopelessness. At the same time, by identifying rooming houses as old women, Lorde is using **personification**, a special kind of comparison, closely related to metaphor, that gives life or human characteristics to inanimate objects or abstract ideas. So closely does equate rooming houses and women in this poem that at times it is difficult to tell which of the two is actually the poem's subject.

Rooming houses are old women (1968)[31]

Rooming houses are old women

rocking dark windows into their whens

waiting incomplete circles

rocking

rent office to stoop to

community bathrooms to gas rings and

under-bed boxes of once useful garbage

city issued with a twice monthly check
and the young men next door
with their loud midnight parties
and fishy rings left in the bathtub
no longer arouse them
from midnight to mealtime no stops inbetween
light breaking to pass through jumbled up windows
and who was it who married the window that Buzzie's son messed with?

To Welfare and insult from the slow shuffle
from dayswork to shopping bags
heavy with leftovers.

Rooming houses
are old women waiting
searching
through darkening windows
the end or beginning of agony
old women seen through half-ajar doors
hoping
they are not waiting
but being
the entrance to somewhere
unknown and desired
but not new.

    Despite the poem's assertion, rooming houses are not old women; however, they are comparable to the old women who live there because their walls enclose a lifetime of disappointments as well as the physical detritus of life. Like the old women, rooming houses are in decline, rocking away their remaining years.

(2) Hyperbole and Understatement

Two additional kinds of figurative language, *hyperbole* and *understatement*, also give poets opportunities to suggest meaning beyond the literal level of language.

Hyperbole is intentional exaggeration — saying more than is actually meant. In the poem "Oh, My love Is like a Red, Red Rose"[32], when the speaker says that he will love his lady until all the seas go dry, he is using hyperbole.

Understatement is the opposite — saying less than it meant. When the speaker in the poem "Fire and Ice"[16], weighing two equally grim alternatives for the end of the world, says that "for destruction ice / Is also great / And would suffice", he is using understatement. In both cases, poets expect their readers to understand that their words are not to be taken literally.

By using hyperbole and understatement, poets enhance the impact of their poems. For example, poets can use hyperbole to convey exaggerated anger or graphic images of horror — and to ridicule and satirize as well as to inflame and shock. With understatement, poets can convey the same kind of powerful emotions subtly, without artifice or embellishment, thereby leading readers to read more closely than they would otherwise do.

Examine the following poem by David Huddle for understatement.

Holes Commence Falling (1979)[33]

The lead & zinc company
owned the mineral rights
to the whole town anyway,
and after drilling holes
for 3 or 4 years,
they finally found the right
place and sunk a mine shaft.
We were proud
of all that digging,
even though nobody from
town got hired. They

were going to dig right
under New River and hook up
with the mine at Austinville.
Then people's wells
started drying up just like
somebody'd shut off a faucet,
and holes commenced falling,
big chunks of people's yards
would drop 5 or 6 feet,
houses would shift and crack.
Now and then the company'd
pay out a little money
in damages; they got a truck
to haul water and sell it
to the people whose wells
had dried up, but most
everybody agreed the
situation wasn't
serious.

Although "Holes Commence Falling[33]" relates a tragic sequence of events, the tone of the poem is matter-of-fact, and the language is understated. The speaker could have overdramatized the events, using inflated rhetoric to denounce big business and to predict disastrous events for the future. At the very least, he could have colored the facts with realistic emotions, assigning blame to the lead and zinc company with justifiable anger. Instead, the speaker is so restrained, so nonchalant, so passive that readers must supply the missing emotions themselves — realizing, for example, that when the speaker concludes "everybody agreed the / situation wasn't / serious? he means exactly the opposite.

(3) Metonymy and Synecdoche

Metonymy and synecdoche are two related figures of speech. **Metonymy** is the substitution of the name of one thing for the name of another thing that most readers associate with the first—for example, using *hired gun* to mean "paid assassin" or *suits* to mean "business executives." A specific kind of metonymy, called **synecdoche**, is the substitution of a part for the whole (for example, using *bread*—as in "Give us this day our daily bread"—to mean "food") or the whole for a part (for example, saying "You can take the boy out of Brooklyn, but you can't take Brooklyn [meaning its distinctive traits] out of the boy"). With metonymy and synecdoche, instead of describing something by saying it is like something else (as in simile) or by equating it with something else (as in metaphor), writers can characterize an object or concept by using a term that evokes it. The following poem illustrates the use of synecdoche.

To Lucasta Going to the Wars (1649)[34]

Tell me not, Sweet, I am unkind
  That from the nunnery
Of thy chaste breast and quiet mind,
  To war and arms I fly.

True, a new mistress now I chase,
  The first foe in the field;
And with a stronger faith embrace
  A sword, a horse, a shield.

Yet this inconstancy is such
  As you too shall adore;
I could not love thee, Dear, so much,
  Loved I not Honor more.

Here, Lovelace's use of synecdoche allows him to condense a number of complex ideas into a very few words. In line 3, when the speaker says that he is flying from his loved one's "chaste breast and quiet mind", he is using "breast" and "mind" to stand for all his loved one's physical and intellectual attributes. In line 8, when he says that he is embracing "A sword, a horse, a shield", he is using these three items to represent the trappings of war—and, thus, to represent war itself.

(4) Apostrophe

With **apostrophe**, a poem's speaker addresses an absent person or thing—for example, a historical or literary figure or even an inanimate object or an abstract concept. In the following poem, the speaker addresses Vincent Van Gogh.

On Passing thru Morgantown, Pa. (1984)[35]

i saw you

vincent van

gogh perched

on those pennsylvania

cornfields communing

amid secret black

bird societies. yes.

i'm sure that was

you exploding your

fantastic delirium

while in the

distance

red indian

hills beckoned.

Expecting her readers to be aware that Van Gogh is a nineteenth-century Dutch postimpressionist painter known for his mental instability as well as for his art, Sanchez is able to give added meaning to a phrase such as "fantastic delirium" as well as to the poem's visual images. Perhaps picturing his 1890 painting *Wheatfield with Crows,* the speaker sees Van Gogh perched like a black bird on a fence, and at the same time she also sees what he sees. Like Van Gogh, then, the speaker sees the Pennsylvania cornfields as both a natural landscape and and "exploding" work of art.

6. Sound

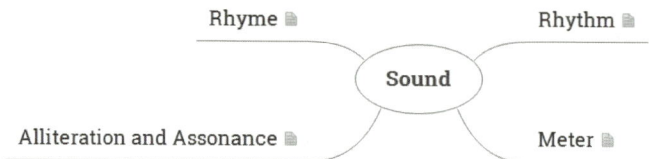

(1) Rhythm

Rhythm — the regular recurrence of sounds — is at the heart of all natural phenomena: the beating of a heart, the lapping of waves against the shore, the croaking of frogs on a summer's night, the whispering of wheat swaying in the wind. In fact, even mechanical phenomena, such as the movement of rush-hour traffic through a city's streets, have a kind of rhythm. Poetry, which explores these phenomena, often tries to reflect the same rhythms.

Effective public speakers frequently repeat key words and phrases to create rhythm. In his speech "I Have a Dream", for example, Martin Luther King Jr. repeats the phrase "I have a dream" to create a cadence that ties the central section of the speech together:

I say to you today, my friends, even though we face the difficulties of today and tomorrow, I still have a dream. It is a dream deeply rooted in the American dream. *I have a dream* that one day this nation will rise up and live out the true meaning of its creed: "We hold these truths to be self-evident, that all men are created equal." *I have a dream* that one day on the red hills of Georgia, the sons of former slaves and the sons of former slave owners will be able to sit down together at the table of brotherhood. *I have a dream* that one day even the state of Mississippi, a state sweltering with the heat of injustice, sweltering with the heat of oppression, will be transformed into an oasis of freedom and justice. *I have a dream* that my four little children will one day live in a nation where they will not be judged by the color of their skin but by the content of their character.

저는 오늘 저의 벗인 여러분께 이 순간의 고난과 좌절에도 불구하고 저에게는 여전히 꿈이 있다는 사실을 말씀 드립니다. 그 꿈은 미국의 건국이념에 깊이 뿌리박힌 꿈입니다. *저에게는 꿈이 있습니다.* 언젠가 이 나라가 떨쳐 일어나 진정한 의미의 국가 이념을 실천하리라는 꿈, 즉 모든 인간은 평등하게 태어났다는 진리를 우리 모두가 자명한 진실로 받아들이는 날이 오리라는 꿈입니다. *저에게는 꿈이 있습니다.* 조지아의 붉은 언덕 위에서 과거에 노예로 살았던 부모의 후손과 그 노예의 주인이 낳은 후손이 식탁에 함께 둘러앉아 형제애를 나누는 날이 언젠가 오리라는 꿈입니다. *저에게는 꿈이 있습니다.* 삭막한 사막으로 뒤덮인 채 불의와 억압의 열기에 신음하던 미시시피 주조차도 자유와 정의가 실현되는 오아시스로 탈바꿈되리라는 꿈입니다. *저에게는 꿈이 있습니다.* 저의 네 자식들이 피부색이 아니라 인격에 따라 평가 받는 나라에서 살게 되는 날이 언젠가 오리라는 꿈입니다.

Poets too create rhythm by using repeated words and phrases, as Gwendolyn Brooks does in the poem that follows.

Sadie and Maud (1945)[36]

Maud went to college.
Sadie stayed home.
Sadie scraped life
With a fine toothed comb.

She didn't leave a tangle in
Her comb found every strand.
Sadie was one of the livingest chicks
In all the land.

Sadie bore two babies
Under her maiden name.
Maud and Ma and Papa
Nearly died of shame.

When Sadie said her last so-long
Her girls struck out from home.
(Sadie left as heritage
Her fine-toothed comb.)

Maud, who went to college,

> Is a thin brown mouse.
> She is living all alone
> In this old house.

Much of the force of this poem comes from its balanced structure and regular rhyme and meter, underscored by the repeated words "Sadie" and "Maud," which shift the focus from one subject to the other and back again ("Maud went to college /Sadie stayed home"). The poem's singsong rhythm recalls the rhymes children recite when jumping rope. This evocation of care free childhood is ironically contrasted with the adult realities that both Sadie and Maud face as they grow up: Sadie stays at home and has two children out of wedlock; Maud goes to college and ends up "a thin brown mouse." The speaker implies that the alternatives Sadie and Maud represent are both undesirable. Although Sadie "scraped her desire to experience life. Maud, who graduated from college, shuts out life and cuts herself off from her roots.

Just as the repetition of words and phrases can create rhythm, so can the arrangement of words in a poem — and even the appearance of words on the printed page. How a poem looks is especially important in **open form poetry**, which dispenses with traditional patterns of verification. In the following excerpt from a poem by E.E. Cummings, for example, an unusual arrangement of words forces readers to slow down and then to speed up, creating a rhythm that emphasizes a key phrase — "The / Lily[37]":

> the moon is hiding
> in her hair.
> The
> lily
> of heaven
> full of all dreams,
> draws down.

Poetic rhythm — the repetition of stresses and pauses — is an essential element in poetry. Rhythm helps to establish a poem's mood, and, in combination with other poetic elements, it conveys the poet's emphasis and helps communicate the poem's meaning.

(2) Meter

Although rhythm can be affected by the regular repetition of words and phrases or by the arrangement of words into lines, poetic rhythm is largely created by **meter**, the recurrence of regular units of stressed and unstressed syllables. A **stress** (or accent) occurs when one syllable is emphasized more than another, unstressed, syllable. In a poem, even one-syllable words can be stressed to create a particular effect. For example, in Elizabeth Barrett Brownig's line "How do I love thee? let me count the ways", the metrical pattern that places stress on "love" creates one meaning; stressing "I" would create another.

The basic unit of meter is a **foot**—a group of syllables with a fixed pattern of stressed and unstressed syllables. The chart below illustrates the most common types of metrical feet in English and American verse.

Foot	Stress Pattern	Example
Iamb	˘ ´	Thĕy páce | iň sleék | chi vál | rĭc cér | taĭn tý (Adrienne Rich)
Trochee	´ ˘	Thóu, whĕn | thóu re | turń'st, wilĭ | telĺ mĕ. (John Donne)
Anapest	˘ ˘ ´	Wĭth ă héy, | ănd ă hó, | ănd ă héy | nŏnĭnó (William Shakespeare)
Dactyl	´ ˘ ˘	Coństăntlў | riśkiňg ăb | súrđitў (Lawrence Ferlinghetti)

Iambic and *anapestic* meters are called **rising meters** because they progress from unstressed to stressed syllables. *Trochaic* and *dactylic* meters are called **falling meters** because they progress from stressed to unstressed syllables.

A metric line of poetry is measured by the number of feet it contains.

Monometer	one foot	**Pentameter**	five feet
Dimeter	two feet	**Hexameter**	six feet
Trimeter	three feet	**Heptameter**	seven feet
Tetrameter	four feet	**Octameter**	eight feet

The name for a metrical pattern of a line of verse identifies the name of the foot used and the number of feet the line contains. For example, the most common foot in English poetry is the **iamb**, most often occurring in lines of three or five feet.

Eight hún | dred óf | the bráve (William Cowper)	Iambic trimeter
Ŏ, hów | mŭch móre | dŏth beáu | tў beáu | tĕous séem (William Shakespeare)	Iambic pentameter

Because iambic pentameter is so well suited to the rhythms of English speech, writers frequently use it in plays and poems. Shakespeare's play, for example, are written in unrhymed lines of iambic pentameter called **blank verse**.

A poet may use one kind of meter — iambic meter, for example — throughout a poem, but may vary line length to relieve monotony or to accommodate the poem's meaning or emphasis. In the following poem, the poet uses iambic lines of different lengths.

> ### I like to see it lap the Miles— (1891)[38]
>
> I like to see it lap the Miles—
> And lick the Valleys up—
> And stop to feed itself at Tanks—
> And then—prodigious, step
>
> Around a pile of mountains—
> And, supercilious, peer
> In Shanties—by the sides of Roads—
> And then a Quarry pare

> To fit its Ribs
> And crawl between
> Complaining all the while
> In horrid — hooting stanza —
> Then chase itself down Hill —
>
> And neigh like Boanerges —
> Then — punctual as a star,
> Stop — docile and omnipotent
> At its own stable door —

This poem is a single sentence that, except for some pauses, stretches unbroken from beginning to end. Iambic lines of varying lengths actually suggest the movements of the train that the poet describes. Lines of iambic tetrameter, such as the first, give readers a sense of the train's steady, rhythmic movement across a flat landscape, and shorter lines ("To fit its Ribs / And crawl between") suggest the train's slowing motion. Beginning with two iambic dimeter lines and progressing to iambic trimeter lines, the third stanza increases in speed just like the train that is racing downhill "In horrid — hooting stanza —".

(3) Alliteration and Assonance

Just as poetry depends on rhythm, it also depends on the sounds of individual words. One of the earliest, and perhaps the most primitive, methods of enhancing sound is **onomatopoeia**, which occurs when the sound of a word echoes its meaning, as it does in common words such as *bang, crash,* and *hiss.* Poets make broad application of this technique by using combinations of words that suggest a correspondence between sound and meaning, as Edgar Allan Poe does in these lines from his poem "The Bells"[39]:

> Hear the sledges with the bells —
> Silver bells!
> What a world of merriment their melody foretells!
> How they tinkle, tinkle, tinkle,

In the icy air of night!
While the stars that oversprinkle
All the heavens, seem to twinkle
With a crystalline delight;
Keeping time, time, time,
In a sort of Runic rhyme,

To the tintinnabulation that so musically wells
From the bells, bells, bells, bells,
Bells, bells, bells —
From the jingling and the tinkling of the bells.

Poe's primary objective in this poem is to re-create the sound of ringing bells.

Alliteration — the repetition of consonant sounds in consecutive or neighboring words, usually at the beginning of words — is another device used to enhance sound in a poem. Alfred, Lord Tennyson in "The Eagle[40]" makes use of alliteration.

The Eagle (1851)[40]

He clasps the crag with crooked hands;
Close to the sun in lonely lands,
Ringed with the azure world, he stands.

The wrinkled sea beneath him crawls:
He watches from his mountain walls,
And like a thunderbolt he falls.

Throughout the poem, *c, l,* and *w* sounds occur repeatedly. The poem is drawn together by the recurrence of these sounds and, as a result, it flows smoothly from beginning to end.

Sometimes **assonance** unifies an entire poem. In the following poem, assonance emphasizes the thematic connections among words and thus links the poem's ideas.

Delight in Disorder (1648)[41]

A sweet disorder in the dress
Kindles in clothes a wantonness;
A lawn about the shoulders thrown
Into a fine distraction;
An erring lace, which here and there
Enthrals the crimson stomacher;
A cuff neglectful, and thereby
Ribbons to flow confusedly;
A winning wave, deserving note,
In the tempestuous petticoat;
A careless shoe-string, in whose tie
I see a wild civility;—
Do more bewitch me, than when art
Is too precise in every part.

Repeated vowel sounds extend throughout this poem—for instance, "sh*ou*lders" and "thr*ow*n" in line 3; and "t*ie*", "w*i*ld", and "prec*i*se" in line 11, 12, and 14. Using **alliteration** as well as **assonance**, Herrick subtly links certain words—"*t*em*p*es*t*uous *p*e*t*ticoat", for example. By connecting these words, he calls attention to the pattern of imagery that helps to convey the poem's theme.

(4) Rhyme

In addition to alliteration and assonance, poets create sound patterns with **rhyme**—the use of matching sounds in two or more words: "tight" and "might"; "born" and "horn"; "sleep" and "deep". Rhyme can be classified according to the position of the rhyming syllables in a line of verse. The most common type of rhyme is **end rhyme**, which occurs at the end of a line:

> Tyger! Tyger! burning <u>bright</u>
> In the forests of the <u>night</u>
>   William Blake, "The Tyger"

Internal rhyme occurs within a line:

> The Sun came up upon the left,
> Out of the sea came he!
> And he shone bright and on the right
> Went down into the sea
>
> Samuel Taylor Coleridge, "The Rime of the Ancient Mariner"

Beginning rhyme occurs at the beginning of a line:

> Red river, red river,
> <u>Slow</u> flow heat is silent
> <u>No</u> will is still as a river
>
> T.S. Eliot, "Virginia"

The conventional way to describe a poem's rhyme scheme is to chart rhyming sounds that appear at that ends of lines. The sound that ends the first line is designated *a,* and all subsequent lines that end in that sound are also labeled *a.* The next sound to appear at the end of a line is designated *b,* and all other lines whose last sounds rhyme with it are also designated *b*— and so on through the alphabet. The rhyme scheme reinforces the poem's meaning and binds lines into structural units, connecting each stanza. Sometimes it reflects the central theme of the poem.

An obvious rhyme scheme can communicate meaning by connecting ideas that are not normally linked. Notice how Alexander Pope uses this technique in the following excerpt from *An Essay on Man:*

> Honour and shame from no condition rise;
> Act well your part, there all the honour lies.
> Fortune in men has some small difference made,
> One flaunts in rags, one flutters in brocade;
> The cobbler aproned, and the parson gowned,
> The friar hooded, and the monarch crowned,
> "What differ more (you cry) than crown and cowl?"
> I'll tell you, friend! a wise man and a fool.

This poem is written in **heroic couplets**, paired iambic pentameter lines with a rhyme scheme of *aa, bb, cc, dd,* and so on. In a heroic couplet, greater stress falls on the second line, usually on the last word. Coming at the end of the line, this word receives double emphasis: it is strengthened both because of its position in the line and because it is rhymed with the last word of the couplet's first line. In this excerpt, rhyme sometimes joins opposing ideas, thereby reinforcing a theme that runs through the passage: the contrast between the high and the low, the virtuous and the immoral. For example, "gowned" and "crowned" in lines 5 and 6 convey the opposite conditions of the parson and the monarch and exemplify the idea expressed in lines 3 and 4 that fortune, not virtue, determines one's station.

7. Form

The **form** of a literary work is its structure or shape, the way its elements fit together to form a whole; **poetic form** is the design of a poem described in terms of rhyme, meter, and stanzaic pattern.

Until the twentieth century, most poetry was written in **closed form** (sometimes called **fixed form**), characterized by regular patterns of meter, rhyme, line length, and stanzaic divisions. Poets tended to favor regular patterns. Many poets have experimented with imagery, figures of speech, allusion, and other techniques, stretching closed form to its limits.

(1) Closed Form

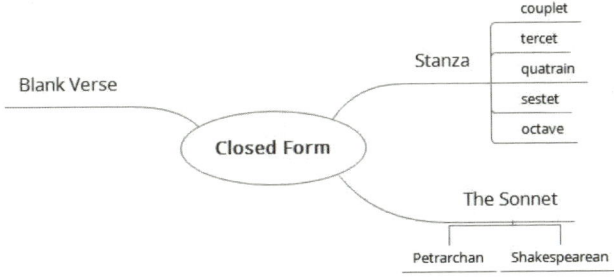

A **closed form** (or *fixed form*) poem looks symmetrical; it has an identifiable, repeated pattern, with lines of similar length arranged in groups of two, three, four, or more. A closed form poem also tends to rely on regular metrical patterns and rhyme schemes.

Sometimes a pattern (such as *blank verse*) simply determines the meter of poem's individual lines. At other times, the pattern extends to the level of the *stanza,* with lines arranged into groups (*couplets, quatrains,* and so on). At still other times, as in the case of traditional closed forms like sonnets, a poetic pattern gives shape to an entire poem.

Blank Verse

Blank verse is unrhymed poetry with each line written in a set pattern of five stressed and five unstressed syllables called **iambic pentameter.** Many passages from Shakespeare's plays, such as the following lines from Hamlet, are written in blank verse.

> To sleep! perchance to dream: — ay, there's the rub;
> For in that sleep of death what dreams may come,
> When we have shuffled off this mortal coil,
> Must give us pause: there's the respect
> That makes calamity of so long life

Stanza

A **stanza** is a group of two or more lines with the same metrical pattern — and often with a regular rhyme scheme as well — separated by blank space from other such groups of lines. Stanzas in poetry are like paragraphs in prose: they group related ideas into units.

A two-line stanza with rhyming lines of similar length and meter is called a **couplet**. The **heroic couplet**, first used by Chaucer and especially popular throughout the eighteenth century, consists of two rhymed lines of iambic pentameter, with a weak pause after the first line and a strong pause after the second. The following example, from Alexander Pope's *An Essay on Criticism*, is a heroic couplet.

> True ease in writing comes from art, not chance,
> As those move easiest who have learned to dance.

A three-line stanza with lines of similar length and a set rhyme scheme is called a **tercet**. Percy Bysshe Shelley's "Ode to the West Wind[5]" is built largely of tercets.

> O wild West Wind, thou breath of Autumn's being,
> Thou, from whose unseen presence the leaves dead
> Are driven, like ghosts from an enchanter fleeing,
>
> Yellow, and black, and pale, and hectic red,
> Pestilence-stricken multitudes: O thou,
> Who chariotest to their dark wintry bed

A four-line stanza with lines of similar length and a set rhyme scheme is called a **quatrain**. The quatrain, the most widely used and versatile unit in English and American poetry, is used by William Wordsworth in the following excerpt from his 1800 poem "She dwelt among the untrodden ways[42]."

> A violet by a mossy stone
>   Half hidden from the eye!
> —Fair as a star, when only one
>   Is shining in the sky.

Quatrains are frequently used by contemporary poets as well—for instance, in Theodore Roethke's "My Papa's Waltz[43]", Adrienne Rich's "Aunt Jennifer's Tigers[44]", and William Stafford's "Traveling through the Dark[45]".

The Sonnet

Perhaps the most familiar kind of traditional closed form poem written in English is the **sonnet**, a fourteen-line poem with a distinctive rhyme scheme and metrical pattern. The English or **Shakespearean sonnet**, which consists of fourteen lines divided into three quatrains and a concluding couplet, is written in iambic pentameter and follows the rhyme scheme *abab cdcd efef gg*. The **Petrarchan sonnet**, popularized in the fourteenth century by the Italian poet Francesco Petrarch, also consists of fourteen lines of iambic pentameter, but these lines are divided into an eight-line unit called an **octave** and a six-line unit (composed of two tercets) called a **sestet**. The rhyme scheme of the octave is *abba abba;* the rhyme scheme of the sestet is *cde cde.*

The conventional structures of these sonnet forms reflect the arrangement of ideas within the poem. In the shakespearean sonnet, the poet typically presents three "paragraphs" of related thoughts, introducing an idea in the first quatrain, developing it in the two remaining quatrains, and summing up in a succinct closing couplet. In the Petrarchan sonnet, the octave introduces a problem that is resolved in the sestet. (Many Shakespearean sonnets also have a problem-solution structure.) Some poets vary the traditional patterns somewhat to suit the poem's language or ideas. For example, they may depart from the pattern to side-step a forced rhyme or unnatural stress on a syllable, or they may shift from problem to solution in a place other than between octave and sestet.

The following Shakespeare's poem has the form of a traditional English sonnet.

When In Disgrace With Fortune And Men's Eyes (1609)[46]

When in disgrace with fortune and men's eyes,
I all alone beweep my outcast state,
And trouble deaf heaven with my bootless cries,
And look upon myself and curse my fate,
wishing me like to one more rich in hope,
Featured like him, like him with friends possessed,
Desiring this man's art, and that man's scope,
With what I most enjoy contented least;
Yet in these thoughts myself almost despising,
Haply I think on thee—and then my state,
Like to the lark at break of day arising
From sullen earth sings hymns at heaven's gate;
  For thy sweet love remembered such wealth brings,
  That then I scorn to change my state with kings.

This sonnet is written in iambic pentameter and has a conventional rhyme scheme: *abab* (eyes-state-cries-fate), *cdcd* (hope-possessed-scope-least), *efef* (despising-state-arising- gate), *gg* (brings-kings). In this poem, in which the speaker explains how thoughts of his loved one can rescue him from despair, each quatrain is unified by subject matter as well as by rhyme. In the first quatrain, the speaker presents his problem: he is down on his luck and out of favor with his peers, isolated in self-pity and cursing his fate. In the second quatrain, he develops this idea further: he is envious of others and dissatisfied with things that usually please him. In the third quatrain, the focus shifts. Although the first two quatrains develop a dependent clause ("When . . .") that introduces a problem, line 9 begins to present the resolution. In the third quatrain, the speaker explains how, in the midst of his despair and self-hatred, he thinks of his loved one, and his spirits soar. The closing couplet sums up the mood transformation the poem describes and explains its significance: when the speaker realizes the emotional riches his loved one gives him, he is no longer envious of others.

(2) Open Form

An **open form** poem may make occasional use of rhyme and meter but has no easily identifiable pattern or design: no conventional stanzaic divisions, no consistent metrical pattern or line length, no repeated rhyme scheme. Still, open form poetry is not necessarily shapeless, untidy, or randomly ordered. All poems have form, and the form of a poem may be determined by factors such as repeated sounds, the appearance of words on the printed page, or pauses in natural speech as well as by a conventional metrical pattern or rhyme scheme.

Open form poetry invites readers to participate in the creative process, to discover the relationship between form and meaning. Some modern poets believe that only open form offers them freedom to express their ideas or that the subject matter or mood of their poetry demands a relaxed, experimental approach to form.

Without a predetermined pattern, however, poets must create forms that suit their needs, and they must continue to shape and reshape the look of the poem on the page as they revise its words. Thus, open form is a challenge, but it is also a way for poets to experiment with fresh arrangements of words and new juxtapositions of ideas.

For some poets, such as Carl Sandburg, open form provides an opportunity to create prose poems, and for other poets like E.E. Cummings[47], it allows an extreme example of open form, which looks almost as if it has spilled out of a box of words.

8. Symbol, Allegory, Allusion

(1) Symbol

A **symbol** is an idea or image that suggests something else — but not in the simple way that a dollar sign stands for money or a flag represents a country. A symbol is an image that transcends its literal, or denotative, meaning in a complex way. For instance, if someone gives a rose to a loved one, it could simply be a sign of love. But in the poem "The Sick Rose[48]", the rose has a range of contradictory and complementary meanings. For what does the rose stand? Beauty? Perfection? Passion? Something else? As this poem illustrates, the distinctive trait of a symbol is that its meaning cannot easily be pinned down or defined.

Such ambiguity can be frustrating, but it is precisely this characteristic of a symbol that enables it to enrich a poem by giving it additional layers of meaning.

Symbols that appear in poetic works can be conventional or universal. **Conventional symbols** are those recognized by people who share certain cultural and social assumptions. For example, national flags evoke a general and agreed-upon response in most people of a particular country and — for better or for worse — American children have for years perceived the golden arches of McDonald's as a symbol of food and fun. **Universal symbols** are those likely to be recognized by people regardless of their culture. The psychologist Carl Jung formulated a theory of **archetypes,** which held that certain images or ideas reside in the subconscious of all people. According to Jung, archetypal symbols include water, symbolizing rebirth: spring, symbolizing growth; and winter, symbolizing death.

How do we know when an idea or image in a poem is a symbol? At what point do you decide that a particular object or idea goes beyond the literal level and takes on symbolic significance? When is a rose more than a rose or a cross more than a cross? Frequently you can recognize a symbol by its prominence or repetition.

It is not enough, however, to identify an image or idea that seems to suggest something else. Your decision that a particular item has symbolic significance must be supported by the details of the poem and make sense in light of the ideas the poem develops. In the following poem, the symbolic significance of the volcano helps readers to understand the poem's central theme. In Emily Dickinson's "Volcanoes be in Sicily[49]", the symbolic significance of the volcano helps readers to understand the poem's central theme.

Volcanoes be in Sicily (1914)[49]

Volcanoes be in Sicily
And South America
I judge from my Geography -
Volcanos nearer here
A Lava step at any time
Am I inclined to climb -
A Crater I may contemplate
Vesuvius at Home.

This poem opens with a statement of fact: volcanoes are located in Sicily and South America. In lines 3 and 4, however, the speaker makes the improbable observation that volcanoes are located near where she is at the moment. Readers familiar with Dickinson know that her poems are highly autobiographical and that she lived in Massachusetts, where there are no volcanoes. This information leads readers to suspect that they should not take the speaker's observation literally and that in the context of the poem volcanoes may have symbolic significance. But what do volcanoes suggest here?

On the one hand, volcanoes represent the awesome creative power of nature; on the other hand, they suggest its destructiveness. The speaker's contemplation

Vesuvius — the volcano that buried the ancient Roman city of Pompeii in A.D. 79 — is therefore filled with contradictory associations. Because Dickinson was a recluse, volcanoes — active, destructive, unpredictable, and dangerous — may be seen as symbolic of everything she fears in the outside world — and, perhaps, within herself. Volcanoes may even suggest her own creative power, which, like a volcano, is something to be feared as well as contemplated. She has a voyeur's attraction to danger and power, but she is also afraid of them. For this reason, she (and her speaker) may feel safer contemplating Vesuvius at home — not traveling to exotic lands but simply reading a geography book.

(2) Allegory

Allegory is a form of narrative that conveys a message or doctrine by using people, places, or things to stand for abstract ideas. **Allegorical figures**, each with a strict equivalent, form an allegorical framework, a set of ideas that conveys the allegory's message or lesson. Thus, allegory takes place on two levels: a **literal level** that tells a story and a **figurative level** on which the allegorical figures in the story stand for ideas, concepts, and other qualities.

Like symbols, allegorical figures suggest other things. But unlike symbols, which have a range of possible meanings, allegorical figures can always be assigned specific meanings. (Because writers use allegory to instruct, they gain nothing by hiding its significance.) Thus, symbols open up possibilities for interpretation, whereas allegories tend to restrict possibilities.

Quite often an allegory involves a journey or an adventure. Within an allegory, everything can have meaning: the road on which the characters walk, the people they encounter, or a phrase that one of them repeats throughout the journey. Once you understand the allegorical framework, your main task is to see how the various elements fit within this system. Some allegorical poems can be relatively straightforward, but others can be so complicated that it takes a great deal of efforts to unlock their meaning. In Christina Rossetii's "Uphill[50]", a journey is central to the allegory.

Uphill (1861)[50]

Does the road wind up-hill all the way?
   Yes, to the very end.
Will the day's journey take the whole long day?
   From morn to night, my friend.

But is there for the night a resting-place?
   A roof for when the slow dark hours begin.
May not the darkness hide it from my face?
   You cannot miss that inn.

Shall I meet other wayfarers at night?
   Those who have gone before.
Then must I knock, or call when just in sight?
   They will not keep you standing at that door.

Shall I find comfort, travel-sore and weak?
   Of labour you shall find the sum.
Will there be beds for me and all who seek?
   Yea, beds for all who come.

This poem uses a question-and-answer structure to describe a journey along an uphill road. Like the one described in John Bunyan's seventeenth-century allegory *The Pilgrim's Progress,* this is a spiritual journey, one that suggests the challenges a person faces throughout life. The day-and-night duration of the journey stands for life and death, and the inn at the end of the road stands for the grave, the final resting place.

(3) Allusion

An **allusion** is a brief reference to a person, place, or event (fictional or actual) that readers are expected to recognize. Like symbols and allegories, allusions enrich a work by introducing associations from another context.

When poets use allusions, they assume that they and their readers have a common body of knowledge. If, when reading a poem, you come across a reference with which you are not familiar, take the time to look it up in a dictionary or an encyclopedia. As you have probably realized by now, **your understanding of a poem** may depend on your ability to interpret an unfamiliar reference.

Allusions can come from any source: history, the arts, other works of literature, the Bible, current events, or even the personal life of the poet. The poem "Dreams of Suicide[51]" by William Meredith uses allusions to prominent literary figures, as well as to myth, to develop its theme.

Dreams of Suicide (1980)[51]

I

I reach for the awkward shotgun not to disarm
You, but to feel the metal horn,
Furred with the downy membrane of dream.
More surely than the unicorn
You are the mythical beast.

II

Or I am sniffing an oven. On all fours
I am imitating a totemic animal
but she is not my totem or the totem
of my people, this is not my magic oven.

III

If I hold you tight by the ankles,
still you fly upward from the iron railing.
Your father made these wings,
after he made his own, and now from beyond
he tells you *fly down,* in the voice
my own father might say *walk, boy.*

This poem is dedicated to the memory of three writers who committed suicide. In each stanza, the speaker envisions in a dream the death of one of the writers.

In the first stanza, he dreams of Ernest Hemmingway, who killed himself with a shotgun. In the second stanza, the speaker dreams of Sylvia Plath, who asphyxiated herself in a gas oven. In the third stanza, the speaker dreams of John Berryman, who leaped to his death. In this poem, the speaker uses allusions to make a point about the difficult lives of writers — and, perhaps, to convey his own empathy for those who could not survive the struggle to reconcile art and life.

9. Themes

A poem can be about anything, from the mysteries of the universe to poetry itself. Although no subject is really inappropriate for poetic treatment, certain conventional subjects — family, nature, love, war, death, the folly of human desires, and the inevitability of growing old — recur frequently.

A poem's *theme,* however, is more than its *subject.* In general terms, theme refers to the ideas that the poet explores, the concerns that the poem examines. More specifically, a poem's **theme** is its main point or idea. Poems "about death", for example, may examine the difficulty of facing one's own mortality, eulogize a friend, assert the need for the acceptance of life's cycles, or cry out against death's inevitability. Or, such poems may explore the **carpe diem theme** — the belief that life is brief, so we must seize the day.

In order to understand the theme of a poem, readers should consider its form, voice, language, images, allusions, sound — all of its individual elements. Together, these elements communicate the ideas that are important in the poem. Keep in mind, however, that a poem may not mean the same thing to every reader. Different readers will bring different backgrounds, attitudes, and experiences to a poem and will therefore see things in various ways. And, poets may approach the same subject in drastically different ways, emphasizing different elements as they view the subject matter from their own unique perspectives. Ultimately, there are as many different themes, and ways to approach these themes, as there are writers (and readers) of poetry.

(1) Poems about Parents

Although a poet's individual experience may be vastly different from the experiences of his or her readers, certain ideas seem universal in poems about **parents.** On the one hand, such poems can express positive sentiments: love, joy, wistfulness, nostalgia, and gratitude for childhood's happy memories and unconditional love. On the other hand, they may express negative emotions: anger, frustration, resentment, regret, and emotional distance. When they write about parents, poets may be curious or apathetic, remorseful or grateful; they may idealize parents or be puzzled by them. Regardless of the particulars of the poem's specific theme, virtually all poems about parents address one general concept: the influence of a parent over his or her child. Although the poems about parents all deal with issues related to parents and family, their styles, voices, and focuses are very different as seen in the following poems.

"My Papa's Waltz" by Theodore Roethke (1908~1963)[43]

"The courage that my mother had" by Edna St. Vincent Millay (1892~1950)[52]

"Do not go gentle into that good night" by Dylan Thomas (1914~1953)[53]

(2) Poems about Nature

Some forms of poetry are dedicated solely to the subject of **nature.** For example, a **pastoral** is a literary form that deals nostalgically with a simple rural life. In the early Greek and Roman pastorals, the shepherd's life was idealized. Thus, the patoral tradition celebrates simple times and the beauty of the rural life. Similarly, and **idyll,** a short work in verse or prose (or a painting or a piece of music), depicts simple pastoral or rural scenes, often in idealized terms.

Certain literary movements also focused on the subject of nature. For example, the **Romantic** poets found in nature a mirror for their own beliefs and sense of identity. They believed that only the sweeping grandeur of nature could reflect the comparable grandeur of humanity as well as a sense of the infinite and the transcendental. Later, the American **Transcendentalists,** including Ralph Waldo Emerson and Henry David Thoreau, examined the relationships between philosophy, religion, and nature. In *walden,* for example, Thoreau wrote about the pleasures and rewards of withdrawing from mainstream life in order to live simply in the woods. While poems about nature deal with the same general subject, their approaches, and their focuses, can differ greatly as in the poems below.

"Summer" by Christina Rossetti (1830~1894)[54]

"The Windhover" by Gerard Manley Hopkins (1844~1889)[55]

(3) Poems about Love

Poetry has long been regarded as a romantic genre. During the Renaissance, a more personal style love poems developed, and poems became vehicles for demonstrating a poet's amorous feelings. Often cloaked in metaphor, simile, or other figures of speech, poems expressed feelings of love in numerous forms. Examples of Renaissance love poems include many of Shakespeare's sonnets, as well as Christopher marlowe's *The Passionate Shepherd to His Love*, a poem in the pastoral tradition, which was answered by Sir Walter Raleigh's *The Nymph's Reply to the Shepherd*.

Although the Renaissance marked a high point in the development of the love poem, love has remained a constant theme in poetry regardless of the literary fads and trends of the day. In fact, in every literary movement — from the seventeenth-century metaphysical poets through today's slam poetry — one can find love poems written in the movement's characteristic style and form. In the following love poems, the poets address the subject of love in their own styles and voices.

"Meeting at Night" by Robert Browning (1812~1889)[56]

"Parting at Morning" by Robert Browning (1812~1889)[57]

"How Do I Love Thee?" by Elizabeth Barrett Browning (1806~1861)[58]

Chapter 02 Poems To Read

01 Summary of Poems To Read

1. "My Arkansas" by Maya Angelou (1928~2014)
2. "Richard Cory" by Edwin Arlington Robinson (1869~1935)
3. "Ballad of Birmingham" by Dudley Randall (1914~2000)
4. "To an Athlete Dying Young" by A.E. Houseman (1859~1936)
5. "Ode to the West Wind" by Percy Bysshe Shelly (1792~1822)
6. "Aubade" by Philips Larkin (1922~1985)
7. "The Names" by Billy Collins (1941~)
8. "Go, lovely rose" by Edmund Waller (1606~1687)
9. "The Passionate Shepherd to His Love" by Christopher Marlowe (1564~1593)
10. "My Last Duchess" by Robert Browning (1812~1889)
11. "Ulysses" by Alfred, Lord Tennyson (1809~1892)
12. "I'm nobody! Who are you?" by Emily Dickinson (1830~1886)
13. "The Chimney Sweeper" by William Blake (1757~1827)
14. "Red Wheelbarrow" by William Carlos Williams (1883~1963)
15. "Negro" by Langston Hughes (1902~1967)
16. "Fire and Ice" by Robert Frost (1874~1963)
17. "The Man He Killed" by Thomas Hardy (1840~1928)
18. "Porphyria's Lover" by Robert Browning (1812~1889)
19. "Ozymandias" by Percy Bysshe Shelley (1792~1822)
20. "War Is Kind" by Stephen Crane (1871~1900)
21. "When I Heard the Learn'd Astronomer" by Walt Whitman (1819~1892)
22. "The City Planners" by Margaret Atwood (1939~)

23. "Amoretti Lxxv: One day I wrote her name upon the strand" by Edmund Spenser (1552~1599)

24. "Stopping by Woods on a Snowy Evening" by Robert Frost (1874~1963)

25. "In a Station of the Metro" by Ezra Pound (1885~1972)

26. "Some Good Things to Be Said for the Iron Age" by Gary Snyder(1930~)

27. "Shall I compare thee to a summer's day? (Sonnet 18)" by William Shakespeare (1564~1616)

28. "I wandered lonely as a cloud[Daffodils]" by William Wordsworth (1770~1850)

29. "Harlem[Dream deferred]" by Langston Hughes (1902~1967)

30. "Constantly Risking Absurdity" by Lawrence Ferlinghetti (1919~)

31. "Rooming houses are old women" by Audre Lorde (1934~1992)

32. "Oh, My love Is like a Red, Red Rose" by Robert Burns (1759~1796)

33. "Holes Commence Falling" by David Huddle (1942~)

34. "To Lucasta Going to the Wars" by Richard Lovelace (1618~1658)

35. "On Passing thru Morgantown, Pa." by Sonia Sanchez (1934~)

36. "Sadie And Maud" by Gwendolyn Brooks (1917~2000)

37. "The Moon Is Hiding In" by Edward Estlin Cummings (1894~1962)

38. "I Like To See It Lap The Miles" by Emily Dickinson (1830~1886)

39. "The Bells" by Edgar Allan Poe (1809~1849)

40. "The Eagle" By Alfred, Lord Tennyson (1809~1892)

41. "Delight In Disorder" by Robert Herrick (1591~1674)

42. "She Dwelt Among The Untrodden Ways" by William Wordsworth (1770~1850)

43. "My Papa's Waltz"by Theodore Roethke (1908~1963)

44. "Aunt Jennifer's Tigers" by Adrienne Rich (1929~2012)

45. "Traveling Through The Dark" by William Stafford (1914~1993)

46. "When In Disgrace With Fortune And Men's Eyes (Sonnet 29)" by William Shakespeare (1564~1616)

47. "the sky was can dy" by Edward Estlin Cummings (1894~1962)

48. "The Sick Rose" by William Blake (1757~1827)

49. "Volcanoes be in Sicily" by Emily Dickinson (1830~1886)
50. "Uphill" by Christina Rossetii (1830~1894)
51. "Dreams of Suicide" by William Meredith (1919~2007)
52. "The courage that my mother had" by Edna St. Vincent Millay (1892~1950)
53. "Do not go gentle into that good night" by Dylan Thomas (1914~1953)
54. "Summer" by Christina Rossetti (1830~1894)
55. "The Windhover" by Gerard Manley Hopkins (1844~1889)
56. "Meeting at Night" by Robert Browning (1812~1889)
57. "Parting at Morning" by Robert Browning (1812~1889)
58. "How Do I Love Thee?" by Elizabeth Barrett Browning (1806~1861)

02   Poems To Read

1. "My Arkansas" by Maya Angelou (1928~2014)

There is a deep brooding

In Arkansas.

Old crimes like moss pend

From poplar trees.

The sullen earth

Is too much

Red for comfort.

Sunrise seems to hesitate

And in that second

Lose its

Incandescent aim, and

Dusk no more shadows

Than the noon.

The past is brighter yet

Old hates and

Ante-bellum lace, are rent

But not discarded

Today is yet to come

In Arkansas.

It writhes. It writhes in awful

Waves of brooding

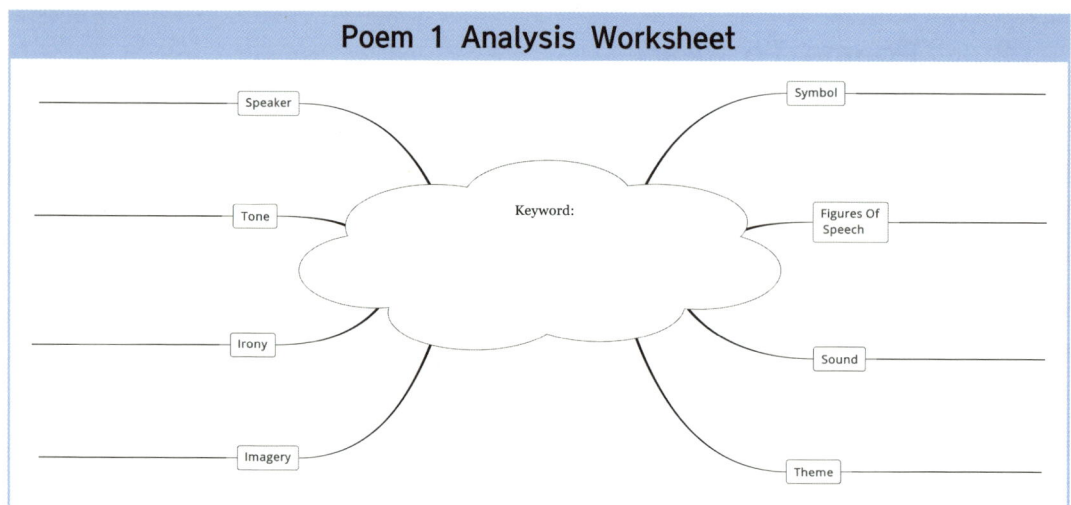

2. "Richard Cory" by Edwin Arlington Robinson (1869~1935)

Whenever Richard Cory went down town,
We people on the pavement looked at him:
He was a gentleman from sole to crown,
Clean favored, and imperially slim.

And he was always quietly arrayed,
And he was always human when he talked;
But still he fluttered pulses when he said,
"Good-morning," and he glittered when he walked.

And he was rich — yes, richer than a king —
And admirably schooled in every grace:
In fine, we thought that he was everything
To make us wish that we were in his place.

So on we worked, and waited for the light,
And went without the meat, and cursed the bread;
And Richard Cory, one calm summer night,
Went home and put a bullet through his head.

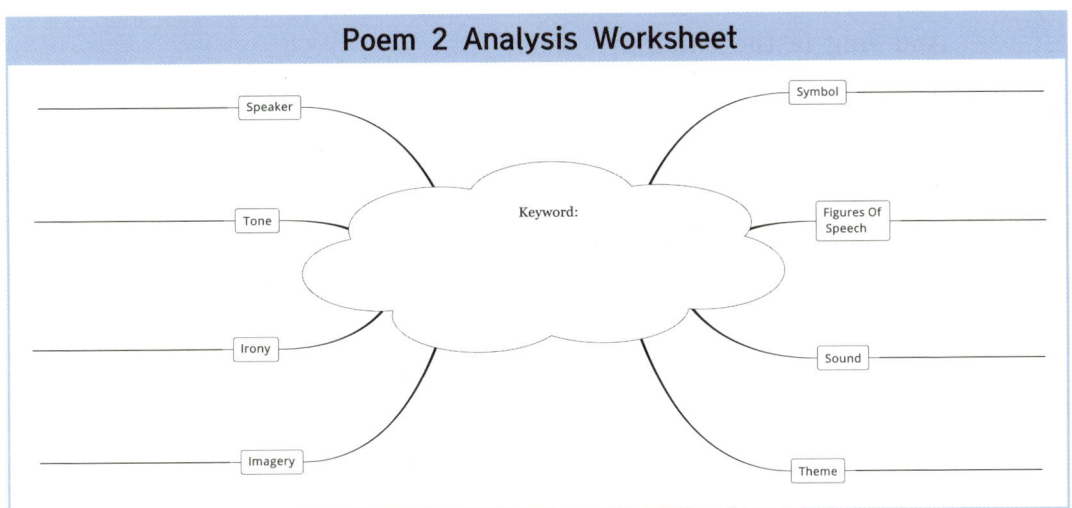

3. "Ballad of Birmingham" by Dudley Randall (1914~2000)

(On the bombing of a church in Birmingham, Alabama, 1963)

"Mother dear, may I go downtown
Instead of out to play,
And march the streets of Birmingham
In a Freedom March today?"

"No, baby, no, you may not go,
For the dogs are fierce and wild,
And clubs and hoses, guns and jails
Aren't good for a little child."

"But, mother, I won't be alone.
Other children will go with me,
And march the streets of Birmingham
To make our country free."

"No, baby, no, you may not go,
For I fear those guns will fire.
But you may go to church instead
And sing in the children's choir."

She has combed and brushed her night-dark hair,
And bathed rose petal sweet,
And drawn white gloves on her small brown hands,
And white shoes on her feet.

The mother smiled to know her child
Was in the sacred place,
But that smile was the last smile
To come upon her face.

For when she heard the explosion,
Her eyes grew wet and wild.
She raced through the streets of Birmingham
Calling for her child.

She clawed through bits of glass and brick,
Then lifted out a shoe.
"O, here's the shoe my baby wore,
But, baby, where are you?"

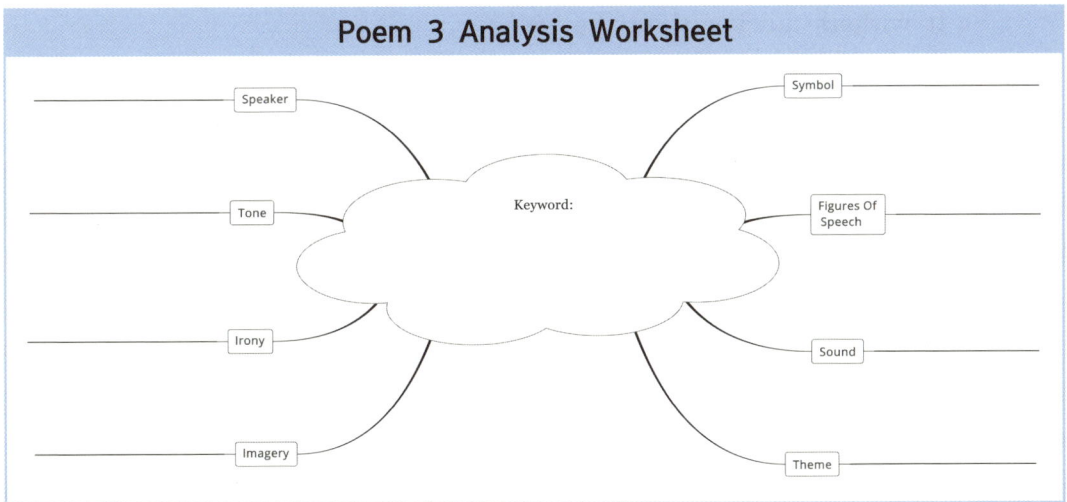

4. "To an Athlete Dying Young" by A.E. Houseman (1859~1936)

The time you won your town the race
We chaired you through the market-place;
Man and boy stood cheering by,
And home we brought you shoulder-high.

Today, the road all runners come,
Shoulder-high we bring you home,
And set you at your threshold down,
Townsman of a stiller town.

Smart lad, to slip betimes away
From fields where glory does not stay,
And early though the laurel grows
It withers quicker than the rose.

Eyes the shady night has shut
Cannot see the record cut,
And silence sounds no worse than cheers
After earth has stopped the ears.

Now you will not swell the rout
Of lads that wore their honours out,
Runners whom renown outran
And the name died before the man.

So set, before its echoes fade,
The fleet foot on the sill of shade,
And hold to the low lintel up
The still-defended challenge-cup.

And round that early-laurelled head
Will flock to gaze the strengthless dead,
And find unwithered on its curls
The garland briefer than a girl's.

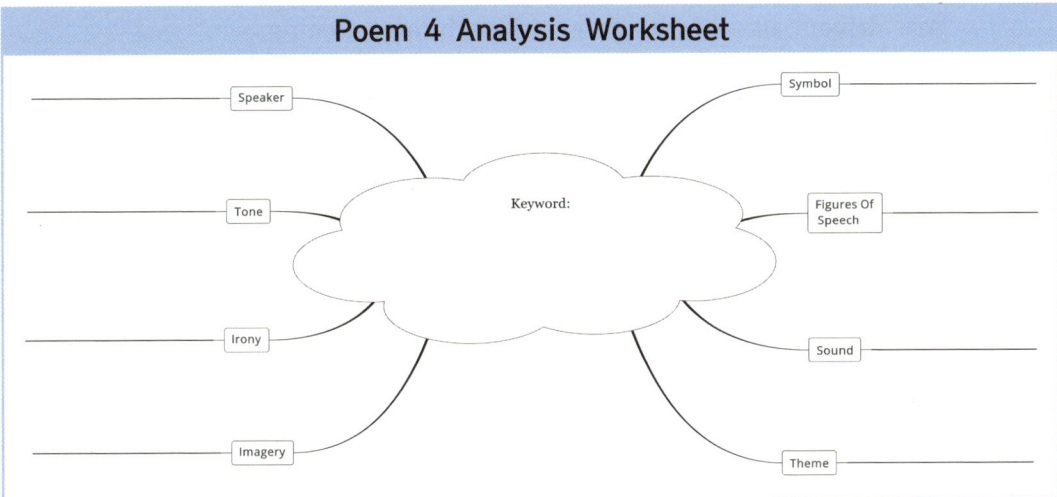

5. "Ode to the West Wind" by Percy Bysshe Shelly (1792~1822)

I

O wild West Wind, thou breath of Autumn's being,
Thou, from whose unseen presence the leaves dead
Are driven, like ghosts from an enchanter fleeing,

Yellow, and black, and pale, and hectic red,
Pestilence-stricken multitudes: O thou,
Who chariotest to their dark wintry bed

The wingèd seeds, where they lie cold and low,
Each like a corpse within its grave, until
Thine azure sister of the Spring shall blow

Her clarion o'er the dreaming earth, and fill
(Driving sweet buds like flocks to feed in air)
With living hues and odours plain and hill:

Wild Spirit, which art moving everywhere;
Destroyer and Preserver; hear, O hear!

IV

If I were a dead leaf thou mightest bear;
If I were a swift cloud to fly with thee;
A wave to pant beneath thy power, and share

The impulse of thy strength, only less free
Than thou, O Uncontrollable! If even
I were as in my boyhood, and could be

The comrade of thy wanderings over Heaven,
As then, when to outstrip thy skiey speed
Scarce seemed a vision; I would ne'er have striven

As thus with thee in prayer in my sore need.
Oh! lift me as a wave, a leaf, a cloud!
I fall upon the thorns of life! I bleed!

A heavy weight of hours has chained and bowed
One too like thee: tameless, and swift, and proud.

V

Make me thy lyre, even as the forest is:
What if my leaves are falling like its own!
The tumult of thy mighty harmonies
Will take from both a deep, autumnal tone,
Sweet though in sadness. Be thou, Spirit fierce,
My spirit! Be thou me, impetuous one!

Drive my dead thoughts over the universe
Like withered leaves to quicken a new birth!
And, by the incantation of this verse,

Scatter, as from an unextinguished hearth
Ashes and sparks, my words among mankind!
Be through my lips to unawakened Earth

The trumpet of a prophecy! O Wind,
If Winter comes, can Spring be far behind?

6. "Aubade" by Philips Larkin (1922~1985)

I work all day, and get half-drunk at night.
Waking at four to soundless dark, I stare.
In time the curtain-edges will grow light.
Till then I see what's really always there:
Unresting death, a whole day nearer now,
Making all thought impossible but how
And where and when I shall myself die.
Arid interrogation: yet the dread
Of dying, and being dead,
Flashes afresh to hold and horrify.

The mind blanks at the glare. Not in remorse
—The good not done, the love not given, time
Torn off unused—nor wretchedly because
An only life can take so long to climb
Clear of its wrong beginnings, and may never;
But at the total emptiness for ever,
The sure extinction that we travel to
And shall be lost in always. Not to be here,
Not to be anywhere,
And soon; nothing more terrible, nothing more true.

This is a special way of being afraid
No trick dispels. Religion used to try,
That vast moth-eaten musical brocade
Created to pretend we never die,
And specious stuff that says No rational being
Can fear a thing it will not feel, not seeing
That this is what we fear—no sight, no sound,

No touch or taste or smell, nothing to think with,
Nothing to love or link with,
The anaesthetic from which none come round.

And so it stays just on the edge of vision,
A small unfocused blur, a standing chill
That slows each impulse down to indecision.
Most things may never happen: this one will,
And realisation of it rages out
In furnace-fear when we are caught without
People or drink. Courage is no good:
It means not scaring others. Being brave
Lets no one off the grave.
Death is no different whined at than withstood.

Slowly light strengthens, and the room takes shape.
It stands plain as a wardrobe, what we know,
Have always known, know that we can't escape,
Yet can't accept. One side will have to go.
Meanwhile telephones crouch, getting ready to ring
In locked-up offices, and all the uncaring
Intricate rented world begins to rouse.
The sky is white as clay, with no sun.
Work has to be done.
Postmen like doctors go from house to house.

7. "The Names" by Billy Collins (1941~)

Yesterday, I lay awake in the palm of the night.

A soft rain stole in, unhelped by any breeze,

And when I saw the silver glaze on the windows,

I started with A, with Ackerman, as it happened,

Then Baxter and Calabro,

Davis and Eberling, names falling into place

As droplets fell through the dark.

Names printed on the ceiling of the night.

Names slipping around a watery bend.

Twenty-six willows on the banks of a stream.

In the morning, I walked out barefoot

Among thousands of flowers

Heavy with dew like the eyes of tears,

And each had a name —

Fiori inscribed on a yellow petal

Then Gonzalez and Han, Ishikawa and Jenkins.

Names written in the air

And stitched into the cloth of the day.

A name under a photograph taped to a mailbox.

Monogram on a torn shirt,

I see you spelled out on storefront windows

And on the bright unfurled awnings of this city.

I say the syllables as I turn a corner —

Kelly and Lee,

Medina, Nardella, and O'Connor.

When I peer into the woods,

I see a thick tangle where letters are hidden

As in a puzzle concocted for children.

Parker and Quigley in the twigs of an ash,

Rizzo, Schubert, Torres, and Upton,
Secrets in the boughs of an ancient maple.
Names written in the pale sky.
Names rising in the updraft amid buildings.
Names silent in stone
Or cried out behind a door.
Names blown over the earth and out to sea.
In the evening—weakening light, the last swallows.
A boy on a lake lifts his oars.
A woman by a window puts a match to a candle,
And the names are outlined on the rose clouds—
Vanacore and Wallace,
(let X stand, if it can, for the ones unfound)
Then Young and Ziminsky, the final jolt of Z.
Names etched on the head of a pin.
One name spanning a bridge, another undergoing a tunnel.
A blue name needled into the skin.
Names of citizens, workers, mothers and fathers,
The bright-eyed daughter, the quick son.
Alphabet of names in a green field.
Names in the small tracks of birds.
Names lifted from a hat
Or balanced on the tip of the tongue.
Names wheeled into the dim warehouse of memory.
So many names, there is barely room on the walls of the heart.

8. "Go, lovely rose" by Edmund Waller (1606~1687)

Go, lovely rose!
Tell her that wastes her time and me
That now she knows,
When I resemble her to thee,
How sweet and fair she seems to be.

Tell her that's young,
And shuns to have her graces spied,
That hadst thou sprung
In deserts, where no men abide,
Thou must have uncommended died.

Small is the worth
Of beauty from the light retired;
Bid her come forth,
Suffer herself to be desired,
And not blush so to be admired.

Then die! that she
The common fate of all things rare
May read in thee;
How small a part of time they share
That are so wondrous sweet and fair!

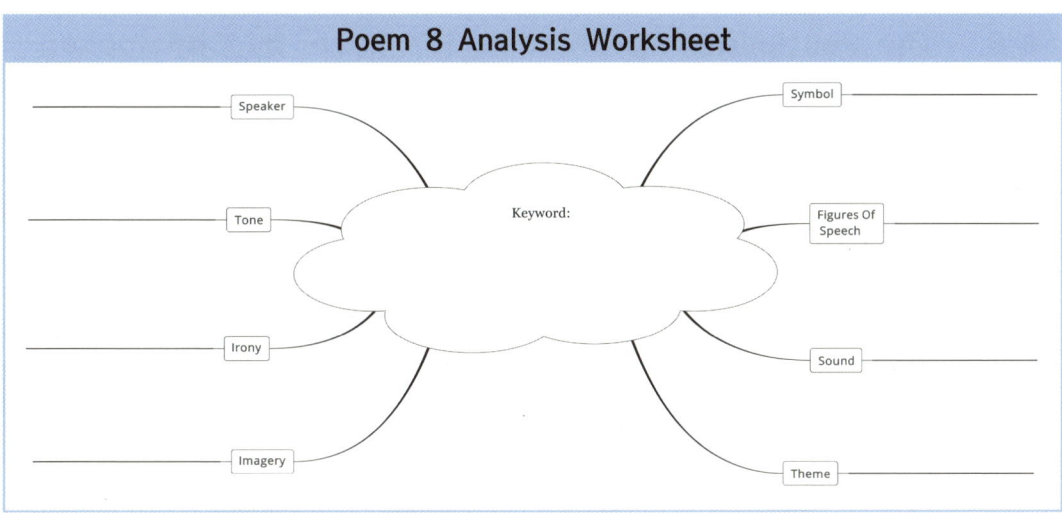

9. "The Passionate Shepherd to His Love" by Christopher Marlowe (1564~1593)

Come live with me and be my love,
And we will all the pleasures prove
That valleys, groves, hills, and fields,
Woods, or steepy mountain yields.

And we will sit upon the rocks,
Seeing the shepherds feed their flocks,
By shallow rivers to whose falls
Melodious birds sing madrigals.

And I will make thee beds of roses
And a thousand fragrant posies,
A cap of flowers, and a kirtle
Embroidered all with leaves of myrtle;

A gown made of the finest wool
Which from our pretty lambs we pull;
Fair lined slippers for the cold,
With buckles of the purest gold;

A belt of straw and ivy buds,
With coral clasps and amber studs:
And if these pleasures may thee move,
Come live with me, and be my love.

10. "My Last Duchess" by Robert Browning (1812~1889)

That's my last Duchess painted on the wall,
Looking as if she were alive. I call
That piece a wonder, now: Fra Pandolf's hands
Worked busily a day, and there she stands.
Will't please you sit and look at her? I said
"Fra Pandolf" by design, for never read
Strangers like you that pictured countenance,
The depth and passion of its earnest glance,
But to myself they turned (since none puts by
The curtain I have drawn for you, but I)
And seemed as they would ask me, if they durst,
How such a glance came there; so, not the first
Are you to turn and ask thus. Sir, 'twas not
Her husband's presence only, called that spot
Of joy into the Duchess' cheek: perhaps
Fra Pandolf chanced to say "Her mantle laps
Over my lady's wrist too much," or "Paint
Must never hope to reproduce the faint
Half-flush that dies along her throat:" such stuff
Was courtesy, she thought, and cause enough
For calling up that spot of joy. She had
A heart—how shall I say?—too soon made glad,
Too easily impressed; she liked whate'er
She looked on, and her looks went everywhere.
Sir, 'twas all one! My favour at her breast,
The dropping of the daylight in the West,
The bough of cherries some officious fool
Broke in the orchard for her, the white mule
She rode with round the terrace—all and each

Would draw from her alike the approving speech,
Or blush, at least. She thanked men,—good! but thanked
Somehow—I know not how—as if she ranked
My gift of a nine-hundred-years-old name
With anybody's gift. Who'd stoop to blame
This sort of trifling? Even had you skill
In speech—(which I have not)—to make your will
Quite clear to such an one, and say, "Just this
Or that in you disgusts me; here you miss,
Or there exceed the mark"—and if she let
Herself be lessoned so, nor plainly set
Her wits to yours, forsooth, and made excuse,
—E'en then would be some stooping; and I choose
Never to stoop. Oh sir, she smiled, no doubt,
Whene'er I passed her; but who passed without
Much the same smile? This grew; I gave commands;
Then all smiles stopped together. There she stands
As if alive. Will't please you rise? We'll meet
The company below, then. I repeat,
The Count your master's known munificence
Is ample warrant that no just pretence
Of mine for dowry will be disallowed;
Though his fair daughter's self, as I avowed
At starting, is my object. Nay, we'll go
Together down, sir. Notice Neptune, though,
Taming a sea-horse, thought a rarity,
Which Claus of Innsbruck cast in bronze for me!

11. "Ulysses" by Alfred, Lord Tennyson (1809~1892)

It little profits that an idle king,
By this still hearth, among these barren crags,
Match'd with an aged wife, I mete and dole
Unequal laws unto a savage race,
That hoard, and sleep, and feed, and know not me.
I cannot rest from travel; I will drink
Life to the lees. All times I have enjoy'd
Greatly, have suffer'd greatly, both with those
That loved me, and alone; on shore, and when
Thro' scudding drifts the rainy Hyades
Vext the dim sea. I am become a name;
For always roaming with a hungry heart
Much have I seen and known,—cities of men
And manners, climates, councils, governments,
Myself not least, but honor'd of them all,—
And drunk delight of battle with my peers,
Far on the ringing plains of windy Troy.
I am a part of all that I have met;
Yet all experience is an arch wherethro'
Gleams that untravell'd world whose margin fades
For ever and for ever when I move.
How dull it is to pause, to make an end,
To rust unburnish'd, not to shine in use!
As tho' to breathe were life! Life piled on life
Were all too little, and of one to me
Little remains; but every hour is saved
From that eternal silence, something more,
A bringer of new things; and vile it were
For some three suns to store and hoard myself,
And this gray spirit yearning in desire
To follow knowledge like a sinking star,
Beyond the utmost bound of human thought. (……)

12. "I'm nobody! Who are you?" by Emily Dickinson (1830~1886)

I'm Nobody! Who are you?
Are you — Nobody — too?
Then there's a pair of us!
Don't tell! they'd advertise — you know!

How dreary — to be — Somebody!
How public — like a Frog —
To tell one's name — the livelong June —
To an admiring Bog!

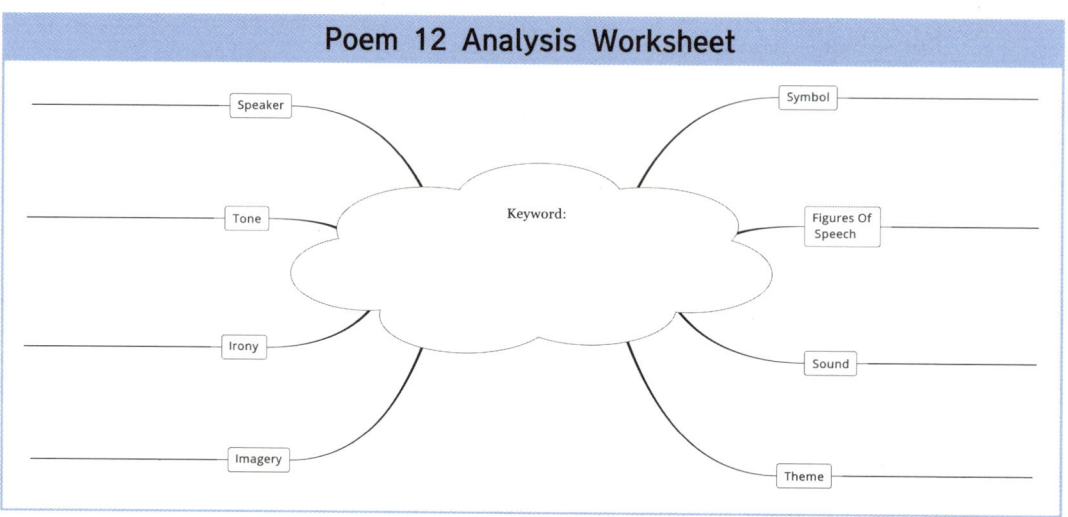

13. "The Chimney Sweeper" by William Blake (1757~1827)

When my mother died I was very young,
And my father sold me while yet my tongue
Could scarcely cry 'Weep! weep! weep! weep!'
So your chimneys I sweep, and in soot I sleep.

There's little Tom Dacre, who cried when his head,
That curled like a lamb's back, was shaved; so I said,
'Hush, Tom! never mind it, for, when your head's bare,
You know that the soot cannot spoil your white hair.'

And so he was quiet, and that very night,
As Tom was a-sleeping, he had such a sight! —
That thousands of sweepers, Dick, Joe, Ned, and Jack,
Were all of them locked up in coffins of black.

And by came an angel, who had a bright key,
And he opened the coffins, and let them all free;
Then down a green plain, leaping, laughing, they run,
And wash in a river, and shine in the sun.

Then naked and white, all their bags left behind,
They rise upon clouds, and sport in the wind;
And the Angel told Tom, if he'd be a good boy,
He'd have God for his father, and never want joy.

And so Tom awoke, and we rose in the dark,
And got with our bags and our brushes to work.
Though the morning was cold, Tom was happy and warm:
So, if all do their duty, they need not fear harm.

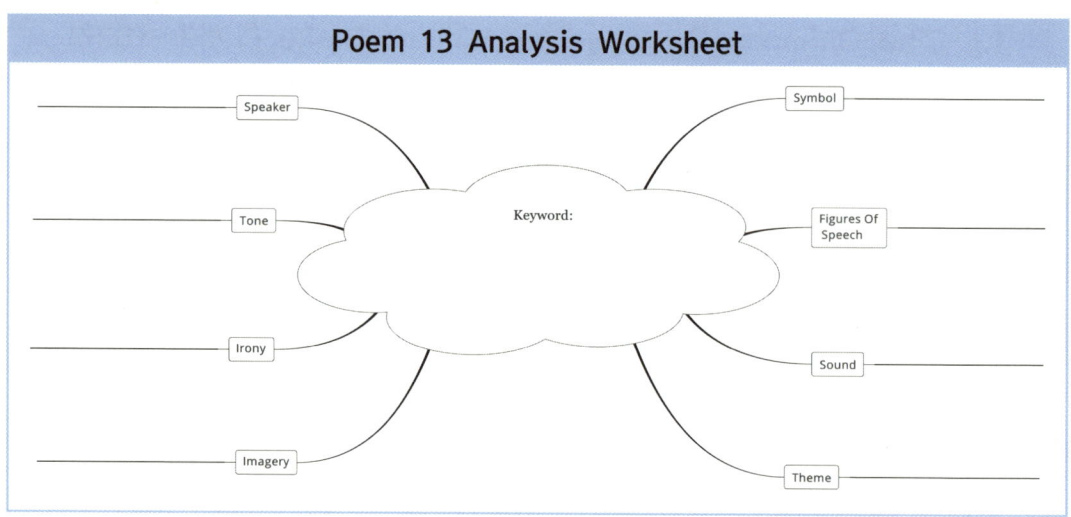

14. "Red Wheelbarrow" by William Carlos Williams (1883~1963)

so much depends
upon

a red wheel
barrow

glazed with rain
water

beside the white
chickens.

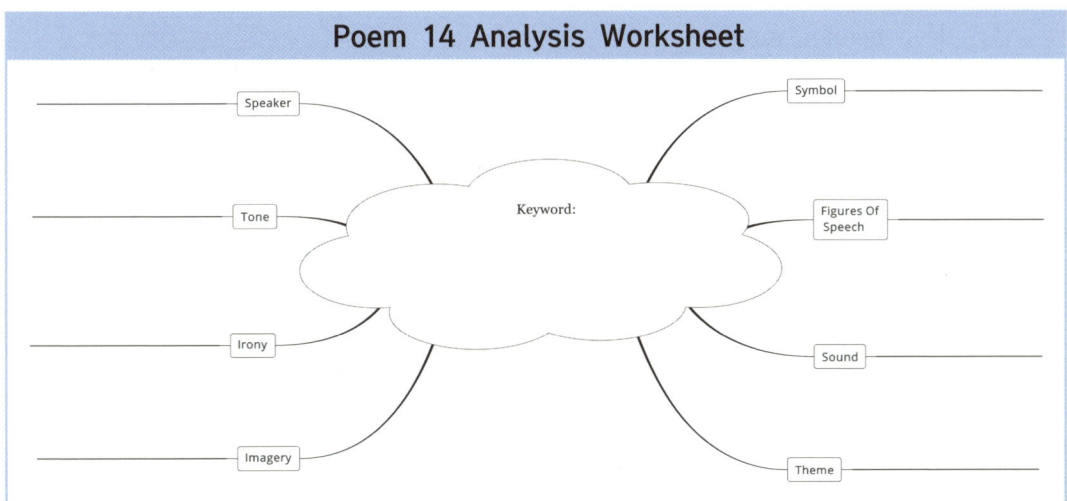

15. "Negro" by Langston Hughes (1902~1967)

I am a Negro:
Black as the night is black,
Black like the depths of my Africa.

I've been a slave:
Caesar told me to keep his door-steps clean.
I brushed the boots of Washington.

I've been a worker:
Under my hand the pyramids arose.
I made mortar for the Woolworth Building.

I've been a singer:
All the way from Africa to Georgia
I carried my sorrow songs.
I made ragtime.

I've been a victim:
The Belgians cut off my hands in the Congo.
They lynch me still in Mississippi.

I am a Negro:
Black as the night is black,
Black like the depths of my Africa.

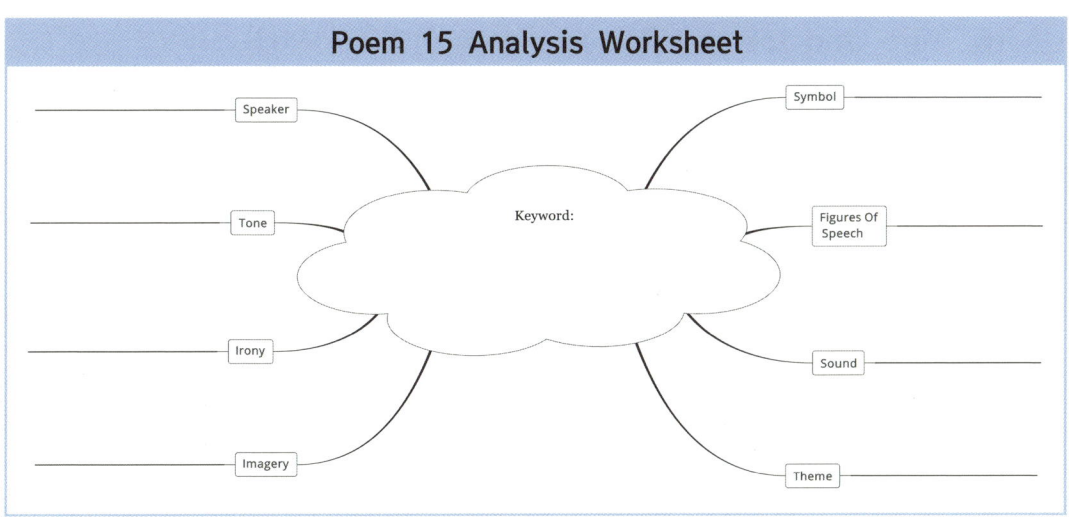

16. "Fire and Ice" by Robert Frost (1874~1963)

Some say the world will end in fire,
Some say in ice.
From what I've tasted of desire
I hold with those who favor fire.
But if it had to perish twice,
I think I know enough of hate
To say that for destruction ice
Is also great
And would suffice.

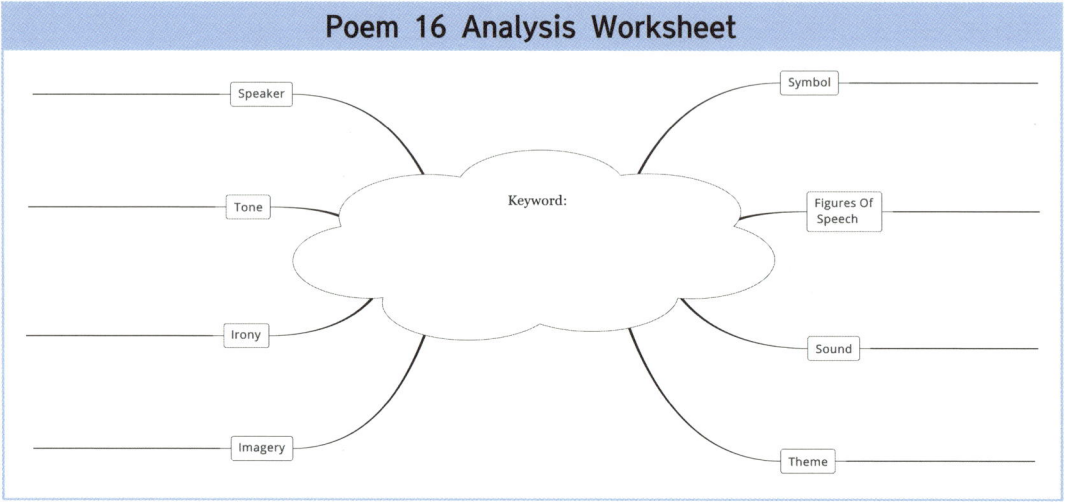

17. "The Man He Killed" by Thomas Hardy (1840~1928)

"Had he and I but met
 By some old ancient inn,
We should have set us down to wet
 Right many a nipperkin!

"But ranged as infantry,
 And staring face to face,
I shot at him as he at me,
 And killed him in his place.

"I shot him dead because —
 Because he was my foe,
Just so: my foe of course he was;
 That's clear enough; although

"He thought he'd 'list, perhaps,
 Off-hand like — just as I —
Was out of work — had sold his traps —
 No other reason why.

"Yes; quaint and curious war is!
 You shoot a fellow down
You'd treat, if met where any bar is,
 Or help to half a crown."

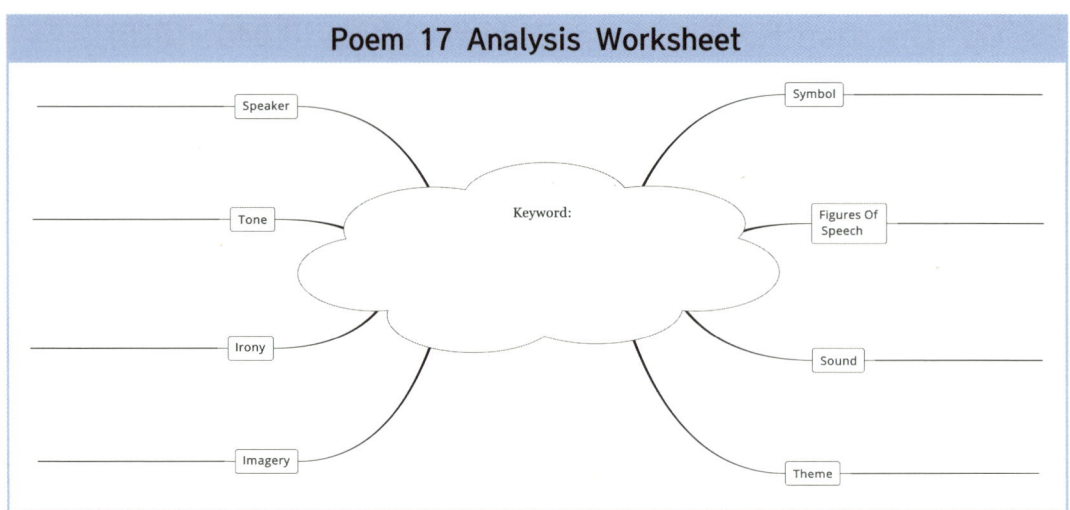

18. "Porphyria's Lover" by Robert Browning (1812~1889)

The rain set early in to-night,
  The sullen wind was soon awake,
It tore the elm-tops down for spite,
  And did its worst to vex the lake:
  I listened with heart fit to break.
When glided in Porphyria; straight
  She shut the cold out and the storm,
And kneeled and made the cheerless grate
  Blaze up, and all the cottage warm;
  Which done, she rose, and from her form
Withdrew the dripping cloak and shawl,
  And laid her soiled gloves by, untied
Her hat and let the damp hair fall,
  And, last, she sat down by my side
  And called me. When no voice replied,
She put my arm about her waist,
  And made her smooth white shoulder bare,
And all her yellow hair displaced,
  And, stooping, made my cheek lie there,
  And spread, o'er all, her yellow hair,
Murmuring how she loved me — she
  Too weak, for all her heart's endeavour,
To set its struggling passion free
  From pride, and vainer ties dissever,
  And give herself to me for ever.
But passion sometimes would prevail,
  Nor could to-night's gay feast restrain
A sudden thought of one so pale
  For love of her, and all in vain:

So, she was come through wind and rain.
Be sure I looked up at her eyes
   Happy and proud; at last I knew
Porphyria worshipped me; surprise
   Made my heart swell, and still it grew
   While I debated what to do.
That moment she was mine, mine, fair,
   Perfectly pure and good: I found
A thing to do, and all her hair
   In one long yellow string I wound
   Three times her little throat around,
And strangled her. No pain felt she;
   I am quite sure she felt no pain.
As a shut bud that holds a bee,
   I warily oped her lids: again
   Laughed the blue eyes without a stain.
And I untightened next the tress
   About her neck; her cheek once more
Blushed bright beneath my burning kiss:
   I propped her head up as before,
   Only, this time my shoulder bore
Her head, which droops upon it still:
   The smiling rosy little head,
So glad it has its utmost will,
   That all it scorned at once is fled,
   And I, its love, am gained instead!
Porphyria's love: she guessed not how
   Her darling one wish would be heard.
And thus we sit together now,
   And all night long we have not stirred,
   And yet God has not said a word!

19. "Ozymandias" by Percy Bysshe Shelley (1792~1822)

I met a traveller from an antique land
Who said: "Two vast and trunkless legs of stone
Stand in the desert … Near them, on the sand,
Half sunk, a shattered visage lies, whose frown,
And wrinkled lip, and sneer of cold command,
Tell that its sculptor well those passions read
Which yet survive, stamped on these lifeless things,
The hand that mocked them, and the heart that fed:
And on the pedestal these words appear:
'My name is Ozymandias, king of kings:
Look on my works, ye Mighty, and despair!'
Nothing beside remains. Round the decay
Of that colossal wreck, boundless and bare
The lone and level sands stretch far away."

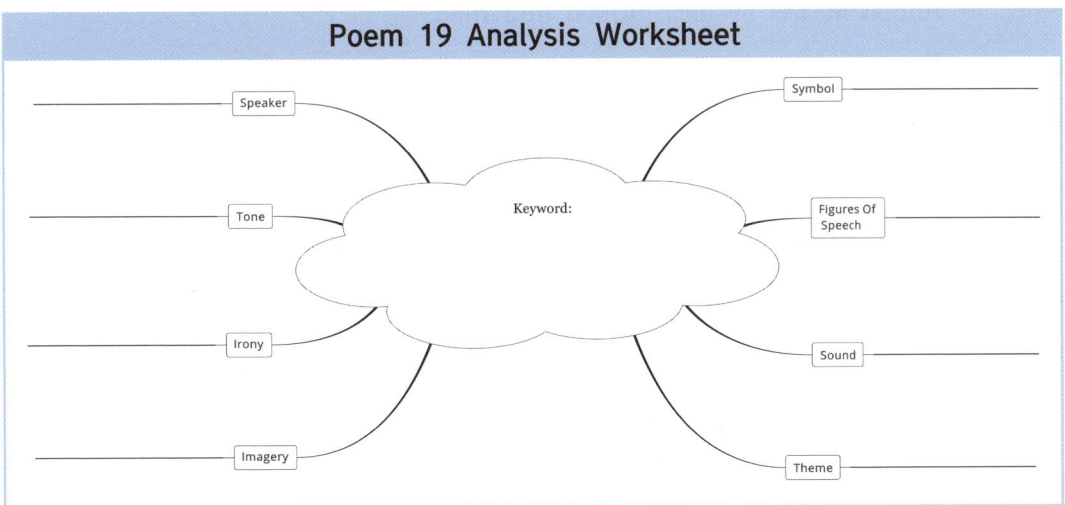

20. "War Is Kind" by Stephen Crane (1871~1900)

Do not weep, maiden, for war is kind.
Because your lover threw wild hands toward the sky
And the affrighted steed ran on alone,
Do not weep.
War is kind.

    Hoarse, booming drums of the regiment
    Little souls who thirst for fight,
    These men were born to drill and die
    The unexplained glory flies above them
    Great is the battle-god, great, and his kingdom —
    A field where a thousand corpses lie.

Do not weep, babe, for war is kind.
Because your father tumbled in the yellow trenches,
Raged at his breast, gulped and died,
Do not weep.
War is kind.

    Swift, blazing flag of the regiment
    Eagle with crest of red and gold,
    These men were born to drill and die
    Point for them the virtue of slaughter
    Make plain to them the excellence of killing
    And a field where a thousand corpses lie.

Mother whose heart hung humble as a button
On the bright splendid shroud of your son,
Do not weep.
War is kind.

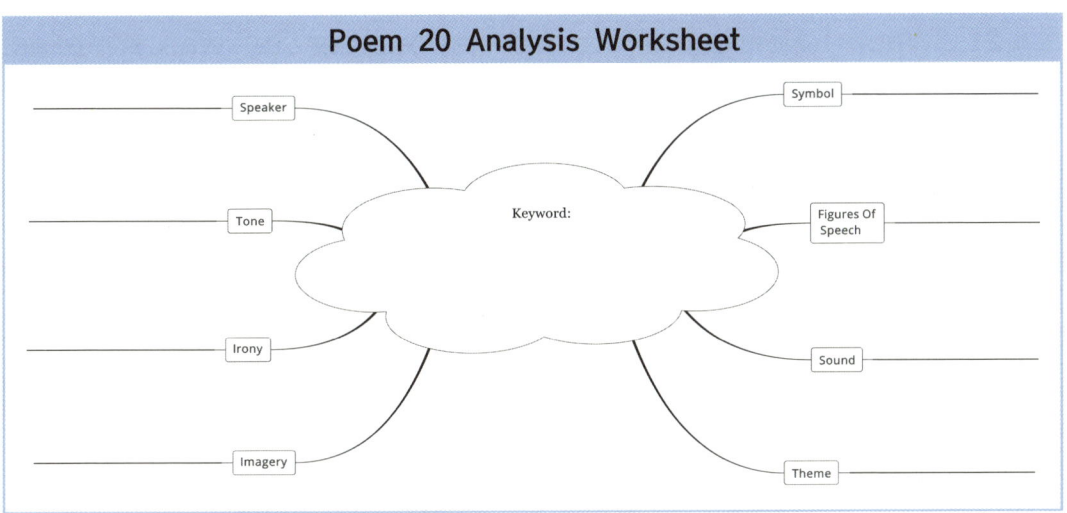

21. "When I Heard the Learn'd Astronomer" by Walt Whitman (1819~1892)

When I heard the learn'd astronomer,
When the proofs, the figures, were ranged in columns before me,
When I was shown the charts and diagrams, to add, divide,
    and measure them,
When I sitting heard the astronomer where he lectured with
    much applause in the lecture-room,
How soon unaccountable I became tired and sick,
Till rising and gliding out I wander'd off by myself,
In the mystical moist night-air, and from time to time,
Look'd up in perfect silence at the stars.

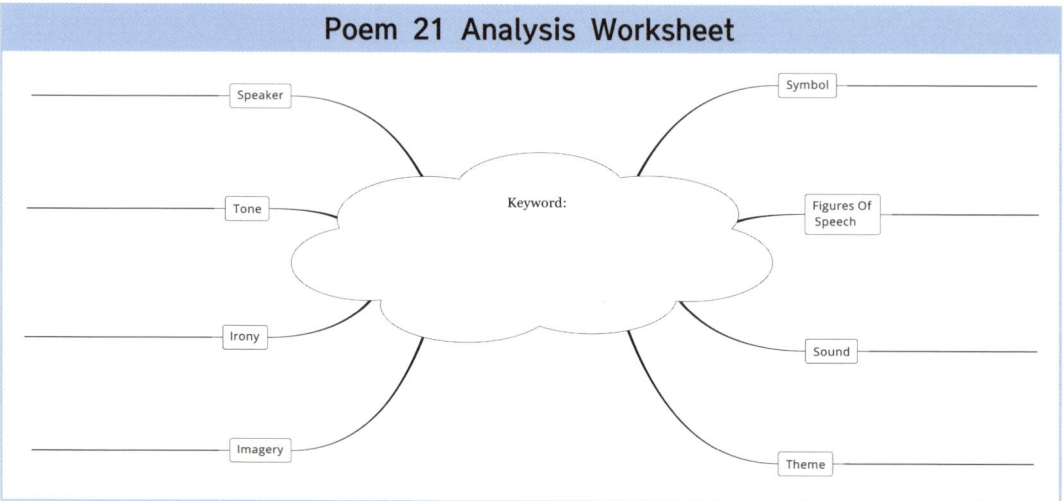

22. "The City Planners" by Margaret Atwood (1939~)

Cruising these residential Sunday
streets in dry August sunlight:
what offends us is
the sanities:
the houses in pedantic rows, the planted
sanitary trees, assert
levelness of surface like a rebuke
to the dent in our car door.
No shouting here, or
shatter of glass; nothing more abrupt
than the rational whine of a power mower
cutting a straight swath in the discouraged grass.

But though the driveways neatly
sidestep hysteria
by being even, the roofs all display
the same slant of avoidance to the hot sky,
certain things:
the smell of spilled oil a faint
sickness lingering in the garages,
a splash of paint on brick surprising as a bruise,
a plastic hose poised in a vicious
coil; even the too-fixed stare of the wide windows

give momentary access to
the landscape behind or under
the future cracks in the plaster

when the houses, capsized, will slide
obliquely into the clay seas, gradual as glaciers
that right now nobody notices.

That is where the City Planners
with the insane faces of political conspirators
are scattered over unsurveyed
territories, concealed from each other,
each in his own private blizzard;

guessing directions, they sketch
transitory lines rigid as wooden borders
on a wall in the white vanishing air

tracing the panic of suburb
order in a bland madness of snows

23. "Amoretti Lxxv: One day I wrote her name upon the strand" by Edmund Spenser (1552~1599)

One day I wrote her name upon the strand,
But came the waves and washed it away:
Again I wrote it with a second hand,
But came the tide, and made my pains his prey.
"Vain man," said she, "that dost in vain assay,
A mortal thing so to immortalize;
For I myself shall like to this decay,
And eke my name be wiped out likewise."
"Not so," (quod I) "let baser things devise
To die in dust, but you shall live by fame:
My verse your virtues rare shall eternize,
And in the heavens write your glorious name:
Where whenas death shall all the world subdue,
Our love shall live, and later life renew."

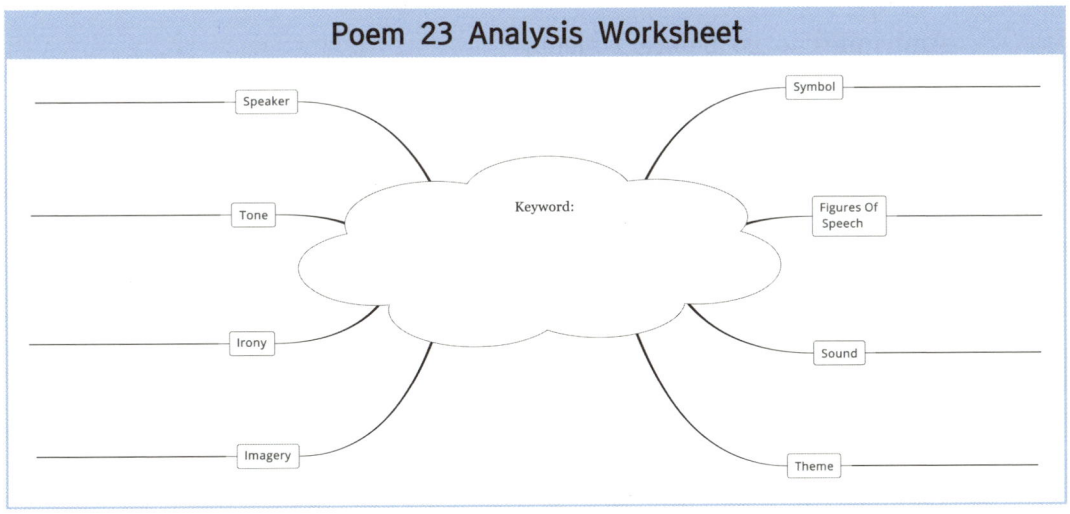

24. "Stopping by Woods on a Snowy Evening" by Robert Frost (1874~1963)

Whose woods these are I think I know.
His house is in the village, though;
He will not see me stopping here
To watch his woods fill up with snow.

My little horse must think it queer
To stop without a farmhouse near
Between the woods and frozen lake
The darkest evening of the year.

He gives his harness bells a shake
To ask if there is some mistake.
The only other sound's the sweep
Of easy wind and downy flake.

The woods are lovely, dark and deep,
But I have promises to keep,
And miles to go before I sleep,
And miles to go before I sleep.

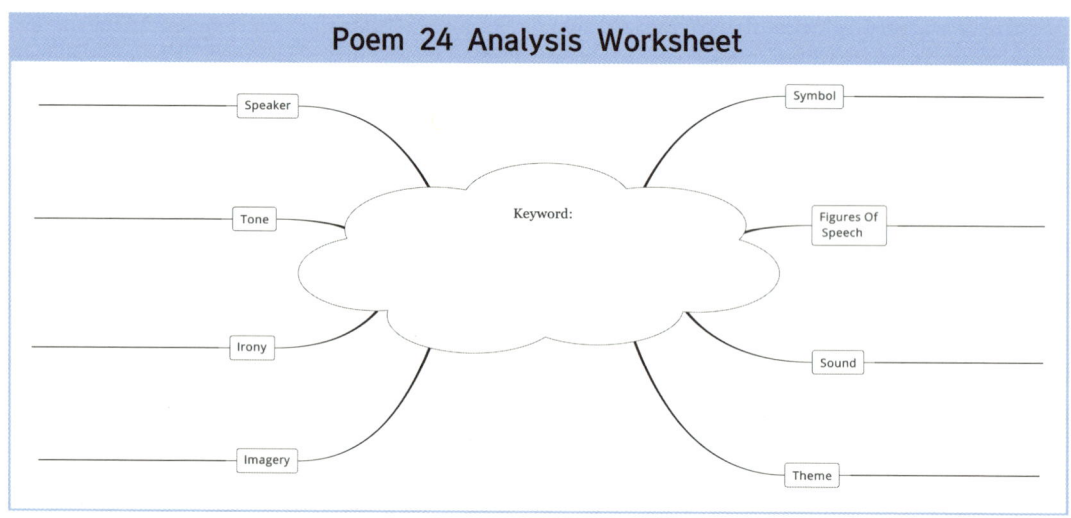

25. "In a Station of the Metro" by Ezra Pound (1885~1972)

The apparition of these faces in the crowd;
Petals on a wet, black bough.

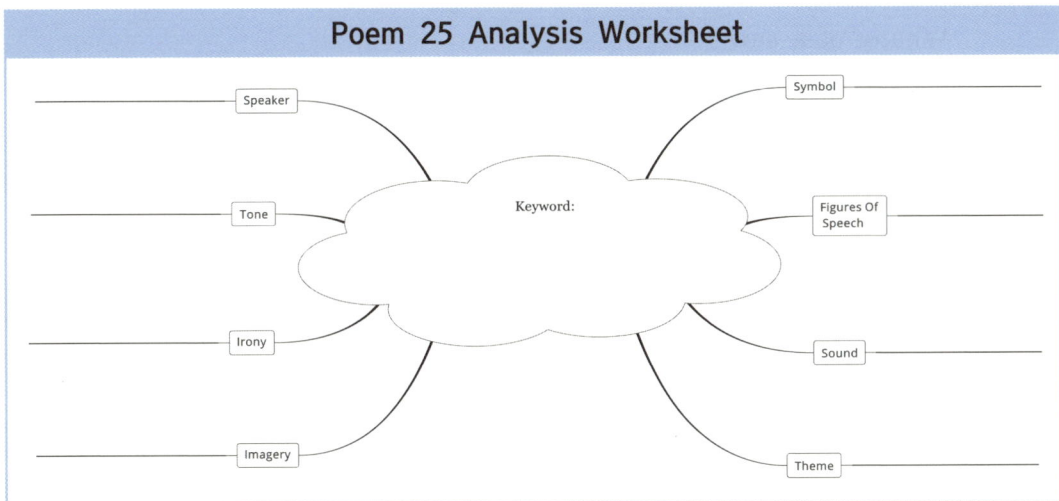

26. "Some Good Things to Be Said for the Iron Age" by Gary Snyder (1930~)

A ringing tire iron
   dropped on the pavement
Whang of a saw
brusht on limbs
the taste
of rust

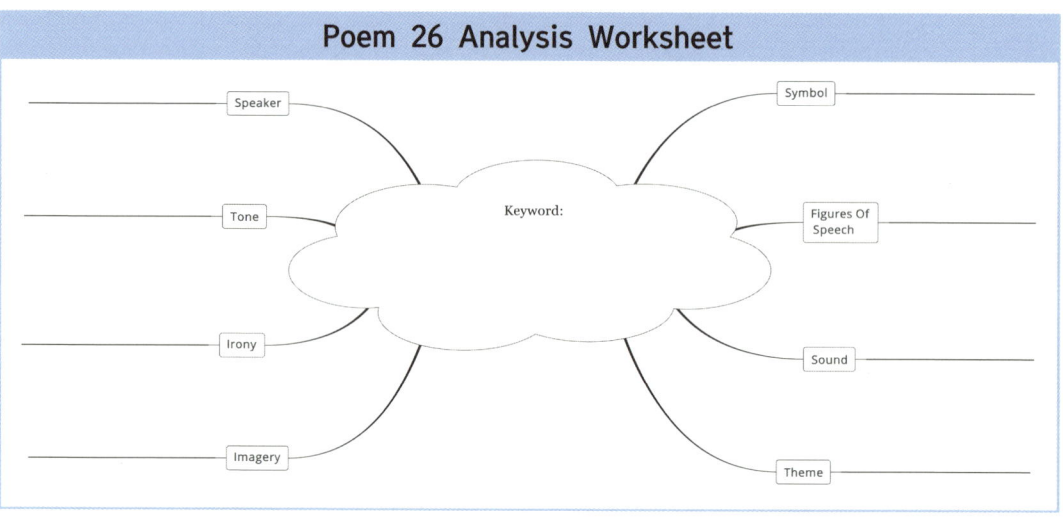

27. "Shall I compare thee to a summer's day? (Sonnet 18)" by William Shakespeare (1564~1616)

Shall I compare thee to a summer's day?
Thou art more lovely and more temperate.
Rough winds do shake the darling buds of May,
And summer's lease hath all too short a date.
Sometime too hot the eye of heaven shines,
And often is his gold complexion dimm'd;
And every fair from fair sometime declines,
By chance or nature's changing course untrimm'd;
But thy eternal summer shall not fade
Nor lose possession of that fair thou ow'st;
Nor shall Death brag thou wander'st in his shade,
When in eternal lines to time thou grow'st:
So long as men can breathe or eyes can see,
So long lives this, and this gives life to thee.

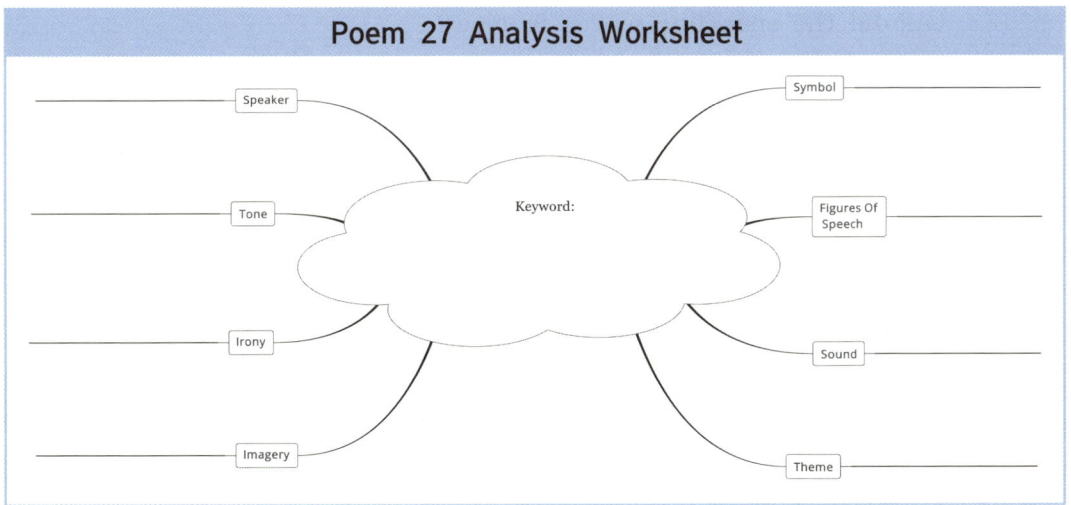

28. "I wandered lonely as a cloud[Daffodils]" by William Wordsworth (1770~1850)

I wandered lonely as a cloud
That floats on high o'er vales and hills,
When all at once I saw a crowd,
A host, of golden daffodils;
Beside the lake, beneath the trees,
Fluttering and dancing in the breeze.

Continuous as the stars that shine
And twinkle on the milky way,
They stretched in never-ending line
Along the margin of a bay:
Ten thousand saw I at a glance,
Tossing their heads in sprightly dance.

The waves beside them danced; but they
Out-did the sparkling waves in glee:
A poet could not but be gay,
In such a jocund company:
I gazed- and gazed- but little thought
What wealth the show to me had brought:

For oft, when on my couch I lie
In vacant or in pensive mood,
They flash upon that inward eye
Which is the bliss of solitude;
And then my heart with pleasure fills,
And dances with the daffodils.

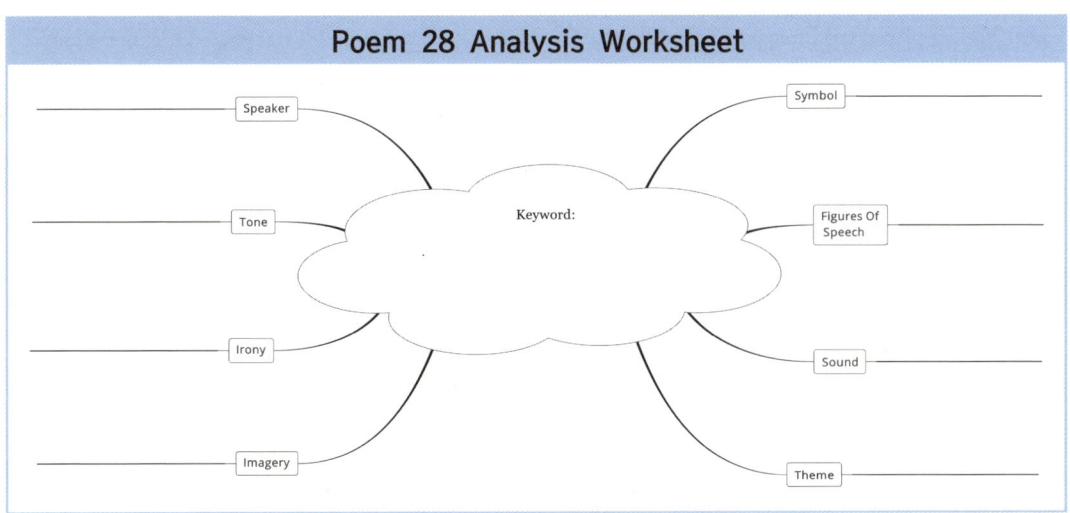

29. "Harlem[Dream deferred]" by Langston Hughes (1902~1967)

What happens to a dream deferred?

Does it dry up
like a raisin in the sun?
Or fester like a sore—
And then run?
Does it stink like rotten meat?
Or crust and sugar over—
like a syrupy sweet?

Maybe it just sags
like a heavy load.

Or does it explode?

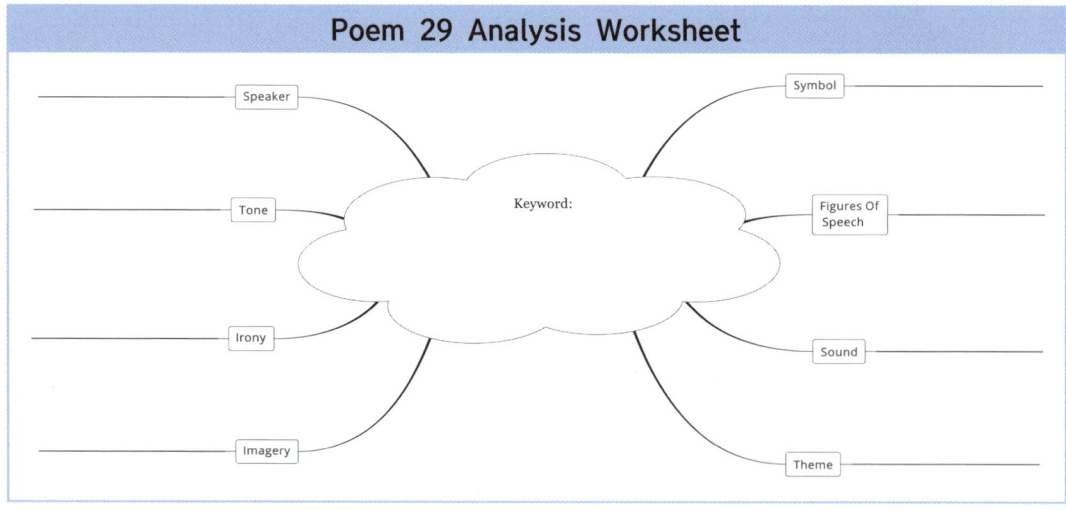

30. "Constantly Risking Absurdity" by Lawrence Ferlinghetti (1919~)

Constantly risking absurdity

and death

whenever he performs

above the heads

of his audience

the poet like an acrobat

climbs on rime

to a high wire of his own making

and balancing on eyebeams

above a sea of faces

paces his way

to the other side of the day

performing entrechats

and sleight-of-foot tricks

and other high theatrics

and all without mistaking

any thing

for what it may not be

For he's the super realist

who must perforce perceive

taut truth

before the taking of each stance or step

in his supposed advance

toward that still higher perch

where Beauty stands and waits

with gravity

to start her death-defying leap

And he
a little charleychaplin man
who may or may not catch
her fair eternal form
spreadeagled in the empty air
of existence

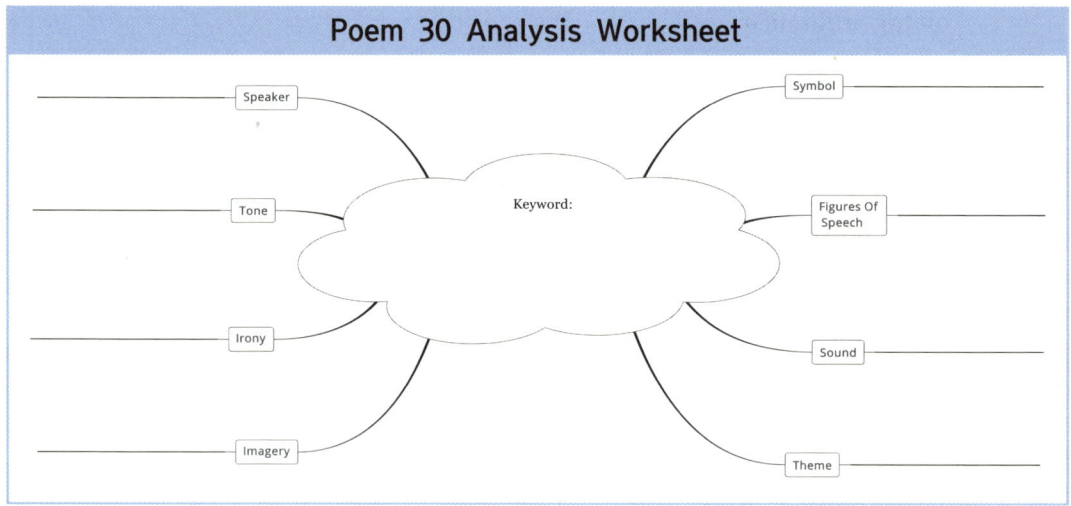

31. "Rooming houses are old women" by Audre Lorde (1934~1992)

Rooming houses are old women
rocking dark windows into their whens
waiting incomplete circles
rocking
rent office to stoop to
community bathrooms to gas rings and
under-bed boxes of once useful garbage
city issued with a twice monthly check
and the young men next door
with their loud midnight parties
and fishy rings left in the bathtub
no longer arouse them
from midnight to mealtime no stops inbetween
light breaking to pass through jumbled up windows
and who was it who married the window that Buzzie's son messed with?

To Welfare and insult from the slow shuffle
from dayswork to shopping bags
heavy with leftovers.

Rooming houses
are old women waiting
searching
through darkening windows
the end or beginning of agony
old women seen through half-ajar doors
hoping
they are not waiting
but being
the entrance to somewhere
unknown and desired
but not new.

32. "Oh, My love Is like a Red, Red Rose" by Robert Burns (1759~1796)

My love is like a red, red rose
   That's newly sprung in June;
My love is like the melody
   That's sweetly played in tune.

As fair art thou, my bonnie lass,
   So deep in love am I;
And I will love thee still, my dear,
   Till a' the seas gang dry.

Till a' the seas gang dry, my dear,
   And the rocks melt wi' the sun;
And I will love thee still, my dear,
   While the sands o' life shall run.

And fare thee weel, my only love,
   And fare thee weel awhile!
And I will come again, my love
   Though it were ten thousand mile.

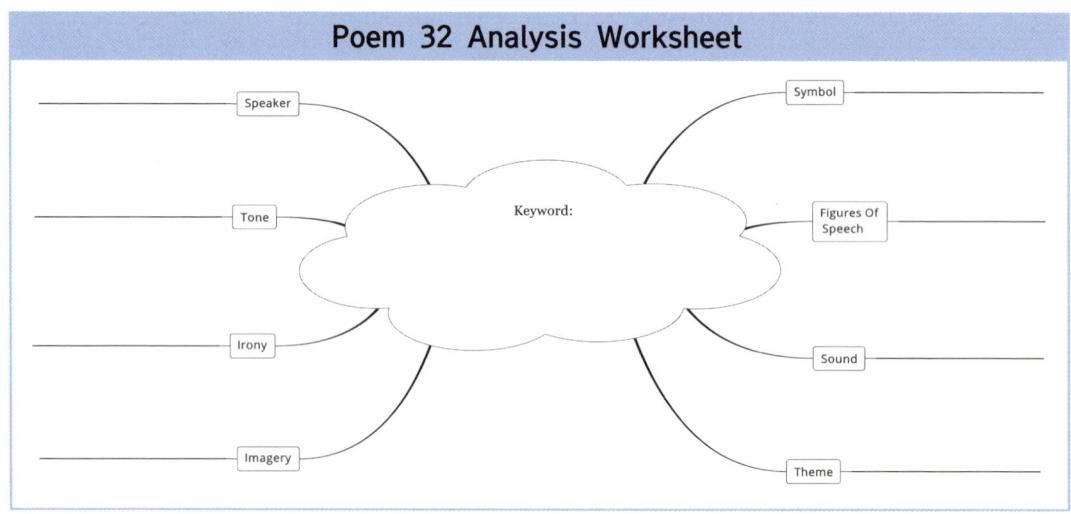

Poem 32 Analysis Worksheet — Speaker, Tone, Irony, Imagery, Keyword:, Symbol, Figures Of Speech, Sound, Theme

33. "Holes Commence Falling" by David Huddle (1942~)

The lead & zinc company
owned the mineral rights
to the whole town anyway,
and after drilling holes
for 3 or 4 years,
they finally found the right
place and sunk a mine shaft.
We were proud
of all that digging,
even though nobody from
town got hired. They
were going to dig right
under New River and hook up
with the mine at Austinville.
Then people's wells
started drying up just like
somebody'd shut off a faucet,
and holes commenced falling,
big chunks of people's yards
would drop 5 or 6 feet,
houses would shift and crack.
Now and then the company'd
pay out a little money
in damages; they got a truck
to haul water and sell it
to the people whose wells
had dried up, but most
everybody agreed the
situation wasn't
serious.

34. "To Lucasta Going to the Wars" by Richard Lovelace (1618~1658)

Tell me not, Sweet, I am unkind
  That from the nunnery
Of thy chaste breast and quiet mind,
  To war and arms I fly.

True, a new mistress now I chase,
  The first foe in the field;
And with a stronger faith embrace
  A sword, a horse, a shield.

Yet this inconstancy is such
  As you too shall adore;
I could not love thee, Dear, so much,
  Loved I not Honor more.

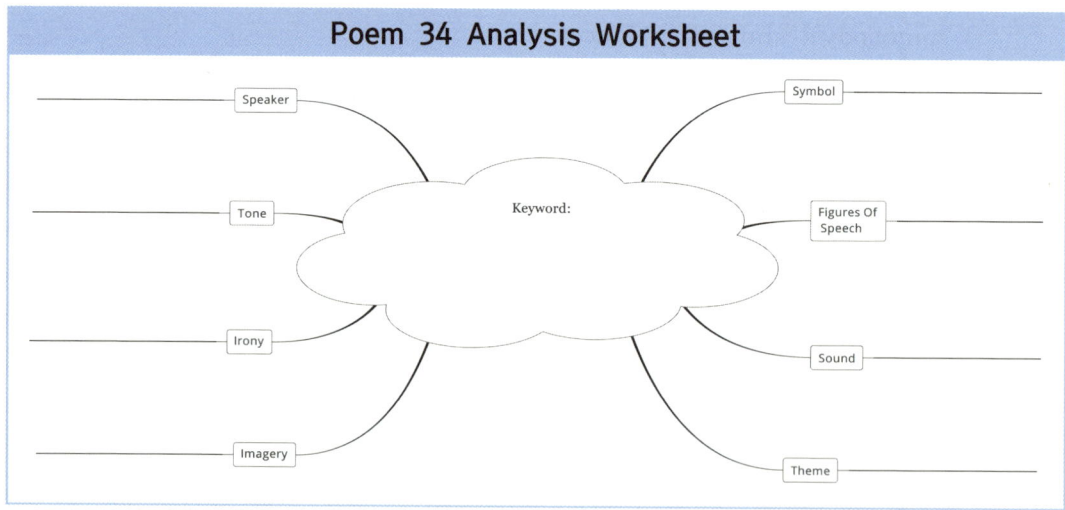

35. "On Passing thru Morgantown, Pa." by Sonia Sanchez (1934~)

i saw you

vincent van

gogh perched

on those pennsylvania

cornfields communing

amid secret black

bird societies. yes.

i'm sure that was

you exploding your

fantastic delirium

while in the

distance

red indian

hills beckoned.

36. "Sadie And Maud" by Gwendolyn Brooks (1917~2000)

Maud went to college.
Sadie stayed home.
Sadie scraped life
With a fine toothed comb.

She didn't leave a tangle in
Her comb found every strand.
Sadie was one of the livingest chicks
In all the land.

Sadie bore two babies
Under her maiden name.
Maud and Ma and Papa
Nearly died of shame.

When Sadie said her last so-long
Her girls struck out from home.
(Sadie left as heritage
Her fine-toothed comb.)

Maud, who went to college,
Is a thin brown mouse.
She is living all alone
In this old house.

37. "The Moon Is Hiding In" by Edward Estlin Cummings (1894~1962)

the moon is hiding in

her hair.

The

lily

of heaven

full of all dreams,

draws down.

cover her briefness in singing

close her with the intricate faint birds

by daisies and twilights

Deepen her,

Recite

upon her

flesh

the rain's

pearls singly-whispering.

38. "I Like To See It Lap The Miles" by Emily Dickinson (1830~1886)

I like to see it lap the Miles —
And lick the Valleys up —
And stop to feed itself at Tanks —
And then — prodigious, step

Around a pile of mountains —
And, supercilious, peer
In Shanties — by the sides of Roads —
And then a Quarry pare

To fit its Ribs
And crawl between
Complaining all the while
In horrid — hooting stanza —
Then chase itself down Hill —

And neigh like Boanerges —
Then — punctual as a star,
Stop — docile and omnipotent
At its own stable door —

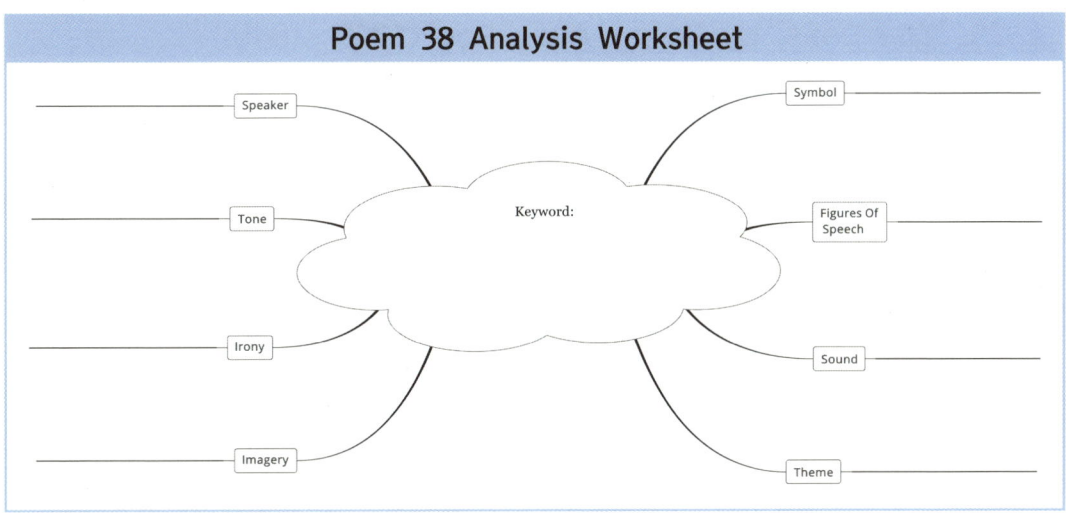

39. "The Bells" by Edgar Allan Poe (1809~1849)

I

Hear the sledges with the bells—

Silver bells!

What a world of merriment their melody foretells!

How they tinkle, tinkle, tinkle,

In the icy air of night!

While the stars that oversprinkle

All the heavens, seem to twinkle

With a crystalline delight;

Keeping time, time, time,

In a sort of Runic rhyme,

To the tintinnabulation that so musically wells

From the bells, bells, bells, bells,

Bells, bells, bells—

From the jingling and the tinkling of the bells.

II

Hear the mellow wedding bells

Golden bells!

What a world of happiness their harmony foretells!

Through the balmy air of night

How they ring out their delight!

From the molten-golden notes,

And all in tune,

What a liquid ditty floats

To the turtle-dove that listens, while she gloats

On the moon!

Oh, from out the sounding cells,

What a gush of euphony voluminously wells!

How it swells!

How it dwells

On the Future! how it tells

Of the rapture that impels

To the swinging and the ringing

Of the bells, bells, bells,

Of the bells, bells, bells, bells,

Bells, bells, bells —

To the rhyming and the chiming of the bells!

40. "The Eagle" by Alfred, Lord Tennyson (1809~1892)

He clasps the crag with crooked hands;
Close to the sun in lonely lands,
Ringed with the azure world, he stands.

The wrinkled sea beneath him crawls:
He watches from his mountain walls,
And like a thunderbolt he falls.

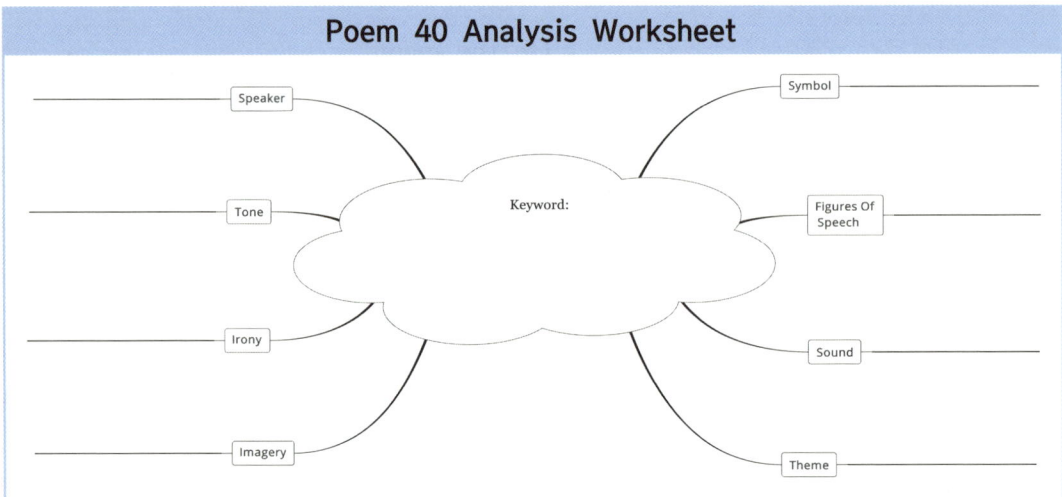

41. "Delight In Disorder" by Robert Herrick (1591~1674)

A sweet disorder in the dress

Kindles in clothes a wantonness;

A lawn about the shoulders thrown

Into a fine distraction;

An erring lace, which here and there

Enthrals the crimson stomacher;

A cuff neglectful, and thereby

Ribbons to flow confusedly;

A winning wave, deserving note,

In the tempestuous petticoat;

A careless shoe-string, in whose tie

I see a wild civility —

Do more bewitch me, than when art

Is too precise in every part.

42. "She Dwelt Among The Untrodden Ways" by William Wordsworth (1770~1850)

She dwelt among the untrodden ways
  Beside the springs of Dove,
A Maid whom there were none to praise
  And very few to love:

A violet by a mossy stone
  Half hidden from the eye!
—Fair as a star, when only one
  Is shining in the sky.

She lived unknown, and few could know
  When Lucy ceased to be;
But she is in her grave, and, oh,
  The difference to me!

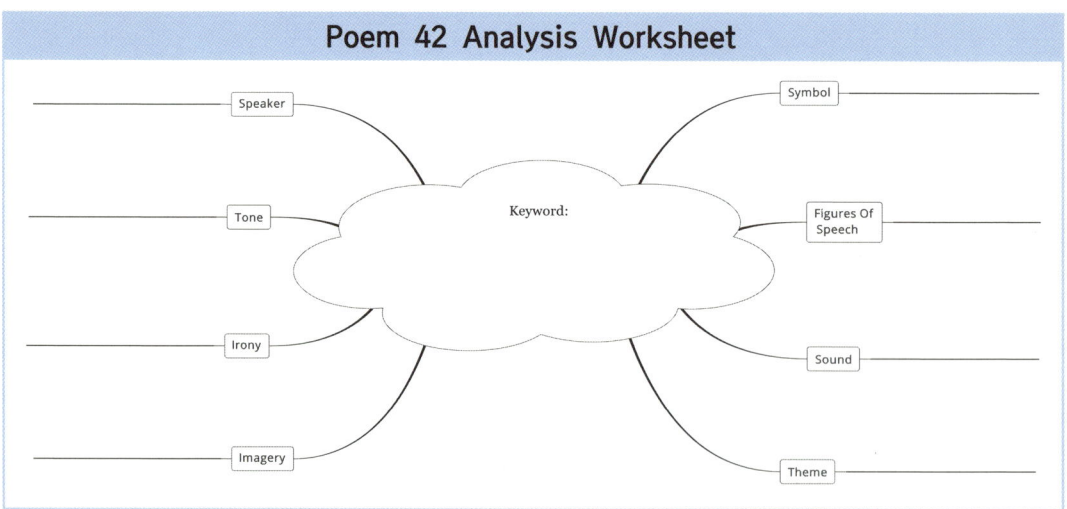

43. "My Papa's Waltz" by Theodore Roethke (1908~1963)

The whiskey on your breath
Could make a small boy dizzy;
But I hung on like death:
Such waltzing was not easy.

We romped until the pans
Slid from the kitchen shelf;
My mother's countenance
Could not unfrown itself.

The hand that held my wrist
Was battered on one knuckle;
At every step you missed
My right ear scraped a buckle.

You beat time on my head
With a palm caked hard by dirt,
Then waltzed me off to bed
Still clinging to your shirt.

44. "Aunt Jennifer's Tigers" by Adrienne Rich (1929~2012)

Aunt Jennifer's tigers prance across a screen,
　Bright topaz denizens of a world of green.
　They do not fear the men beneath the tree;
　They pace in sleek chivalric certainty.

Aunt Jennifer's finger fluttering through her wool
　Find even the ivory needle hard to pull.
　The massive weight of Uncle's wedding band
　Sits heavily upon Aunt Jennifer's hand.

When Aunt is dead, her terrified hands will lie
　Still ringed with ordeals she was mastered by.
　The tigers in the panel that she made
　Will go on prancing, proud and unafraid.

45. "Traveling Through The Dark" by William Stafford (1914~1993)

Traveling through the dark I found a deer
dead on the edge of the Wilson River road.
It is usually best to roll them into the canyon:
that road is narrow; to swerve might make more dead.

By glow of the tail-light I stumbled back of the car
and stood by the heap, a doe, a recent killing;
she had stiffened already, almost cold.
I dragged her off; she was large in the belly.

My fingers touching her side brought me the reason —
her side was warm; her fawn lay there waiting,
alive, still, never to be born.
Beside that mountain road I hesitated.

The car aimed ahead its lowered parking lights;
under the hood purred the steady engine.
I stood in the glare of the warm exhaust turning red;
around our group I could hear the wilderness listen.

I thought hard for us all — my only swerving —,
then pushed her over the edge into the river.

46. "When In Disgrace With Fortune And Men's Eyes (Sonnet 29)" by William Shakespeare (1564~1616)

When in disgrace with fortune and men's eyes,
I all alone beweep my outcast state,
And trouble deaf heaven with my bootless cries,
And look upon myself and curse my fate,
wishing me like to one more rich in hope,
Featured like him, like him with friends possessed,
Desiring this man's art, and that man's scope,
With what I most enjoy contented least;
Yet in these thoughts myself almost despising,
Haply I think on thee—and then my state,
Like to the lark at break of day arising
From sullen earth sings hymns at heaven's gate;
  For thy sweet love remembered such wealth brings,
  That then I scorn to change my state with kings.

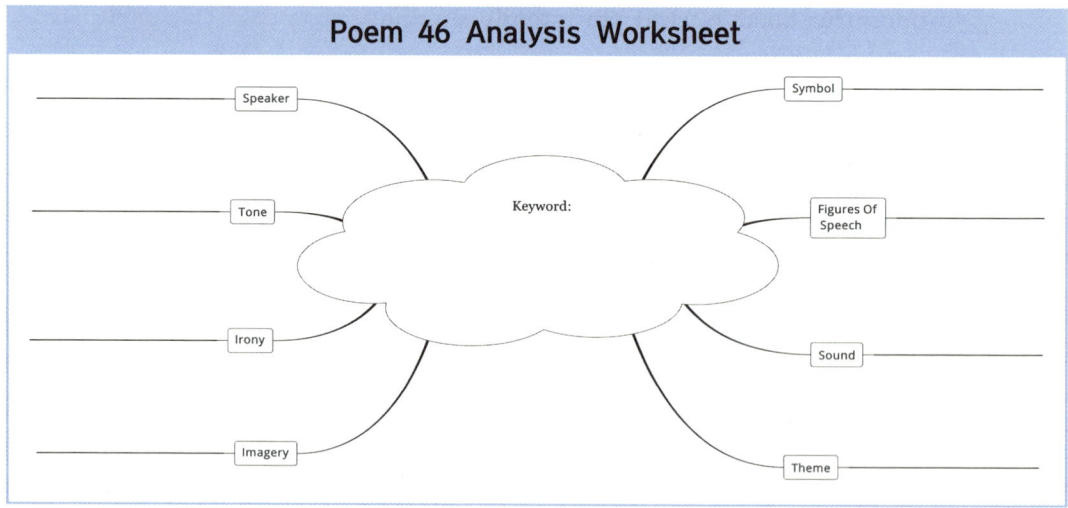

47. "the sky was can dy" by Edward Estlin Cummings (1894~1962)

the
    sky
        was
can   dy   lu
minous
      edible
spry
    pinks shy
lemons
greens coo l choc
olate
s.

  un der,
  a lo
co
mo
   tive   s pout
        ing
       vi
      o
      lets

48. "The Sick Rose" by William Blake (1757~1827)

O Rose, thou art sick!
The invisible worm
That flies in the night,
In the howling storm,

Has found out thy bed
Of crimson joy:
And his dark secret love
Does thy life destroy.

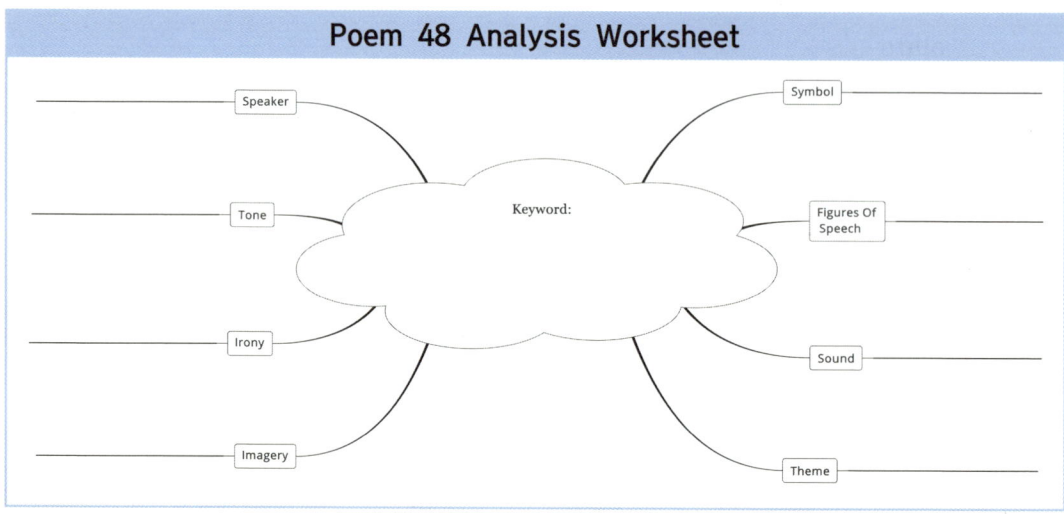

49. "Volcanoes be in Sicily" by Emily Dickinson (1830~1886)

Volcanoes be in Sicily

And South America

I judge from my Geography —

Volcanos nearer here

A Lava step at any time

Am I inclined to climb —

A Crater I may contemplate

Vesuvius at Home.

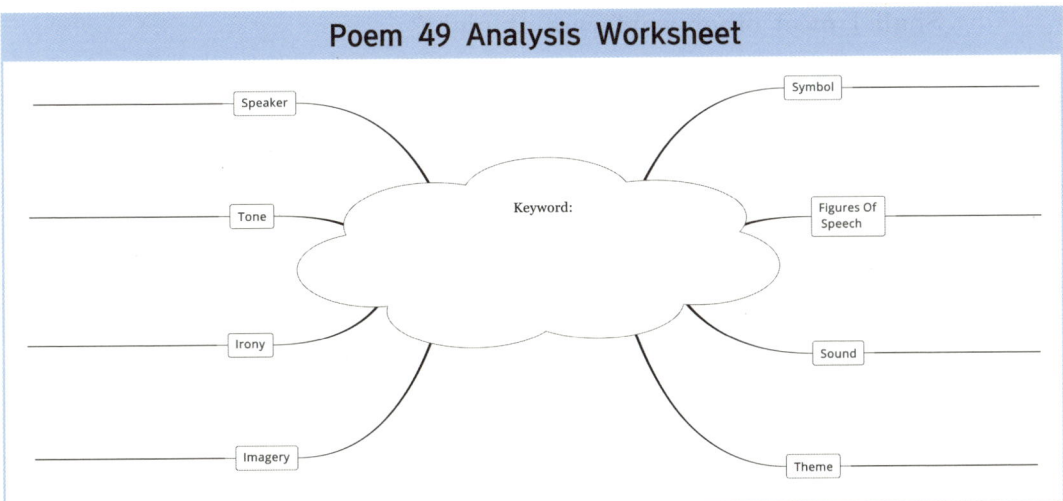

50. "Uphill" by Christina Rossetii (1830~1894)

Does the road wind up-hill all the way?
  Yes, to the very end.
Will the day's journey take the whole long day?
  From morn to night, my friend.

But is there for the night a resting-place?
  A roof for when the slow dark hours begin.
May not the darkness hide it from my face?
  You cannot miss that inn.

Shall I meet other wayfarers at night?
  Those who have gone before.
Then must I knock, or call when just in sight?
  They will not keep you standing at that door.

Shall I find comfort, travel-sore and weak?
  Of labour you shall find the sum.
Will there be beds for me and all who seek?
  Yea, beds for all who come.

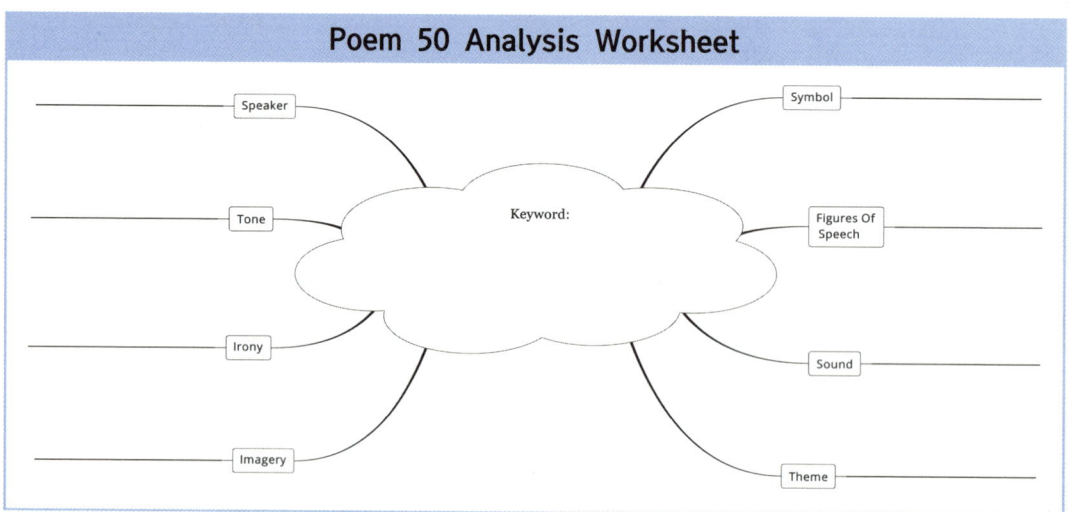

51. "Dreams of Suicide" by William Meredith (1919~2007)

I

I reach for the awkward shotgun not to disarm

You, but to feel the metal horn,

Furred with the downy membrane of dream.

More surely than the unicorn

You are the mythical beast.

II

Or I am sniffing an oven. On all fours

I am imitating a totemic animal

but she is not my totem or the totem

of my people, this is not my magic oven.

III

If I hold you tight by the ankles,

still you fly upward from the iron railing.

Your father made these wings,

after he made his own, and now from beyond

he tells you *fly down,* in the voice

my own father might say *walk, boy.*

52. "The courage that my mother had" by Edna St. Vincent Millay (1892~1950)

The courage that my mother had
Went with her, and is with her still:
Rock from New England quarried;
Now granite in a granite hill.

The golden brooch my mother wore
She left behind for me to wear;
I have no thing I treasure more:
Yet, it is something I could spare.

Oh, if instead she'd left to me

The thing she took into the grave!—
That courage like a rock, which she
Has no more need of, and I have.

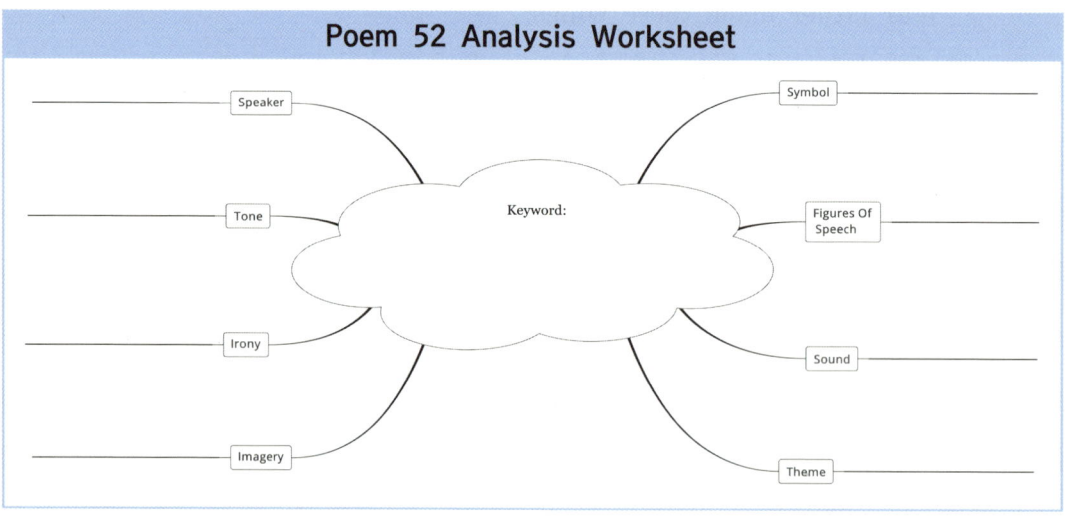

53. "Do not go gentle into that good night" by Dylan Thomas (1914~1953)

Do not go gentle into that good night,
Old age should burn and rave at close of day;
Rage, rage against the dying of the light.

Though wise men at their end know dark is right,
Because their words had forked no lightning they
Do not go gentle into that good night.

Good men, the last wave by, crying how bright
Their frail deeds might have danced in a green bay,
Rage, rage against the dying of the light.

Wild men who caught and sang the sun in flight,
And learn, too late, they grieved it on its way,
Do not go gentle into that good night.

Grave men, near death, who see with blinding sight
Blind eyes could blaze like meteors and be gay,
Rage, rage against the dying of the light.

And you, my father, there on the sad height,
Curse, bless, me now with your fierce tears, I pray.
Do not go gentle into that good night.
Rage, rage against the dying of the light.

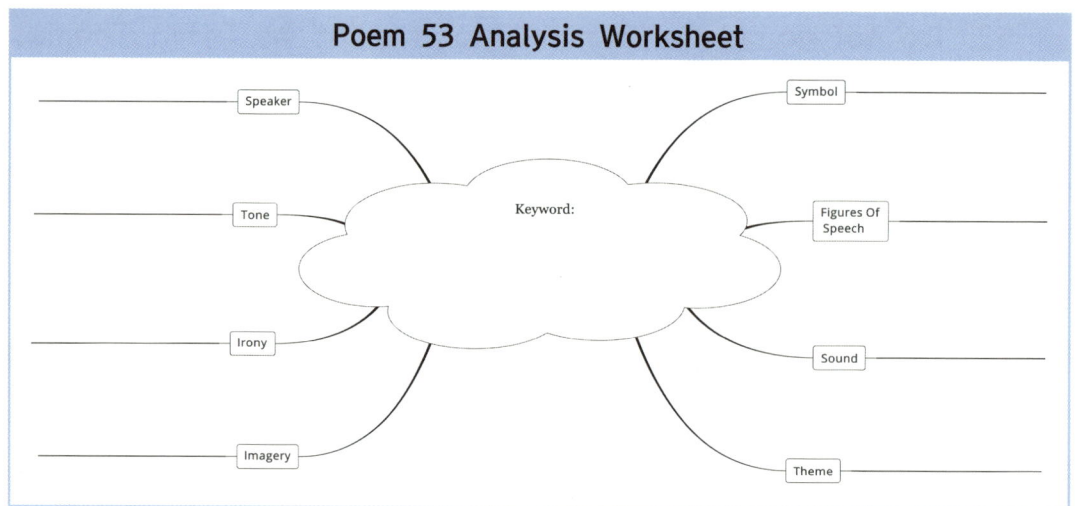

54. "Summer" by Christina Rossetti (1830~1894)

Winter is cold-hearted
Spring is yea and nay,
Autumn is a weather-cock
Blown every way:
Summer days for me
When every leaf is on its tree;

When Robin's not a beggar,
And Jenny Wren's a bride,
And larks hang singing, singing, singing,
Over the wheat-fields wide,
And anchored lilies ride,
And the pendulum spider
Swings from side to side,

And blue-black beetles transact business,
And gnats fly in a host,
And furry caterpillars hasten
That no time be lost,
And moths grow fat and thrive,
And ladybirds arrive.

Before green apples blush,
Before green nuts embrown,
Why, one day in the country
Is worth a month in town;
Is worth a day and a year
Of the dusty, musty, lag-last fashion
That days drone elsewhere.

55. "The Windhover" by Gerard Manley Hopkins (1844~1889)

To Christ our Lord

I caught this morning morning's minion, king—
dom of daylight's dauphin, dapple-dawn-drawn Falcon, in his riding
Of the rolling level underneath him steady air, and striding
High there, how he rung upon the rein of a wimpling wing
In his ecstasy! then off, off forth on swing,
As a skate's heel sweeps smooth on a bow-bend: the hurl and gliding
Rebuffed the big wind. My heart in hiding
Stirred for a bird,—the achieve of, the mastery of the thing!

Brute beauty and valour and act, oh, air, pride, plume, here
Buckle! AND the fire that breaks from thee then, a billion
Times told lovelier, more dangerous, O my chevalier!

No wonder of it: shéer plód makes plough down sillion
Shine, and blue-bleak embers, ah my dear,
Fall, gall themselves, and gash gold-vermillion.

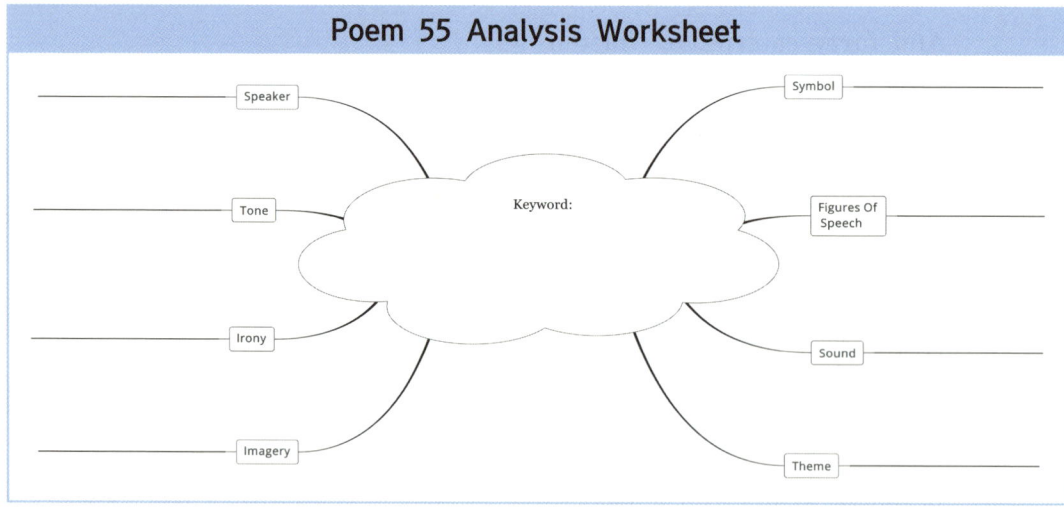

56. "Meeting at Night" by Robert Browning (1812~1889)

The grey sea and the long black land;
And the yellow half-moon large and low;
And the startled little waves that leap
In fiery ringlets from their sleep,
As I gain the cove with pushing prow,
And quench its speed i' the slushy sand.

Then a mile of warm sea-scented beach;
Three fields to cross till a farm appears;
A tap at the pane, the quick sharp scratch
And blue spurt of a lighted match,
And a voice less loud, thro' its joys and fears,
Than the two hearts beating each to each!

57. "Parting at Morning" by Robert Browning (1812~1889)

Round the cape of a sudden came the sea,
And the sun looked over the mountain's rim:
And straight was a path of gold for him,
And the need of a world of men for me.

58. "How Do I Love Thee?" by Elizabeth Barrett Browning (1806~1861)

How do I love thee? Let me count the ways.
I love thee to the depth and breadth and height
My soul can reach, when feeling out of sight
For the ends of Being and ideal Grace.
I love thee to the level of every day's
Most quiet need, by sun and candlelight.
I love thee freely, as men strive for Right;
I love thee purely, as they turn from Praise.
I love with a passion put to use
In my old griefs, and with my childhood's faith.
I love thee with a love I seemed to lose
With my lost saints,—I love thee with the breath,
Smiles, tears, of all my life!—and, if God choose,
I shall but love thee better after death.

03 Analysis of Poems To Read

1. "My Arkansas" by Maya Angelou (1928~2014)

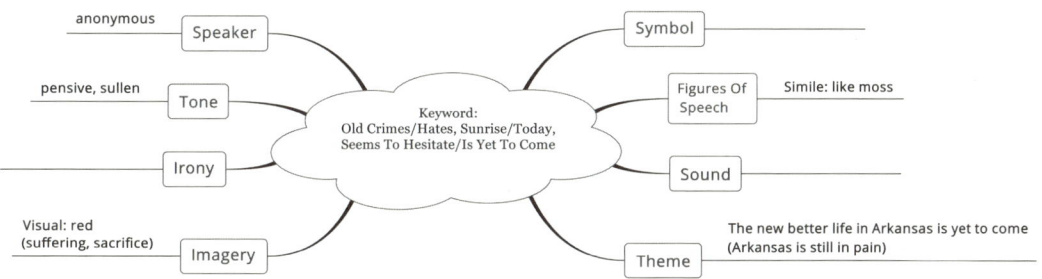

2. "Richard Cory" by Edwin Arlington Robinson (1869~1935)

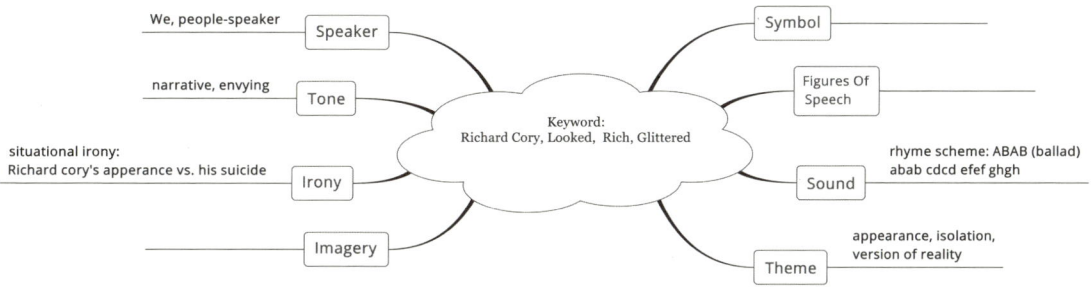

3. "Ballad of Birmingham" by Dudley Randall (1914~2000)

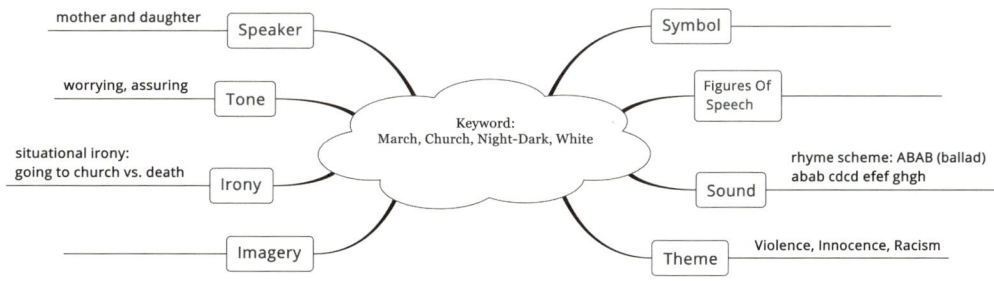

4. "To an Athlete Dying Young" by A.E. Houseman (1859~1936)

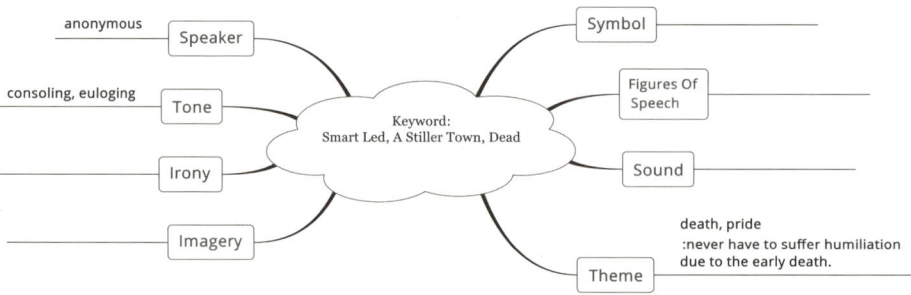

8. "Go, lovely rose" by Edmund Waller (1606~1687)

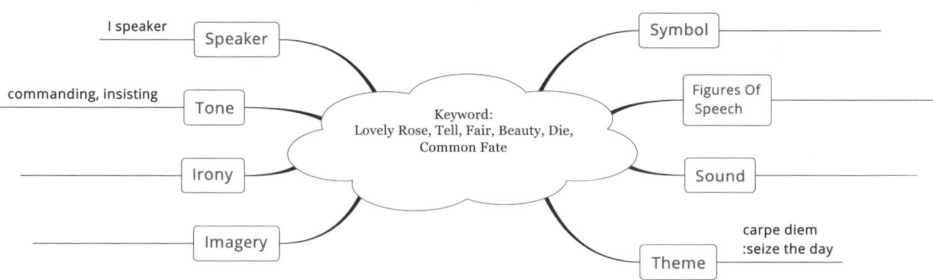

12. "I'm nobody! Who are you?" by Emily Dickinson (1830~1886)

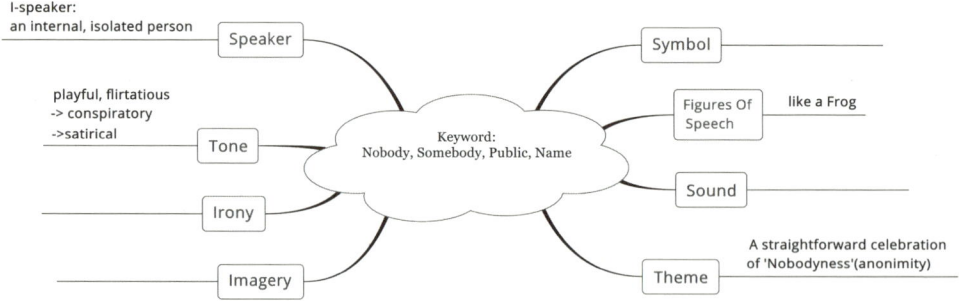

13. "The Chimney Sweeper" by William Blake (1757~1827)

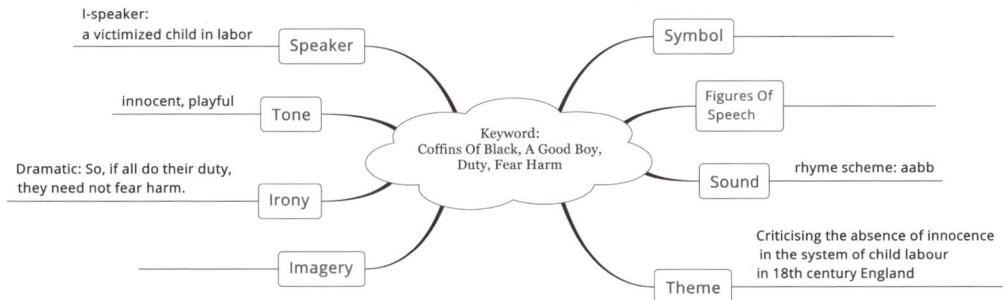

14. "Red Wheelbarrow" by William Carlos Williams (1883~1963)

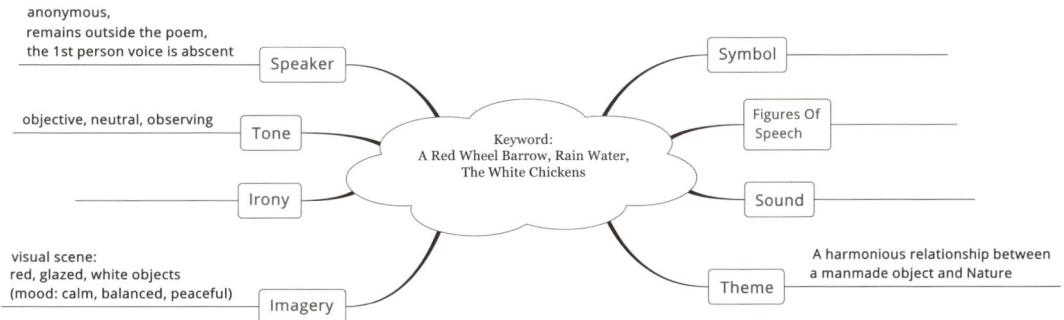

15. "Negro" by Langston Hughes (1902~1967)

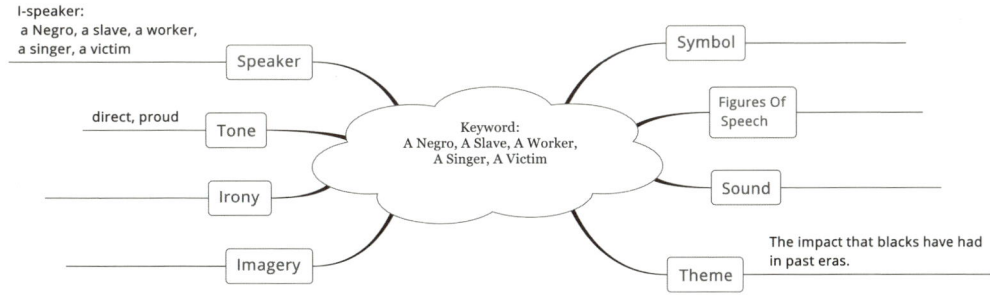

16. "Fire and Ice" by Robert Frost (1874~1963)

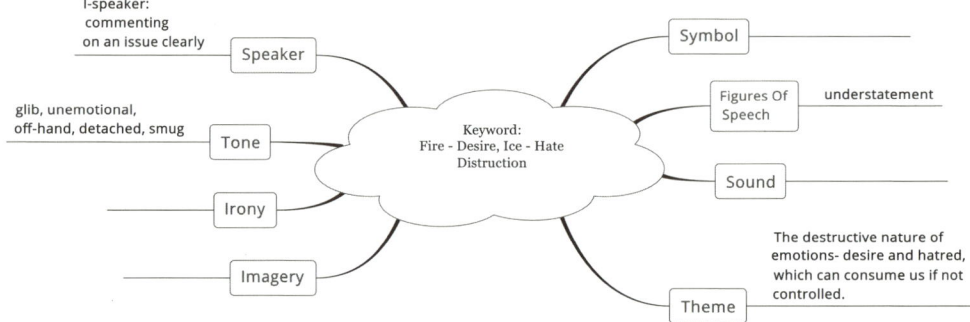

17. "The Man He Killed" by Thomas Hardy (1840~1928)

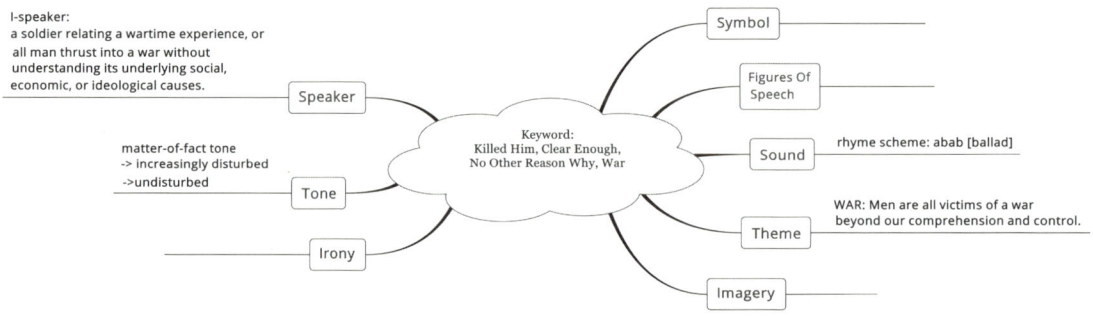

19. "Ozymandias" by Percy Bysshe Shelley (1792~1822)

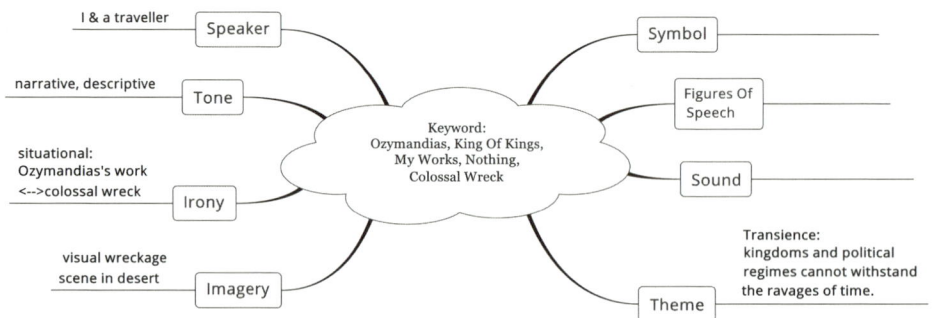

20. "War Is Kind" by Stephen Crane (1871~1900)

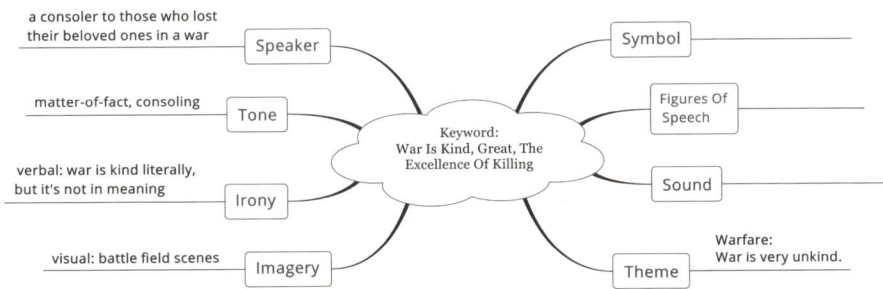

21. "When I Heard the Learn'd Astronomer" by Walt Whitman (1819~1892)

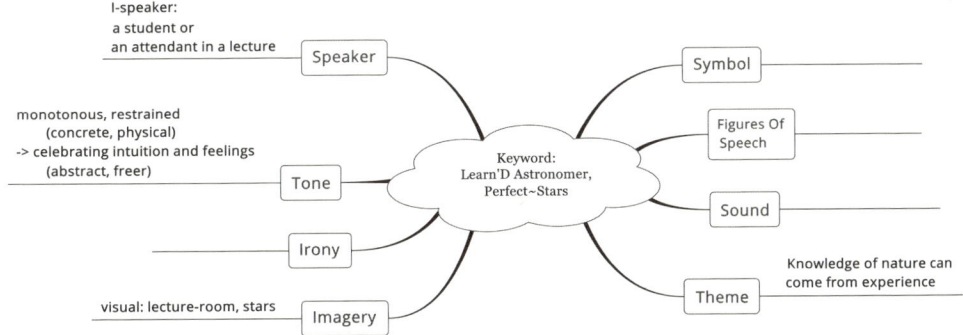

23. "Amoretti Lxxv: One day I wrote her name upon the strand" by Edmund Spenser (1552~1599)

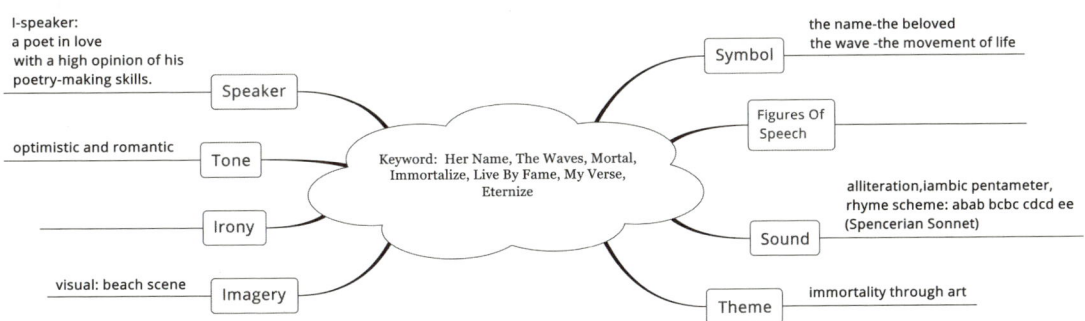

24. "Stopping by Woods on a Snowy Evening" by Robert Frost (1874~1963)

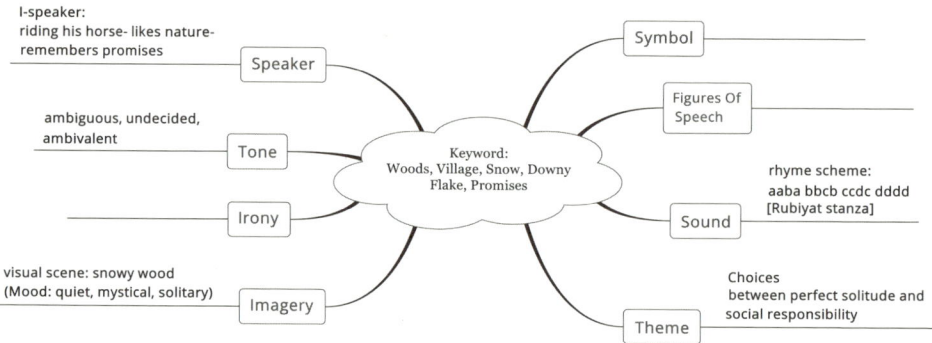

25. "In a Station of the Metro" by Ezra Pound (1885~1972)

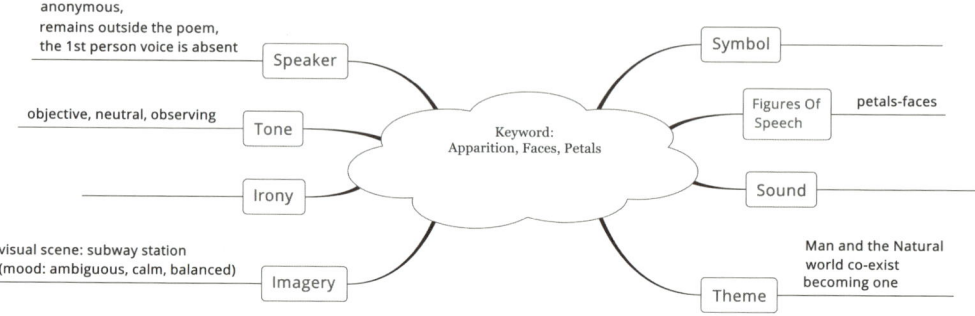

26. "Some Good Things to Be Said for the Iron Age" by Gary Snyder (1930~)

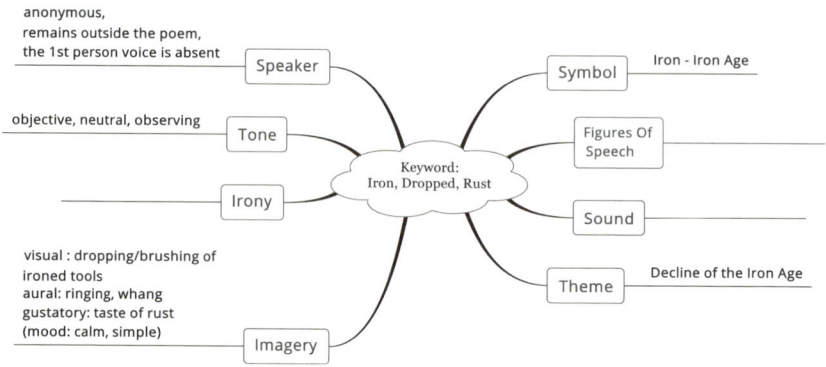

27. "Shall I compare thee to a summer's day?" by William Shakespeare (1564~1616)

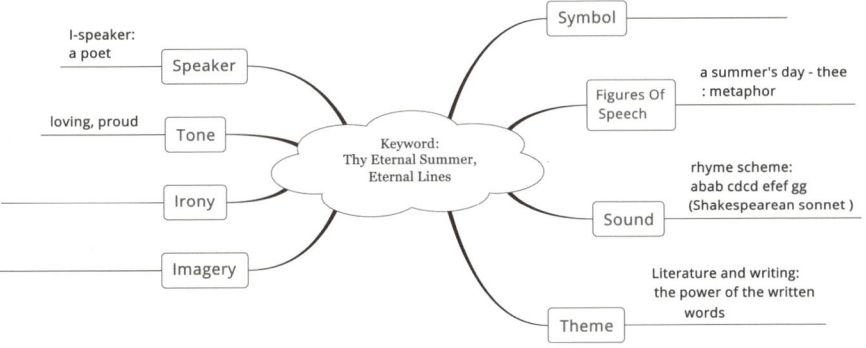

28. "I wandered lonely as a cloud[Daffodils]" by William Wordsworth (1770~1850)

29. "Harlem[Dream deferred]" by Langston Hughes (1902~1967)

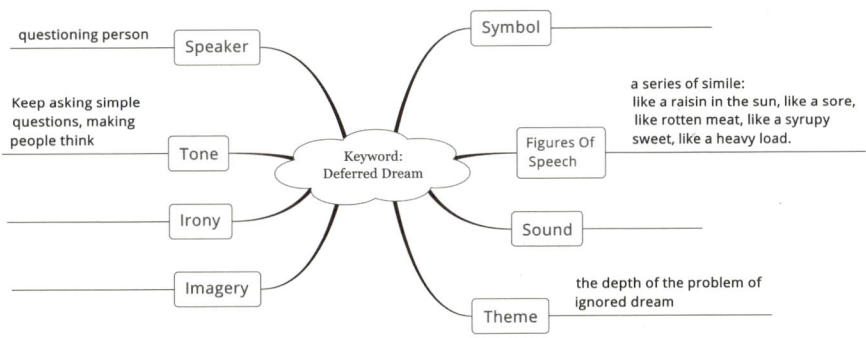

30. "Constantly Risking Absurdity" by Lawrence Ferlinghetti (1919~)

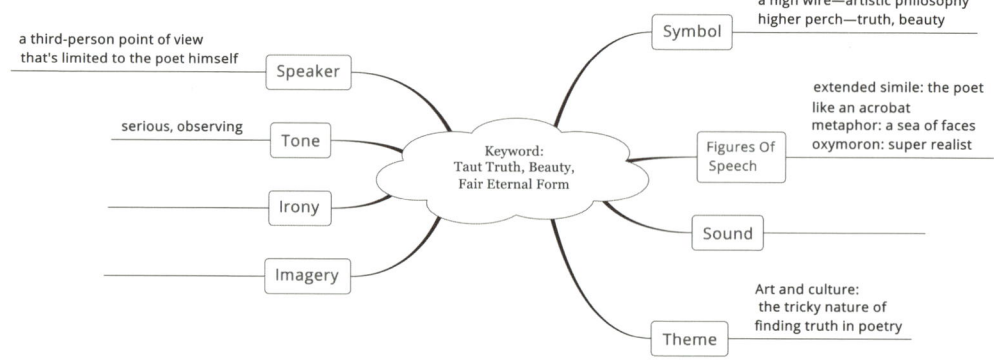

32. "Oh, My love Is like a Red, Red Rose" by Robert Burns (1759~1796)

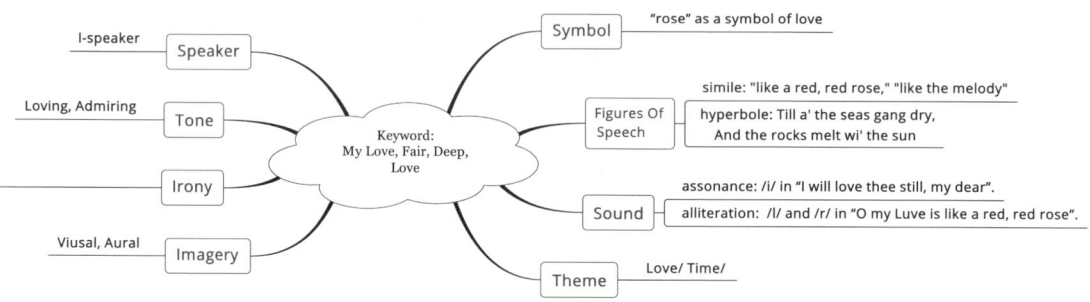

34. "To Lucasta Going to the Wars" by Richard Lovelace (1618~1658)

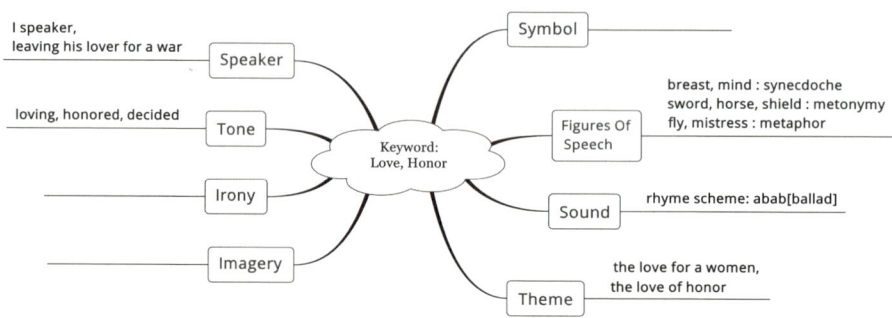

38. "I Like To See It Lap The Miles" by Emily Dickinson (1830~1886)

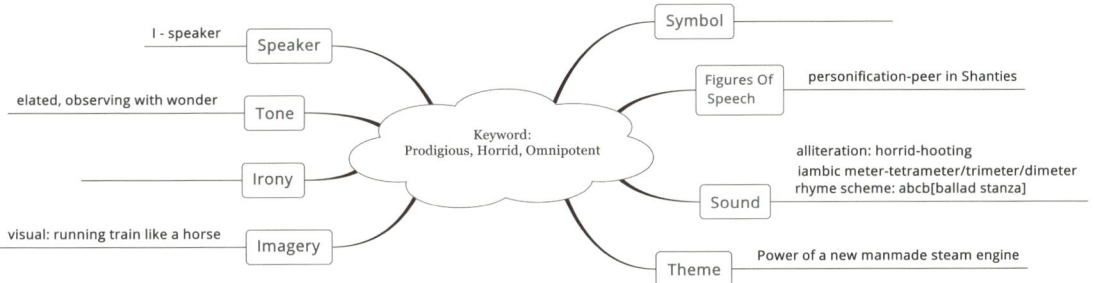

40. "The Eagle" by Alfred, Lord Tennyson (1809~1892)

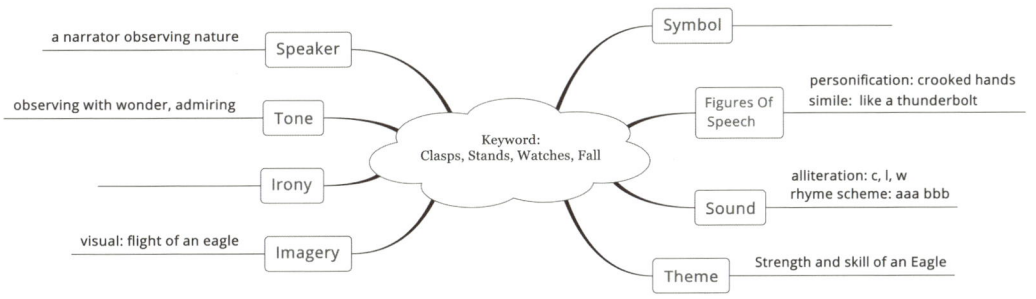

42. "She Dwelt Among The Untrodden Ways" by William Wordsworth (1770~1850)

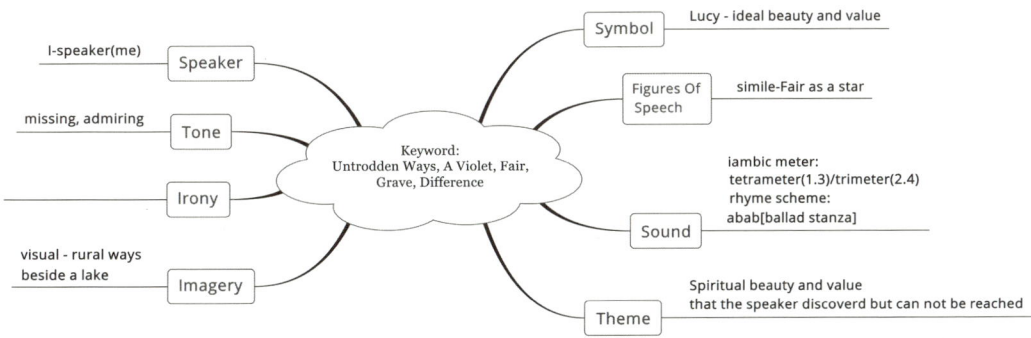

46. "When In Disgrace With Fortune And Men's Eyes (Sonnet 29)" by William Shakespeare (1564~1616)

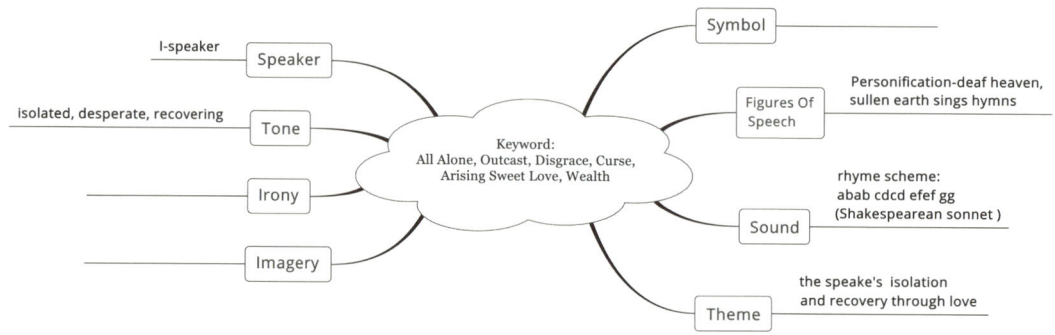

48. "The Sick Rose" by William Blake (1757~1827)

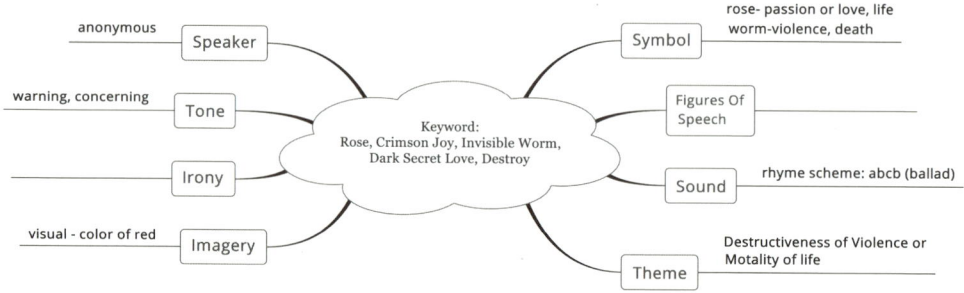

49. "Volcanoes be in Sicily" by Emily Dickinson (1830~1886)

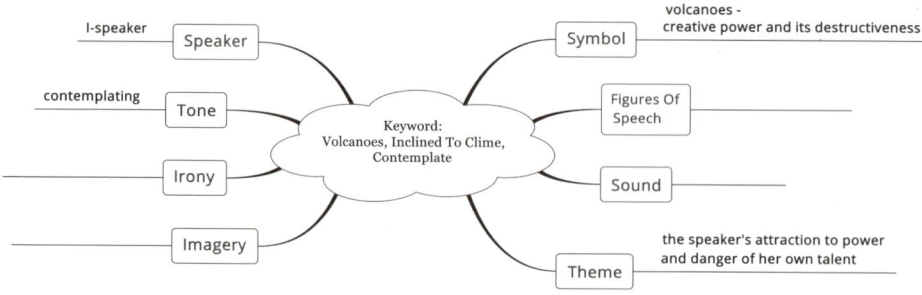

50. "Uphill" by Christina Rossetii (1830~1894)

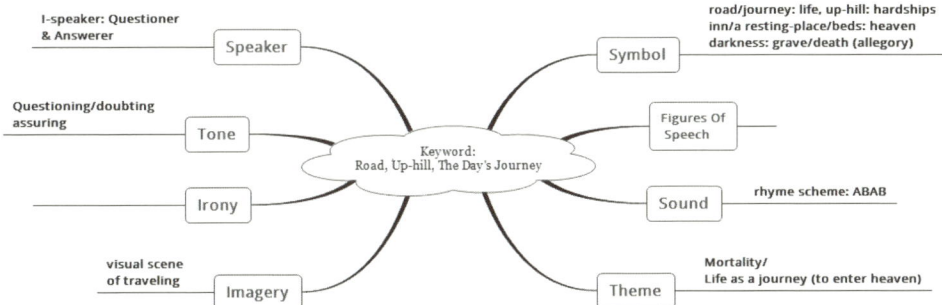

52. "The courage that my mother had" by Edna St. Vincent Millay (1892~1950)

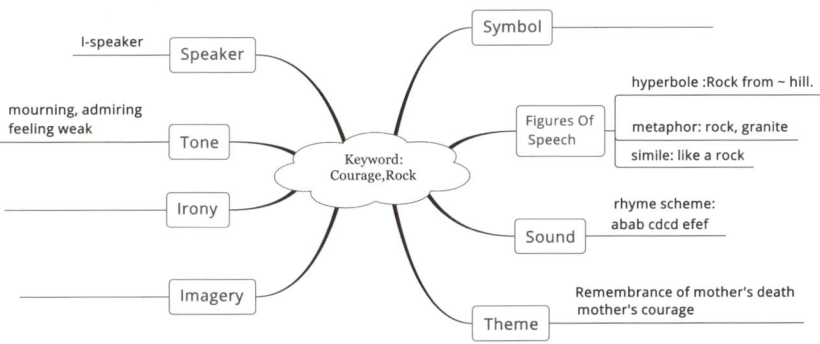

53. "Do not go gentle into that good night" by Dylan Thomas (1914~1953)

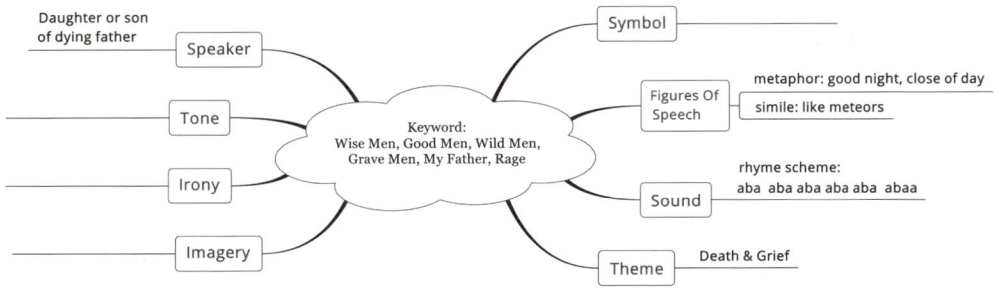

55. "The Windhover" by Gerard Manley Hopkins (1844~1889)

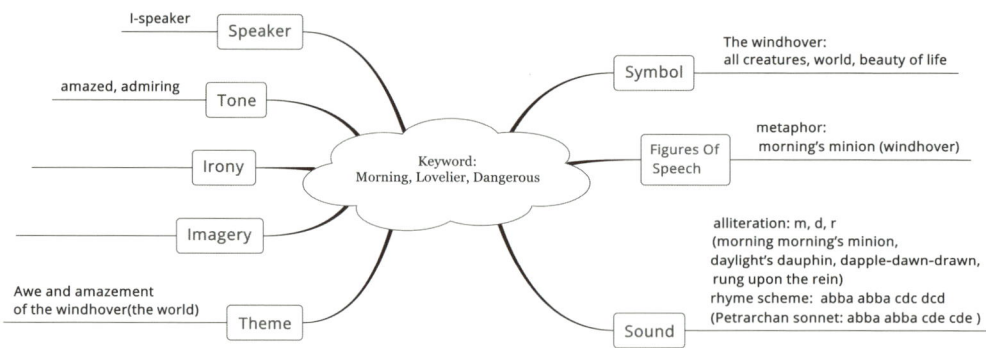

04 Translated Poems to Read

1. "My Arkansas" by Maya Angelou (1928~2014)

깊은 음울함이 있네
알칸사스에는.
이끼와 같은 오래된 범죄가 붙어있네
포플러 나무로부터.
음울한 대지는
너무도
붉어 안식이 없네.

일출도 머뭇거리는 듯하고
또한 그 순간에
빛을 내야 하는 그 목적을
잃어버리고,
그림자를 만들지 못하니
정오와 마찬가지라
예전이 더 밝았다네.

오래된 증오와
남북 전쟁 때의 끈은, 지금은 잠시
사용하지 않지만 완전히 없어지지 않았으니
오늘은 아직 오지 않다네
알칸사스에는.
극심한 고통으로 몸을 비튼다. 몸을 비튼다
끔찍한 음울함의 파도 속에서

VOCA
brooding a. 음울한
pend v. 매달리다, 미해결인 채로 있다, 현안(懸案)인 채 있다
incandescent a. 백열성의, 밝은, 강렬한; 열정적인
dusk v. 땅거미 어둑하게 하다, (날이) 저물어가다
writhe v. (흔히 극심한 고통으로) 온몸을 비틀다
antebellum a. (특히 미국 남북) 전쟁 전의
awful a. 끔찍한, 지독한

2. "Richard Cory" by Edwin Arlington Robinson (1869~1935)

리처드 코리가 시내를 내려갈 때는 언제나,
길 위에 있는 우리들은 그를 바라보았다.
그는 발끝부터 정수리까지 신사였다,
말끔히 면도하고, 정말 날씬하였다.

그리고 그는 언제나 조용히 차려입었고,
대화를 할 때는 언제나 인간적이었다.
그렇지만 그는 "안녕하세요"라고 말할 때에 가슴이 뛰어 안절부절 못하였다,
그리고 그는 걸을 때 빛이 났다.

그리고 그는 부유하였다, 정말, 왕보다 더 부유하였다.
그리고 모든 점에서 교육받은 세련미가 있었다.
요컨대, 우리는 그가 전부를 가진 자이고,
우리도 그의 위치에 오르기를 바랐다.

우리는 계속 일하였고, 빛을 기다렸다.
그리고 고기 없이 지냈고, 빵을 저주하였다.
그런데 리처드 코리는, 어느 조용한 여름날 밤,
집으로 돌아와 그의 머리에 총을 쏘았다.

3. "Ballad of Birmingham" by Dudley Randall (1914~2000)

"엄마, 바깥에 가서 노는 대신
시내에 가서,
버밍햄 거리에서 있는
자유의 행진에 참여해도 될까요?"

"안돼, 애야, 안된단다, 거기 가서는 안돼,
격렬하고 사나운 군중들이나,
곤봉과 호스와 총과 잡혀가는 것을 보는 건
너 같은 아이에게는 안 좋단다."

"그렇지만 엄마, 저 혼자가 아니예요.
다른 애들도 저와 같이 가는걸요,
그리고 버밍햄 거리를 행진하는 것은
우리 나라를 자유롭게 하기 위한 것이예요."

"안돼, 얘야, 안된단다, 거기 가서는 안돼,
총을 쏠까봐 겁난단다.
그렇지만 대신 교회에는 가도 좋단다
교회 유년부 성가대에서 노래를 하거라."

엄마는 딸의 밤처럼 까만 머리를 빗질해주고,
장미꽃 향으로 씻겨주고,
딸의 작은 갈색 두 손에 하얀 장갑을 끼워주고
발에는 하얀 신발을 신겨주었네.

엄마는 아이에게 미소지었네
성스러운 곳으로 가는 것을 알기에
그러나 그 미소는 마지막 미소가 되었네
그녀의 얼굴에서 볼 수 있는.

그녀는 폭발하는 소리를 듣자,
눈가가 젖어오면서 격정적이 되었네.
그녀는 버밍햄 거리를 마구 달려가며
아이의 이름을 불렀네.

그녀는 유리와 벽돌조각에 긁힌 채
신발을 하나 들어 올렸네.
"오, 내 아이가 신었던 신이구나,
그런데 아가 너는 어디에 있니?"

VOCA fierce a. 사나운, 험악한, 격렬한, 맹렬한, 극심한, 맹렬한   claw v. (손톱·발톱으로) 할퀴다[긁다]

4. "To an Athlete Dying Young" by A.E. Houseman (1859~1936)

이 고장에서 그대가 경주에서 우승했을 때
저자거리를 가로질러 그대를 들쳐 업고 돌아다녔네.
어른과 아이들이 환호하며 맞이하고,
우리는 어깨 높이 자넬 떠메고 집으로 갔었지.

오늘은 모든 주자들이 나온 그 길로
그대를 어깨에 메고 집으로 데려와
그대의 문지방에 내려놓네.
고요한 도시의 주민이 된 그대를.

지혜롭다 젊은이여, 때맞춰 떠났으니
영광이 지속되지 않는 그곳,
월계수는 일찍 자라지만
장미보다 빨리 시드는 들판을.

어두운 밤이 눈을 닫으면 그대는
기록이 깨지는 것을 보지 못할 것이요,
정적도 환호보다 나쁘지 않으리,
흙이 그대의 귀를 막아버리면.

이제는 그대 앞에서는 뽐내지 못하리라.
영예를 소진해 버린 젊은이 무리나,
명성이 앞서 달려
이름이 사람보다 먼저 죽은 주자들이

그러니 영광의 메아리가 사라지기 전에
날렵한 발로 어둠의 문지방을 딛고 서서
낮은 상인방까지 들어 올리라,
아직 방어하고 있는 그대의 우승컵을.

이른 월계관을 쓴 그대 머리 주위로
힘없는 망자를 보러 모여들어 보리라,
그대 머리에서는 아직 시들지 않았음을
소녀의 화환보다도 빨리 시드는 화환이.

5. "Ode to the West Wind" by Percy Bysshe Shelly (1792~1822)

I
오 거센 서풍, 너 가을의 숨결이여!
너의 눈에 보이지 않는 존재로부터 죽은 잎사귀들은
마치 마법사에게서 도망치는 유령처럼 쫓겨다니누나,

누렇고, 검고, 창백하며, 열병에 걸린 듯 빨간
역병에 걸린 무리들. 날개 달린 씨앗을
검은 겨울의 잠자리로 전차로 몰아가서,

산과 들을 신선한 색깔과 향기로
가득히 채울 때까지, 무덤 속의 송장들처럼
차가운 곳에 누워있게 하는 오 너 서풍.

봄의 하늘색 동생이 꿈꾸는 대지 위에
나팔을 부네 (향기로운 봉오리를 몰아
양떼처럼 대기속에 방목하며,)

거센 정신이여, 너는 어디서나 움직이누나.
파괴자인 동시 보존자여, 들으라, 오 들어라!

IV
만일 내가 네가 몰아갈 수 있는 하나의 낙엽이라면,
만일 내가 너와 함께 날을 수 있는 한 점의 빠른 구름이라면,
네 힘 밑에 헐떡이며, 네 힘의 충동을 같이 할 수 있고

다만, 오 통제할 수 없는 자여, 너보다 덜
자유로운 한 파도라면, 만일 내가
내 소년 시절 때 같다면, 그래서 너의 하늘을 나는 속도를
능가하는 것이 거의 공상이 아니었던 그때처럼
하늘의 네 방랑의 친구가 될 수 있다면,
나는 결코 이와 같이 심한 괴로움 속에서 기도를 하며

너와 겨루지 않았으리라.
오 나를 일으켜 다오, 파도처럼, 잎새처럼, 구름처럼!
나는 인생의 가시 위에 쓰러져 피를 흘리노라!

세월의 무거운 압박이 사슬로 묶고 굴복하게 했다,
길들일 수 없는, 날쌔고 자존심 강한, 너와 같았던 나를.

V
나를 너의 수금으로 삼아다오, 바로 저 숲처럼.
내 잎새들이 숲의 잎새처럼 떨어진들 어떠리!
너의 억센 조화의 동란은

나와 저 숲으로부터 슬프지만 감미로운
깊은 가을의 가락을 얻으리. 거센 정신이여, 너는
나의 정신이 되라! 맹렬한 자여! 너는 내가 되라,

내 죽은 사상을 온 우주에 뿌려 다오,
새로운 출생을 재촉하는 시든 잎사귀처럼!
그리고 이 시의 주문으로

흐트려 다오, 꺼지지 않은 화로의
재와 불꽃처럼, 인류 사이에 나의 말을!
내 입술을 통해 잠 깨지 않은 대지에

예언의 나팔이 되어 다오! 오 바람이여,
겨울이 오면 봄이 멀 수 있으랴?

6. "Aubade" by Philips Larkin (1922~1985)

나는 하루 종일 일한다, 그리고 밤에 반쯤 취한다.
네 시에 소리 없는 어둠에 깨어, 응시한다.
시간 맞춰 커튼 가장자리가 희붐해질 것이다.
그때까지 내가 보는 것은 실제로 늘 거기 있는 것:
쉬지 않는 죽음, 이제 꽉 찬 하루 더 가까워진,
모든 생각 불가능하게 만들며, 오로지 어떻게
그리고 어디서 그리고 언제 내 자신 죽게 될까 생각 말고는 말이지.
무미건조한 심문: 하지만 그 두려움,
죽어감의, 그리고 죽어 있음의 그것이,
번쩍여 새롭게 다시 쥐고 몸서리치게 만든다.

마음이 멍해진다 그 섬광에. 회한으로 아니라
—행하지 않은 선, 주지 않은 사랑, 쓰지 않고
찢어버린 시간—또한 비참하게도 아니라,
하나의 유일 생이 잘못 시작을 벗는 데
그렇게 오래 걸릴 수 있고, 영영 못할 수 있다는 비참 때문 아니라;
바로 그 전적인 영영 텅 비어 있음에,
그 확실한 절멸, 우리가 여행해 가서
언제나 필경 상실될 그것에. 여기 있지 않는 것,
아무 데도 있지 않는 것,
그것도 곧; 더 끔찍한 게 없다, 더 진실된 게 없다.

이것은 특수한 방식의 겁내기다,
어떤 속임수로도 떨쳐낼 수 없는. 종교가 기를 쓰곤 했지,
저 방대한, 좀먹은, 음악의 양단,
우리가 결코 안 죽을 것처럼 굴게끔 창조된,
그리고 허울만 그럴듯한 것들, 어느 이성적인 존재도 자기가
느끼지 않으려는 것을 두려워할 수 없다 운운하는, 못 보거든
우리가 두려워하는 것은 이것인데—보임 없음, 소리 없음,
촉감도 맛도 냄새도 없음, 생각할 수단 없음,
사랑하거나 연결할 것 없음,
마취, 아무도 그것으로부터 돌아올 수 없는.

그리하여 그것은 딱 시야 가장자리에 머문다,
작은 초점 안 맞은 흐릿한 형체 하나, 상설(常設) 냉기,
각각의 충돌을 둔화, 우유부단으로까지 내려뜨리는.
대개의 일들은 한 번도 벌어지지 않을 수 있다: 이 일은 벌어질 터,
그리고 그 사실 깨달음 분통 터진다
용광로―두려움으로, 우리가 사람들도
술도 없이 사로잡힐 때, 용기는 아무 소용 없다:
그것은 남들을 겁주려는 의도가 아니다. 용감하다는 것
아무도 떼어놓지 못한다 무덤한테서.
죽음은 다를 바 없다 그것에 징징대든 그것을 견디든.

천천히 빛이 강해지고, 방이 구체화한다.
그것은 서 있다 옷장처럼 명백하게, 우리가 아는 것,
늘 알았던 것, 스스로 피할 수 없음을 아는 것,
그렇지만 받아들일 수 없는 것. 한쪽은 가야 할 터.
그러는 동안 전화들 몸을 쭈그린다, 벨 울릴 준비 하느라
문단속한 사무실에서, 그리고 온갖 무정한
복잡한 임대한 세계가 깨우기 시작한다.
하늘은 찰흙처럼 희다, 태양이 전혀 없이.
사무가 처리되어야 한다.
우체부들 의사처럼 이 집 저 집 다닌다.

7. "The Names" by Billy Collins (1941~)

어제, 한 밤중에 나는 깬 채 누워있었네.
어느새 조용한 비가 바람 한 점 없는 가운데 내리고,
은색의 창문틀에 시선이 멈췄을 때
마침 Ackerman으로 A부터 시작해서
그 다음으로는 Baxter와 Calabro,
Davis와 Eberling으로 이름들이
작은 물방울처럼 어둠속으로 떨어졌네.
밤의 천장에 인쇄된 이름들.
젖은 강둑을 돌아나가는 이름들.
시냇가에 있는 스물여섯 그루의 버드나무들.

아침에 나는 맨발로
눈 속에 맺힌 눈물 같은 무거운 이슬이 맺힌,
그리고 각자 이름을 가진
수천 송이의 꽃 사이를 걸었네—
Fiori라고 노란 꽃잎에 새겨져 있었다네.
그리고 Gonzalez와 Han, Ishikawa와 Jenkins라고.
이름들은 공기 중에도 쓰여 있었고
낮의 옷 속으로 수놓아졌다네.
한 장의 사진 아래에 있는 이름은 우체통에 붙여진 채로.
찢어진 셔츠 위의 모노그램,
나는 당신이 전면 창문들에 그리고
이 도시의 밝게 펼쳐진 차양 위에
철자로 써져있는 것을 보네.
나는 모퉁이를 돌면서 음절들을 소리 내어 말해보네—
Kelly와 Lee,
Medina, Nardella, 그리고 O'Connor.

내가 숲을 살짝 보았을 때,
아이들 용으로 일부러 만든 수수께끼 속에 있듯이
글자가 숨겨진 두꺼운 뭉치가 보이네.
Parker와 Quigley는 재가 된 잔가지 속에,
Rizzo, Schubert, Torres와 Upton는

고대 단풍나무의 나뭇가지 속에 있는 비밀들.
창백한 하늘에 써진 이름들.
빌딩들 사이를 수직으로 올라가는 이름들.
돌 속에 말이 없는
혹은 문 뒤에서 울부짖는 이름들.
대지 위로 그리고 바다로 바람에 날려 간 이름들.
밤에는—약해지는 불빛이 마지막 이름을 삼키네.
호수위에 한 소년이 노를 들어 올리네.
창문 옆에 한 여인이 초에 불을 켜고,
그리고 이름들이 장밋빛 구름 위에 줄지어 있네—
Vanacore와 Wallace,
(할 수만 있다면 찾지 못한 이름들에는 X를 세워두었으면)
그리고 Young과 Ziminsky, 마지막으로 가슴 철렁하게 하는 Z.

이름들이 핀 머리에 새겨져 있었네.
이름 하나는 다리 하나에 걸쳐 있고, 다른 이름 하나가 터널을 통과하네.
파란 이름 하나가 하늘 속으로 새겨지네.
평범한 시민들, 노동자들, 엄마와 아빠들의 이름들이,
눈을 반짝이던 그 딸, 그 재치있던 아들.
푸른 들판에 이름들의 철자.
작은 새들의 발자국에 있는 이름들.
모자에서 올라오는 이름들이나
또는 혀끝에서 머물고 있는 이름들.
이름들이 희미한 기억의 창고 속으로 운반되네.
너무나 이름이 많아서, 마음의 벽에는 거의 붙일 자리가 없네.

※ This poem is dedicated to the victims of September 11 and to their survivors.

VOCA

- **steal in** v. 몰래 들어가다; 밀수하다
- **as it happens/happened** 마침[공교롭게도]
- **droplet** n. 작은 (물)방울
- **willows** n. (농업) 버드나무류(類)
- **unfurl** v. (동그랗게 말린 것이) 펼쳐지다[펴지다]; 펼치다, 펴다
- **awning** n. (창이나 문 위의) 차양, 비[해] 가리개
- **concoct** v. (특히 음식이나 음료를 이것저것 섞어) 만들다
- **twig** n. (나무의) 잔가지
- **jolt** n. (특히 강한 충격·놀람으로) 가슴이 철렁하는 느낌
- **etch** v. (유리·금속 등에) 식각(蝕刻)[에칭]하다, 아로새기다

8. "Go, lovely rose" by Edmund Waller (1606~1687)

가라, 사랑스러운 장미여!
그녀의 시간과 나를 낭비하는 그녀에게 말하라
이제야 아느냐고
내가 그녀를 너에게 비길 때
얼마나 사랑스럽고 아름답게 그녀가 보이는 가를.

젊고 우아함을 보이기,
꺼리는 그녀에게 말하라,
만일 네가 사람 하나 살지 않는
사막에서, 피었었더라면,
넌 분명히, 사람들의 칭찬을 받지 못하고 죽었으리라는 것을.

빛으로부터 물러난
아름다움의 가치는 적다;
그녀에게 나오라고 말하라,
사랑 받도록 허락하고,
찬미 받기를 그토록 얼굴 붉히지 말도록.

그리고 죽어라! 그래서 그녀가
너에게서 희귀한 모든 공통된
운명을 읽을 수 있도록;
놀랍도록 달콤하고 아름다운
시간의 몫이 얼마나 짧은 가를.

9. "The Passionate Shepherd to His Love" by Christopher Marlowe (1564~1593)

이리와 내 애인이 되어 함께 살자꾸나,
그리하여 골짜기, 나무숲, 언덕, 들판,
산림, 또는 험한 산이 주는
온갖 환희를 맛보자꾸나.

바위 위에 나가 앉아
얕은 물가에서 목동들이
양치는 걸 보자꾸나 ─ 강물 내리치는
소리에 새들은 고운 가락으로 노래하고

난 장미로 그대 잠자리 마련하고
향기로운 꽃다발 수없이 엮으리라.
꽃으로 모자와 치마를 엮어서
도금양 잎 새로 수를 놓으려니;
우리 귀여운 양들한테서 뽑은 상품의 털로 나들이옷을 만들고
좋은 안감을 댄 추울 때 신발을 만들려니,
순금의 장식을 달아서;

풀줄기와 담장이 순으로 띠를 만들어주려니
산호로 된 꺾쇠와 호박을 못을 박아서,
이 같은 환희에 내 마음이 끌린다면
이리 와서 내 애인이 되어 함께 살지 않을래.

목동들은 그대 기쁨을 위해
5월 아침마다 노래하고 춤추나니,
이 같은 환희에 그대 마음 끌린다면
내 애인이 되어 함께 살자꾸나.

10. "My Last Duchess" by Robert Browning (1812~1889)

저것은 벽에 걸린 내 전(前) 공작부인의 그림이오,
마치 살아있는 것처럼 보이지요. 작품이
참으로 경이롭지 않소. 판돌프 수사가 화필을
하루 동안 바쁘게 움직였고, 그녀는 서 있었소.
앉아서 그녀를 보지 않겠소? 나는
일부러 "판돌프 수사"라고 말했소, 왜냐하면
당신처럼 그려져 있는 표정, 진지한 반짝임의 깊이와 열정을
처음 보는 자들은 절대로 읽지 못하기 때문이오.
그러나 그들이 내 쪽으로 돌아서서 (그 누구도
내가 당신을 위해 걷었던 커튼을 걷지 못하오, 나 말고는)
으레 그들이 감히 어떻게 저런 시선이 저기에서 나오는지
감히 내게 묻고는 했던 것처럼 보였소. 그러니 당신이
돌아서서 물어보는 첫 번째 사람은 아니었소.
경, 공작부인의 뺨에 홍조라고 불리는 그것은
그녀의 남편에게만 보였던 것이 아니었소. 아마도
판돌프 수사는 어쩌다가 "부인의 망토가 너무 많이
부인의 손목을 덮고 있습니다." 또는 "그림은
부인의 목 주변에 감도는 저 희미한 붉은 빛을
다시 만들어 낼 수 있기를 바라서는 안 됩니다." 라고 말했던 것이오.
그 따위 것이 공손한 태도라고 그녀는 생각했고, 그 말은
그녀가 기뻐하며 홍조를 띠울 수 있을 만큼 충분했던 거요. 그녀는
마음을 갖고 있었소—내가 어떻게 말해야 좋을까?—그녀는 그녀가 보는
것마다 좋아했고, 그녀의 눈길은 모든 곳에 닿아 있었소.
너무 쉽게 기뻐하고 너무 쉽게 감동을 받았던 거요.
경, 그것은 모두 동일하였소! 그녀의 가슴 위에 단 내 정표(브로치 등)와
서쪽으로 태양이 지는 것과
어떤 주제넘게 나서는 바보가 그녀를 위해
과수원에서 꺾어다 준 벚나무 가지와
그녀가 테라스 주변에서 타던 흰 노새—모든 것이 혹은 각각의 것이
그녀로부터 똑같이 만족스러운 말이 나오게 하거나
최소한 얼굴이 붉어지게 했소. 그녀는 사람들에게 감사해했소—좋소! 그러나
어떻게 해서든지 감사해했소—난 어떻게 인지는 모르오—마치 그녀는
내가 선물한 900년의 명예와 아무 것도 아닌 사람들의 선물을

동등하게 생각했던 것 같소. 누가 이런 사소한 것을 탓하려고
자존심을 굽히려 하겠소? 설령 당신이 말하는 데에 있어서
기술을 갖고 있다고 해도—(난 갖고 있지 않는)—당신의 의지를
그런 것에게 꽤 확실하게 할 것이고, "당신의 이것이나
저것은 나를 싫증나게 하오. 당신의 이것은 모자라고,
저것은 지나치오."라고 말할 것이오—그리고 만약 그녀가
그녀 자신을 그렇게 교육받게 한다면, 정말로 그녀는
당신의 말에 반박하지 않고, 참으로 변명하지 않을 것이오.
—그렇다 하더라도 자존심을 굽히는 일일 것이고, 나는 절대로
자존심을 굽히는 쪽을 택하지 않소. 오, 경, 내가 그녀를 지나칠 때마다
그녀는 의심할 여지없이 미소를 지었소. 하지만 그 똑같이 환한 미소 없이
누가 지나쳤겠소? 이것은 늘어났소. 나는 명령을 내렸고,
그리고 나서 모든 미소가 함께 멈췄소. 저기 그녀가
마치 살아있는 것처럼 서 있소. 일어서지 않겠소? 아래층에 있는
사람들을 만날 것이오. 다시 한 번 말하지만
당신의 주인인 백작의 알려진 후한 씀씀이는
결혼지참금에 대한 나의 정당한 요구를 거절하지 않을 거라는
충분한 보증이오.
비록 그의 아름다운 따님 자체가, 내가 처음에 얘기했다시피,
나의 목적이기는 하지만. 아니, 우리 함께 아래로
내려갑시다, 경. 그런데, 잠깐 바다말을 길들이는
바다신 상을 봐주시오. 정말 진귀한 것이라오.
저건 인스부르크의 클라우스가 나를 위해 주조한 것이라오!

11. "Ulysses" by Alfred, Lord Tennyson (1809~1892)

하릴없는 왕으로서 이 적막한 화롯가,
불모의 바위 틈서리
늙은 아내와 짝하여
먹고 자고 욕심만 부리는 야만 족속에게
어울리지 않는 법이나 베푼다는 것,
쓸모없는 짓이다
나는 죽어도 모험을 그만둘 수는 없도다
내 삶의 마지막 찌꺼기라도 다 마셔 버리겠도다
나는 즐거움도, 고통도 마음껏 즐겨 본 사람
때로는 나를 따르는 부하들과 함께,
때로는 혼자서
해변에서 폭풍우가 몰아쳐 캄캄한 바다를 성나게 만들었을 때
자연히 내 이름은 사해(四海)에 떨치게 되었도다
채워질 줄 모르는 호기심으로 세상을 떠돌다 보니
보기도 많이 보았고, 배우기도 많이 배웠도다
신기한 사람들이 사는 도시들, 이상한 풍속, 기후, 정치제도
어디에서나 항상 귀빈으로 대접받았도다.
바람 휘몰아치는 트로이 평원에서도
나는 동료들과 함께 전쟁을 만끽 했도다.
나는 그 모든 경험의 한 부분이다.
그러나 모든 체험은 하나의 홍예문
그 너머로 가보지 못한 세계가 힐끗 보이나
다가갈수록 그 변경은 사라져버린다.
일을 하지 않고 쉰다는 것, 정지한다는 것, 얼마나 지루한 일인가
쓰지 않고 녹슬고 빛을 잃는다는 것, 얼마나 지루한 일인가
숨만 쉰다면 그것이 사는 것인가
남보다 몇 배의 삶을 살아도 부족하다 하겠는데
이제는 나 하나의 생애마저 남은 것이 얼마 없구나.
그러나 한 시간 한 시간은
영원한 정적에서 구해낼 수 있는 것,
정적만이 아닌 새로운 것을 가져오는 것,
3년 동안이나 몸을 살찌우고 있는 것,
추악한 짓이라,

이 늙어가는 영혼을
인간 사상의 아득한 변경 너머로
침몰하는 별처럼 지식을 추구하려 몸살하는데.(……)

12. "I'm nobody! Who are you?" by Emily Dickinson (1830~1886)

나는 무명인! 당신은 누구신가요?
당신도 ― 무명인 ― 인가요?
그렇다면 우린 참 잘 만났군요.
말하지 마세요! 우리를 쫓아낼지도 모르니!

얼마나 끔찍한지요 ― 유명인이 ― 된다는 것은!
세상 사람들이 다 알잖아요 ― 개구리처럼 말입니다 ―
자기이름을 ― 기나긴 유월 내내 ―
늪에 대고 자랑하니 말입니다!

13. "The Chimney Sweeper" by William Blake (1757~1827)

어머니께서 돌아가셨을 적 나는 매우 어렸답니다.
아버지는 나를 팔았죠, 아직 나는 입으로
'―청소! ―청소! ―청소! ―청소!'를 제대로 외치지도 못할 때 말이에요.
그래서 굴뚝청소를 하며 검댕 속에서 잠이 들지요.

꼬마 톰 다크레가 있는데요, 양 털처럼 곱슬곱슬한
머리칼이 잘리자 그는 울었지요, 그래서 내가 말해주었답니다,
'뚝, 톰! 신경쓰지 마, 머리칼이 없으면
검댕이 네 하얀 머리칼을 더럽힐 수 없어 좋잖아.'

그러자 그는 잠잠해졌습니다. 바로 그날 밤이었습니다,
그가 잠결에 이런 광경을 보게 된 것은!
딕, 조, 네드, 잭 등 수천 명에 달하는 청소부 모두가
검은 관 속에 갇혀있었습니다.

그런데 빛나는 열쇠를 가진 천사가 다가오더니
관을 열고 모두를 해방시켜주었습니다.
그들은 푸른 들판을 폴짝거리며, 웃으며 달려갑니다.
강에서 몸을 씻자 모두가 햇빛 속에 밝게 빛을 발합니다.

그들은 발가벗은 흰 몸으로, 청소가방을 모두 내팽개쳐 두고
구름위로 솟아올라 바람을 타고 장난치며 놉니다.
천사가 톰에게 말했습니다, 착한 소년이 되면
하나님을 아버지로 모실 수 있고 언제나 기쁨이 넘칠 것이라고.

그러다가 톰은 잠에서 깨어났습니다. 우리들도 어둠 속에서 일어났지요.
우리 모두 가방과 솔을 챙겨 일터로 향했답니다.
비록 아침은 차가웠지만 톰은 행복하고 따뜻함을 느낄 수 있었답니다.
그러니 모두 자기 임무를 다하면 다칠까 두려워할 필요가 없다는 것이지요.

14. "Red Wheelbarrow" by William Carlos Williams (1883~1963)

매우 많은 것들이 기대고
있는 것은

빨간색 외바퀴
손수레

빗물에 반짝이고
있는

하얀 닭들 옆에
놓인
(흰 병아리 옆
빗물로 씻긴
빨간 외바퀴수레에
너무 많은 것이 의존하네.)

15. "Negro" by Langston Hughes (1902~1967)

나는 흑인이네.
검은 밤처럼 검고,
내 아프리카의 깊은 곳처럼 검네.

나는 노예였네.
시저가 그의 현관문을 깨끗하게 유지하라고 말하였네.
나는 워싱턴의 구두를 닦았네.

나는 노동자였네.
내 손 아래 피라미드들이 만들어졌네.
나는 울워스 빌딩을 위해 회반죽을 만들었네.

나는 가수였네.
아프리카에서 조지아까지
내 슬픔의 노래를 가져갔네.
나는 래그타임 노래를 만들었네.

나는 희생자였네.
벨기에인들이 콩고에서 내 손을 잘랐네.
그들은 여전히 미시시피에서 나에게 폭행을 가하네.

나는 흑인이네.
검은 밤처럼 검고,
내 아프리카의 깊은 곳처럼 검네.

16. "Fire and Ice" by Robert Frost (1874~1963)

어떤 이는 이 세상이 불로 망할 것이라 말하고,
또 어떤 이는 얼음으로 끝날 것이라고 말하네.
내가 맛본 욕망이라는 것을 생각해볼 때
나는 불의 종말을 지지한다네.
그러나 세상에 두 번의 종말이 있다면
얼음도 파괴하는 데는 대단한 힘을 가지고 있고
그것으로 충분하다고 말할 만큼
나는 증오에 대해서도 잘 알고 있다고 생각한다네.

17. "The Man He Killed" by Thomas Hardy (1840~1928)

"그와 내가
어떤 오래된 선술집에서 만났더라면,
함께 앉아서 술잔을 기울였을 텐데
단번에 여러 잔의 맥주를!

"그러나 보병이 되어
서로의 얼굴을 노려보며,
그가 나를 쏘듯 나도 쏘아
그를 죽이고 말았네.

"나는 그를 죽였네 —
그가 나의 적이었으므로,
그렇지, 물론 그는 나의 적이었어,
그것은 매우 분명한 사실이었어, 그렇지만

"그도 나처럼 별다른 생각이 없었을게야
군인이나 되겠다고 생각했겠지 — 나처럼 —
일자리도 잃었겠다 — 세간도 다 처분했겠다
아마 그 외에 다른 이유가 있었겠나.

"그렇네. 전쟁이란 참으로 이상하지!
선술집에서 만났었더라면
술도 사고 돈도 좀 보태주었을 사람을
총으로 쏴 죽이니 말이야."

18. "Porphyria's Lover" by Robert Browning (1812~1889)

곧 음산한 바람이 불어대며
느릅나무 꼭대기가 원한으로 찢겨지고
호수를 어지럽힌다
나는 부서진 심장으로 듣고 있었다
포피리아가 혹한과 폭풍을 뚫고
미끄러지듯이 안으로 들어왔을 때
그녀는 무릎을 꿇고 활기 없는 쇠창살을
불태워, 오두막 안을 따뜻하게 했을 때
그리고 그녀는 일어나, 잘 차려 입은 옷으로부터
물이 떨어지는 망토와 숄을 벗어두고
그녀의 더럽혀진 장갑을 벗고
모자를 벗어 습기찬 그녀의 머리카락이 흘러내리게 했다
그리고 마지막으로, 내 옆에 앉아
나를 불렀다. 내가 대답하지 않자
그녀는 내 팔을 그녀 허리춤에 두르고
그녀의 부드럽고 하얀 어깨를 드러내어
그녀의 금발 대신
상체를 굽혀, 내 볼을 거기에 닿게 했다
그리고, 그녀의 금발로 모두 덮었다
어떻게 그녀가 나를 사랑하는지 속삭이면서 — 그녀는
그녀 가슴의 노력에도 불구하고, 너무 약해서
갈등하는 열정을 자존심으로부터
자유롭게 하지 못했고, 공허한 유대감을 잘라내지 못했다
그리고 그녀 자신을 나에게 영원히 주지 못했다
그러나 때때로 열정은 승리하곤 했다
오늘 밤 즐거웠던 향연에서

갑자기 그녀를 사랑해서 너무나도 창백해진
한 사람이 갑자기 생각났고, 그것을 떨쳐 버리지 못했다.
그래서 그녀는 바람과 비를 뚫고 왔다.
나는 그녀의 행복하고 자랑스러워하는 눈을
보았다고 확신한다. 마침내 나는 알았다.
포피리아가 날 숭배했다는 것을. 놀라움은
내 가슴을 북받쳐 오르게 하고, 그것을 더해갔다.
내가 할 일을 생각하는 동안
그 순간 그녀는 나의 것, 나의 것, 깨끗하고
완전히 순수하고 좋은 나는 해야 할 일을 찾았다.
나는 그녀의 머리카락을 모두
하나의 길고 노란 끈으로 만들어
그녀의 작은 목 주위를 세 번 감았다.
그리고 그녀를 목졸라 죽였다. 그녀는 고통을 느끼지 않았다.
나는 정말로 그녀가 고통을 느끼지 않았다고 확신한다
마치 닫힌 꽃봉오리가 한 마리의 벌을 붙잡듯이
나는 주의 깊게 그녀의 눈꺼풀을 열었다.
파란 눈이 다시 티 없이 웃었다.
그리고 나는 머리카락 옆의 목 부근을
느슨하게 하였다. 나의 불타는 키스에
그녀의 뺨이 다시 한 번 밝게 붉어졌다.
나는 이전처럼 그녀의 머리를 들어올려
이번에는 내 어깨로 지탱하였다
그녀의 머리는 여전히 그 위에 늘어져있다.
웃고 있는 발그레한 작은 머리가
그녀는 경멸하고 있던 모든 것이 사라지고
대신에 그녀의 사랑인 나를 얻게 되어
그녀의 궁극적인 의지를 갖게 되었음에 기뻐했다.
포피리아의 사랑, 그녀는 그녀가 바랐던 하나의 소망이
어떻게 이루어지게 되었는지 알지 못했다.
우리는 지금 함께 앉아있다.
그리고 긴 밤 동안 우리는 움직이지 않았고
아직 신은 한 마디도 하지 않았다

19. "Ozymandias" by Percy Bysshe Shelley (1792~1822)

옛 땅에서 온 여행자를 만났네.
그가 말하기를, "몸통이 없는 두 개의 거대한 돌로 된 발이
사막에 서있었소, 그 주위 모래 위에는,
반쯤 파묻힌 채, 산산 조각난 얼굴이 놓여있었소. 그 얼굴의 찡그림,
그리고 주름진 입술, 잔혹한 명령을 내리는 냉소는,
조각가가 그 열정을 잘 읽었음을 말해주는 바.
그 열정은, 이 생명 없는 물체에 찍힌 채로
그 열정을 조롱했던 손과 불러 일으켰던 마음보다도 더 오래 살아있었소.
또한 조각상의 받침대에는 이러한 문구가 새겨져있었소.
'내 이름은 오지만디아스, 왕 중 왕이로다,
그대 강자들이여, 내 업적을 보라, 그리고 절망하라!'
폐허뿐인 주위에는 아무것도 남아 있지 않았소.
그 거대한 잔해의 주위에는, 끝없이 그리고 풀 한포기 없이
황량하고 평평한 사막이 멀리 펼쳐져 있을 뿐."

20. "War Is Kind" by Stephen Crane (1871~1900)

울지 말아요, 그대여, 전쟁은 친절하다오.
당신의 연인은 격렬한 두 손을 하늘을 향해 던지고
겁에 질린 말에 혼자 올라타 있으니,
울지 말아요.
전쟁은 친절하다오.

쉰 소리로, 연대에서는 쾅쾅거리는 드럼
싸움에 목마른 젊은이들,
이 사내들은 훈련하고 죽기위해 태어났던 게지.
그들 위로 이유 없는 아름다운 광경이 날아가는데
위대하다 전쟁의 신이여, 위대하다, 그의 왕국도—
천 개의 시체가 누워있는 들판.

울지 마라, 아가야, 전쟁은 친절하단다.
네 아비는 노란 참호들 속을 굴렀고,
가슴에 격렬함을 품고 겁에 질려 침을 꿀떡 삼키며 죽었으니,
울지 마라.
전쟁은 친절하단다.

빠르게, 연대에서는 맹렬한 깃발
빨간색과 금색으로 장식한 독수리,
이 사내들은 훈련하고 죽기위해 태어났던 게지.
그들에게 중요한 것은 살육의 미덕
탁월한 살인이 뭔지 그들에게 잘 알려주는
그리고 천 개의 시체가 누워있는 들판도.

아들의 밝고 빛나는 수의(壽衣)의 단추처럼
그 심장이 아주 조그라져 있는 어머니여,
울지 말아요.
전쟁은 친절하답니다.

VOCA

weep v. 울다, 눈물을 흘리다	**babe** n. 아기
affright v. 두려워하게 하다	**trench** n. 도랑, 해자(垓子), (전장의) 참호
steed n. (문예체 또는 유머) (승마용) 말	**rage** a. 격렬한 분노, 격노
hoarse a. 사람·목소리가 (목) 쉰	**gulp** v. (특히 공포·놀라움에 질려) 침을 꿀떡 삼키다
boom v. 쾅[탕] 하는 소리를 내다	**blazing** a. 타는 듯이 더운, 맹렬한, 격렬한
regiment n. (군대의) 연대	**slaughter** n. (특히 전쟁에서의) 대량 학살, 살육
unexplained a. 설명되지 않은, 이유가 밝혀지지 않은	**excellence** n. 뛰어남, 탁월함
corpse n. 시체, 송장	**shroud** n. 수의(壽衣)

21. "When I Heard the Learn'd Astronomer" by Walt Whitman (1819~1892)

내가 그 박식한 천문학자의 말을 들었을 때,
증거와 숫자들이 내 앞에 줄지어 나열되었을 때,
더하고 나누고 측정하는 차트와 일람표가 내 눈앞에 제시되었을 때,
천문학자가 큰 강단 안에서 사람들의 큰 호응을 받으며 강의하는 것을 앉아서 들었을 때,
나는 왠지 모르게 금방 따분하고 지루해져서
자리에서 일어나 밖으로 빠져 나와
홀로 신비로운 밤의 촉촉한 대기 속을 거닐며
이따금 조용한 가운데 별들을 올려다보았다.

22. "The City Planners" by Margaret Atwood (1939~)

8월의 건조한 볕 아래서
이 주택 단지의 일요일 거리를 천천히 다닐 때:
우리에겐 불쾌하게
몇 가지가 눈에 들어왔다:
지나치게 규칙적으로 열 지어 있는 집들, 깨끗이
심겨진 나무들은, 겉 표면의
평평함을 드러내고 있어 마치
우리 차 문이 찌그러진 것을 비난하는 것 같다
큰 소리도 여기는 나지 않고, 혹은
유리 깨짐도 없고; 어떤 갑작스런 소리도 없이
축 쳐진 잔디를 싹 베어낸
힘센 잔디 깎는 기계의 일률적인 소리 외엔.

그러나 차도는 솜씨 좋게도
똑같은 모양으로 만들어져
사고와 혼란의 위험성을 피했어도, 지붕들은 모두 똑같은
방향으로 비스듬히 누워 뜨거운 하늘을 피하며
다른 것을 보여준다:
엎질러진 기름 냄새 희미하게

차고에서 풍기는 매스꺼움,
상처 자국처럼 깜짝 놀라게 하는 벽돌에 묻은 페인트 자국,
마구 감겨진 플라스틱
호스; 너무도 고정된 시선을 주는 저 넓은 창문들조차

미래에 있을 회반죽의
갈라진 틈 뒤에나 밑에 있을
광경을 잠시 보여 준다
집들이, 뒤집혀서, 비스듬하게
진흙 바다로, 빙하처럼 천천히 기울어 들어가는 것을
지금은 아무도 알아채지 못하지만.

거기에 도시 계획가들이
정치 음모 공범자들의 정신 나간 얼굴을 하고는
조사도 하지 않은 영토에
흩어져서, 서로서로 숨어서
각각 자기 자신의 눈보라에 숨은 채;

방향을 추측하며, 덧없는 선들을
나무 목재로 경계를 엄격히 세우듯이
하얗게 사라져가는 벽 위에 그린다

교외의 복잡한 모습을 추적하면서
눈의 단조로움의 광기 위에다

VOCA

city planner n. 도시 계획가
cruise v. 천천히 달리다[돌아다니다]
residential a. 거주하기 좋은, 주택지의
sanity n. 온전한 정신 (상태)
pedantic a. 지나치게 규칙을 찾는
sanitary a. 위생의, 위생적인, 깨끗한
levelness n. 평평함, 수평임, 동등함
rebuke n. 힐책, 꾸짖음
dent n. 움푹 들어간[찌그러진] 곳
abrupt a. 돌연한, 갑작스런
whine n. 끼익끽 하는 소리
mower n. (잔디) 깎는[풀 베는] 기계

swath n. (목초·보리 등의) 한 번 낫질한 자취
hysteria n. 히스테리, 과잉 흥분[반응]
neatly adv. 깔끔하게, 말쑥하게, 맵시 있게; 솜씨 있게
slant n. 비스듬함
poise v. (특정한) 태세를 취하다
plaster n. 회[석고]반죽
capsize v. (배가) 뒤집히다; (배를) 뒤집다
obliquely adv. 비스듬히 (기울어져);
conspirator n. 공모자, 음모 가담자
blizzard n. 눈보라, (위압적일 정도로) 많은 양
transitory a. (격식) 일시적인, 덧없는
bland a. 특징 없는, 단조로운, 특별한 맛이 안 나는

23. "Amoretti Lxxv: One day I wrote her name upon the strand" by Edmund Spenser (1552~1599)

어느 날 해변에다 그녀의 이름 써 두었더니
파도가 와서 씻어가 버리기에 또 다시 써 놓았건만
조수가 밀려와서 나의 수고를 삼켜 버렸다.
그녀 말하길 "부질없는 임이여,
필멸의 존재를 불멸케 하려 하시니 헛되고 헛되오이다.
이 한 몸도 이처럼 사라질 것이오
이내 이름 또한 사라질 테니까요."
나는 대답 했었네: "그렇지 않아. 비천한 자들이야 사멸케 두구려.

그러나 당신은 명성으로 살아남게 하리이다.
나의 시가 그대 영광된 이름을 천국에 써두어
그대의 귀한 덕을 영원케 하리이다.
그리하여 죽음이 온 세상 지배할 때, 저 천국에서
우리네 사랑은 살아서 호세를 새로이 누리게 하리이다."

24. "Stopping by Woods on a Snowy Evening" by Robert Frost (1874~1963)

이 숲의 주인이 누군지 알만 하다.
그러나 그의 집이 마을에 있으니
내가 여기, 갈 길 멈추고 서서
눈 덮이는 숲을 감상함을 보진 못하리.

나의 조랑말은 이상히 여기는가
가까이 인가도 없는 숲과
얼은 호수 사이에서 발길 멈춘 것을
일 년 중에도 제일 어두운 저녁에.

방울을 흔들어
잘못된 게 아니냐고 묻는다.

달리 소리라곤
눈송이 몰고 있는 연한 바람 스치는 소리뿐.

숲은 아름답고 깊고 깊은데,
내겐 지켜야 할 약속이 있고
자기 전에 가야할 수 십리 길이 있다,
자기 전에 가야할 수 십리 길이.

25. "In a Station of the Metro" by Ezra Pound (1885~1972)

군중 속의 환영 같은 이 얼굴들,
젖은 검은 나뭇가지 위의 꽃잎들.

26. "Some Good Things to Be Said for the Iron Age" by Gary Snyder (1930~)

쇠 지렛대가 울리면서
        길가에 떨어졌네
톱이 부딪히며 닿더니
나뭇가지들에 닿았네
녹의 맛이
나네

VOCA
tire iron n. (자동차의) 타이어를 떼어내는 지렛대
whang n. 강타; 그 소리; 음경; 철썩 치다, 세게 때리다(beat, whack)
brusht (=brushed) n. (…의 위에) 가볍게 닿음
Iron Age n. 철기 시대

27. "Shall I compare thee to a summer's day?" by William Shakespeare (1564~1616)

당신을 여름날과 비교한다면
당신이 훨씬 아름답고 평화로워요.
(여름엔) 오월의 귀여운 꽃봉오릴 세찬 바람이 흔들고
여름이 누릴 날 수는 너무도 짧아요.
하늘의 눈, 태양은 너무 뜨겁게 쬐기도 하고
하늘의 황금빛 얼굴은 흐려지기도 하지요.
아름다운 모든 것이 우연이나 자연의 변화에 따라 일그러져
아름다움이 언젠가는 사라지지요.
그러나 당신은 영원한 시 속에서 시간과 동행하게 될 때
당신의 영원한 여름은 사라지지 않을 것이요.
당신이 누리는 그 아름다움을 잃지 않을 것이요,
죽음도 당신에게 제 그늘에 논다고 떠벌이진 못하리이다.
사람들이 숨 쉴 수 있고 눈으로 볼 수 있는 한은
이 시도 살아서 당신께 생명을 부여할 것이기에.

28. "I wandered lonely as a cloud[Daffodils]" by William Wordsworth (1770~1850)

계곡과 산 위에 고고히 떠도는 구름처럼
나도 정처 없이 떠돌 적에
홀연히 눈에 띄는
무리지은 황금 수선화
호반의 나무들 아래에서
미풍에 당실당실 춤을 추고 있었네.

은하수에 반짝이는 별들처럼
끝없이 줄을 잇고
호반 따라 늘어서
한 눈에 들어오는 수만 송이 수선화
고개를 하늘대며 사뿐사뿐 춤을 췄네.

은물결도 신바람에
춤을 췄지만 수선화 춤가락이 더욱 흥겨워
이 즐거운 벗님 틈에
신이 안 나면 시인이랴.
넋 잃은 구경 결에 생각조차 못했었네—
구경도 좋았거늘 선물까지 챙긴 줄은—

어쩌다 긴 의자 자리하고
하염없이 누웠거나 생각에 잠길 때면
고독만이 누리는
심안에
수선화 떠오르고 금세 가슴은 즐거움 넘쳐
어울려 춤을 추네.

29. "Harlem[Dream deferred]" by Langston Hughes (1902~1967)

미뤄진 꿈은 어떻게 될까?

햇볕아래의 건포도처럼
말라버릴까?
아니면 상처처럼 곪을까?—
그리고는 짓물러 터질까?
썩어가는 고기처럼 악취가 날까?
아니면 설탕가루로 뒤덮힐까—
끈적이는 과자처럼?

아마도 축 처져서
무거운 짐짝처럼 될 거야.

아니면 혹시 폭발할는지도?

30. "Constantly Risking Absurdity" by Lawrence Ferlinghetti (1919~)

계속해서 무릅쓰네 부조리와
죽음을
관중들의
머리위로
그가 공연할 때마다
시인은 곡예사처럼
서리 위에서
높은 줄로 올라가
균형을 잡고 얼굴들의 바다 위에 있는
눈빛들을 보며
그 날의 다른 쪽으로
속도를 맞추어 나가네
앙트르샤를 하고
발로 날랜 솜씨의 트릭을 보이고
고단수의 연출을 보이고
모든 것을 실수 없이
무엇이든
무엇이든지 간에 하네
왜냐하면 대단한 현실주이자이기 때문이오
부득이하게도 팽팽한(긴장된) 진실을
인식해야 한다오
더 높이 있는 쉴 곳
아름다운 여인이 서서 중력의 무게로
기다리는 곳에
가기위해 그가 내딛어야 하는
각 스텝이
죽음에 반항하는 뛰기를 하기 위해
그리고 그는
작은 찰리 채플린이라네
아마도 그녀의 아름답고 영원한 형태를
잡을 수도 혹은 못 잡을 수도 있지만
존재의 빈 공간에서
팔 다리를 쫙 벌린다네

VOCA

absurdity n. 부조리, 불합리, 모순
acrobat n. 곡예사
rime n. (문예체) 서리
entrechat n. (pl. ~s[~]) (발레) 앙트르샤 (뛰어오른 동안에 발뒤축을 여러 번 교차시키는 동작)
sleight n. 숙련; 날랜 솜씨; 교묘한 수완
perforce adv. 필요해서; 부득이
taut a. (밧줄 따위가) 팽팽한, (팽팽하게) 긴장된
spreadeagled (←spreadeagle) a. 팔다리를 벌린 (자세의)

31. "Rooming houses are old women" by Audre Lorde (1934~1992)

하숙집들은 노파들
어두운 창문들을 흔들어 그들의 때가 되도록
불완전한 일상들을 감내하며 기다리네
임대 사무실을 흔들어 구부려
공동 화장실이 되고 가스가열판과
그리고 한 달에 두 번 시에서 지급하는
한 때는 쓸모 있던 쓰레기를 담은
침대아래 박스가 되도록
그리고 한 밤중 파티로 시끄럽고
욕조에는 수상한 반지들이 남겨져있는
옆집 젊은 남자들이 되도록
그들을 더 이상 깨우지 마시오
한 밤중부터 식사 때까지 멈추지 않고 그 사이에
빛이 뒤섞인 창문들을 통과해 가네
그러면 누가 버지의 아들이 엉망이 되어 있는
저 창문을 못쓰게 만들어 놨는가?

느릿한 걸음으로부터 안락과 모욕으로
낮의 노동으로부터 남은 음식들로
묵직한 쇼핑백까지.
하숙집들은 노파들
기다리고 있네
어두워지는 창문을 통해
고통의 끝이나 시작을
찾으면서

반쯤 열린 문으로 보인 노파는
바라네
자신들이 기다리고 있기 보다는
새롭지는 않으나
미지의 그리고 열망하는
어떤 곳으로 가는
입구이기를.

VOCA

rooming house n. (가구가 딸린) 방을 세 놓는 건물, (식사를 제공하지 않는) 하숙집(lodging house)
stoop v. 몸을 굽히다, (자세가) 구부정하다, 구부정하게 서다[걷다]
gas ring n. 원반형 가스 가열판
issue with v. …을 지급하다
fishy a. 생선 냄새[맛]가 나는, (비격식) 수상한 (냄새가 나는)
mealtime n. (하루 중의) 식사 시간
arouse v. (느낌·태도를) 불러일으키다[자아내다]

inbetween 중간에
mar v. -rr- (좋은 것을) 손상시키다[망치다]
mess with somebody/something v. (보통 부정문에 쓰여) (해로울지도 모르는) ~와 관계를 맺다[~에 얽혀 들다]
welfare n. (개인·단체의) 안녕, 복지, 후생
shuffle n. 발을 끌며 느릿느릿 걷기
leftover n. (주로 복수로) (식사 후에) 남은 음식
ajar a. (명사 앞에는 안 씀) 문이 약간 열린

32. "Oh, My love Is like a Red, Red Rose" by Robert Burns (1759~1796)

오, 내 사랑은 유월에 갓 핀 장미처럼
붉고 붉어라.
오, 내 사랑은 아름답게 연주되는 선율처럼
감미로워라.

내 사랑스런 소녀여, 그대 아름다움만큼
나 그댈 그윽이 사랑하노니
바다가 다 마르도록
변함없이 그대를 사랑하리.

내 사랑이여, 생명의 모래가 흐르는 한은,
바다가 마르고
바위가 햇빛에 녹아내릴 때까지
변함없이 그대를 사랑하리.

그러니 하나뿐인 내 사랑이여,
안녕, 잠시 동안만 안녕!
천만리 먼 길이래도
내 다시금 찾아오리!

33. "Holes Commence Falling" by David Huddle (1942~)

납과 아연 회사는
온 시내에 어쨌든
생수를 공급하는 권리가 있었네.
그래서 3년인가 4년 동안을
구멍을 뚫더니,
마침내 적당한 곳을 발견해
갱도를 내렸네.
우리는 그렇게 뚫는 것을
아주 자랑스럽게 여겼지,
아무도 도시에서
고용되어 일한 사람이 없었는데도. 그들은
뉴 리버 바로 아래를 파려고 했고
어스턴빌에 있는 탄광과 연결되었지.
그러고 나서 사람들의 우물이
누군가 수도꼭지를 잠근 것처럼
마르기 시작했고,
구멍이 생겨 파이기 시작했고,
사람들 땅이 큰 덩어리로
5피트나 6피트 아래로 들어가더니
집들이 흔들리고 갈라지곤 했어.
이따금씩 그 회사는
약간의 돈을 피해금으로
지급하곤 했지; 그들은
트럭으로 물을 끌고 와서
우물이 말라 붙어버린
사람들에게 그것을 팔았지,
그런데 대부분 모두가
그 상황이 심각하지 않다는 데
동의를 했었지.

VOCA			
zinc	n. Zn 아연(금속 원소)	faucet	n. (수도)꼭지
mine shaft	n. (산업안전) 갱도(坑道)	haul	v. (아주 힘들여) 끌다, (몸을) 간신히 움직이다, (억지로) 끌고가다
New River	n. a river in the southeastern United States that flows northward from North Carolina to West Virginia where it empties into the Kanawha River		

34. "To Lucasta Going to the Wars" by Richard Lovelace (1618~1658)

(루카스타에게 전쟁으로 떠나며)

나에게 말하지 마시오, 내 사랑이여, 내가 박정하다고
순결한 가슴과 평온한 마음이라는
수녀원으로부터
전쟁과 무기가 있는 곳으로 내가 떠난다고.

그래요, 나는 지금 새로운 연인을 쫓아가오,
바로 전장에서 처음 만나는 적이라오;
그리고 더 강한 신뢰를 가지고 껴안는다오
칼과, 말과 방패를.

그러나 이러한 변덕을
당신도 아주 좋아할 것이라오;
내 사랑이여, 나는 당신을 그렇게도 많이 사랑할 수 없을 것이오,
내가 명예를 이렇게 더 많이 사랑하지 않았다면 말이오.

VOCA			
nunnery	n. 수녀원(cf. MONASTERY); 수녀 사회	adore	v. 흠모하다, 아주 좋아하다
chaste	a. (육체적으로) 순결한, 순수한, 담백한(성적 의도가 없음을 나타냄)	• could not love thee, Dear, so much, Loved I not Honor more.	
inconstancy	n. 변하기 쉬움, 변덕스러운 행위	= I couldn't love you as much as I does if I didn't love honor even more.	

35. "On Passing thru Morgantown, Pa." by Sonia Sanchez (1934~)

나는 당신을 봅니다
빈센트 반 고흐가
펜실베니아 옥수수밭에
비밀스러운 찌르레기
무리와 교감하며
앉아 쉬고
있는 것을. 그래.
나는 확신하네
바로 당신이지
환상적인 섬망을
터뜨려버린 것이
저 멀리서
인디언 언덕들이
손짓하며 불렀을 때.

VOCA
- **perch** v. 새가 나뭇가지 등에 앉아 있다[쉬다]
- **blackbird** n. (유럽산)검은새, (북미산) 찌르레기
- **commune** v. 교감하다
- **delirium** n. (병으로 인한) 섬망[망상/헛소리]
- **red indian** n. 〈아메리카 원주민을 가리키는 대단히 모욕적인 말〉
- **beckon** v. (오라고) 손짓하다, (손짓으로) 부르다

36. "Sadie And Maud" by Gwendolyn Brooks (1917~2000)

모드는 대학에 갔습니다.
사디는 집에 남았고요.
사디는 촘촘한 참빗으로
삶을 빗질했습니다.

엉킨 곳 하나 남기지 않고
참빗은 머리카락을 한 올 한 올 지나갔습니다.
사디는 세상에서
가장 생명력이 넘치는 아이였습니다.

사디는 아이 둘을 낳았습니다.
결혼도 하지 않고.
모드와 엄마와 아빠는
창피해 죽을 지경이었습니다.

사디가 마지막 작별 인사를 했을 때
두 딸은 집을 나갔고
(사디는 유품으로
그녀의 참빗을 남겼습니다.)

대학에 간 모드는
깡마르고 겁이 많은 생쥐입니다.
모드는 이 낡은 집에서.
혼자 살고 있습니다.

37. "The Moon Is Hiding In" by Edward Estlin Cummings (1894~1962)

달이 숨어 있네 그녀의
머리카락 속에.
그
하늘
백합이
온갖 꿈으로 가득 찬 채로,
아래로 드리웠네.

그녀의 짧음을 노래하며 덮어라
그녀를 데이지 꽃들 옆에 있는 복잡하고 희미한 새들처럼
여기고 땅거미가
그녀를 더 깊게 하라,

그녀의
살 위에서
울려퍼지네
비의 진주방울이

노래하는 듯한 속삭임이.

VOCA
intricate a. (여러 부분·내용으로 되어 있어) 복잡한　　**daisy** n. 데이지 꽃
faint a. (빛·소리·냄새 등이) 희미한[약한]

38. "I Like To See It Lap The Miles" by Emily Dickinson (1830~1886)

나는 즐겨 보노라 그것이 수십 리를 핥고—
계곡을 핥아—
물탱크에서 배를 채우고—
다시금—큰 걸음을 디뎌

이산 저산을 돌아—
오만한 눈빛으로
길가의 오두막집을 들여다보는 것을—
그리곤 바위를 뚫어

제 옆구리에 맞도록
그 틈을 비집고 기어 나오면서
줄곧 끙끙거리는 것을
소름끼치는 괴성으로—
그리곤 산을 좇아 내려와서는—

천둥의 아들처럼 울어대며—
그리곤—별처럼 시간을 맞춰
멈춘다—유순하고 전능한 모습으로
자신의 마구간 문 앞에—

39. "The Bells" by Edgar Allan Poe (1809~1849)

I

종을 매달은 썰매의 소리를 들어보시오—
은종들!
그 멜로디는 즐거움의 나라를 예언해주네!
밤의 얼음 공기 속에서,
얼마나 쨍그렁거리는 소리가 나는지!
하늘에 온통 흩뿌려놓은 별들이
수정 같은 기쁨으로
쨍그렁, 쨍그렁, 쨍그렁 울리는 듯,
고대의 북유럽식의 압운으로,
너무도 잘 기고 있게 딸랑거리는 소리로
종, 종, 종, 종으로부터
종, 종, 종—
종에서 나오는 댕그랑 소리와 딸랑대는 소리에서 시작하여.

II

부드러운 결혼의 종소리를 들어보시오
금종들!
그 하모니는 행복의 나라를 예언해주네!
밤의 아늑한 공기 속으로
얼마나 그 기쁨을 울려내는지!
녹은 금색의 음표들부터,
그리고 모두 음을 맞추어
액체로 된 짧은 노래가
달에게 이긴 듯 의기양양해하면서
듣고 있는 멧비둘기에게
흘러가듯!
오, 소리가 울리고 있는 수도원들 밖으로
듣기 좋은 음조가 풍성하게 솟구쳐 흐른다!
커지며!
미래에 머물며!
황홀감을 말하며

흔들거리며 울리며
종, 종, 종, 종들의
종소리, 종소리, 종소리—
종에서 나오는 압운과 차임벨 소리로!

VOCA

sledge n. 썰매
foretell v. (특히 마술을 이용하여) 예언하다
tinkle v. 쨍그랑[짤랑/딸랑]하는 소리가 나다
oversprinkle = sprinkle over v. 뿌리다
crystalline a. 크리스털[수정] 같은
runic a. 룬 문자(rune)의, 고대 북유럽식의
tintinnabulation n. (격식) 딸랑[따르릉] (하고 울리는 소리)
jingle n. 딸랑, 짤랑, 댕그랑
balmy a. (호감) 공기·날씨 등이 아늑한, 훈훈한
in/out of tune 곡조[음]가 맞는/안 맞는
ditty n. (흔히 유머) 짤막한 노래
turtle-dove n. 멧비둘기(암수가 사이 좋기로 유명한 야생 비둘기)
gush n. (액체가 많은 양이) 솟구침[분출]
gloat v. (자신의 성공에) 흡족해 하다, (남의 실패를) 고소해 하다
euphony n. 듣기 좋은 음조(opp. cacophony); [언어] 활(滑)음조, 음운 변화
well v. 솟아 나오다[흐르다], 샘솟다
rapture n. 황홀(감)
impel v. ~비 ~ sb (to sth) (생각·기분이) …해야만 하게 하다
chime v. 종이나 시계가 울리다; (차임벨 소리로) 시간을 알리다

Summary

(I~II) The silver bells of the sleds are merry and keep time in the winter nights while the sky twinkles happily. The golden bells of weddings are delightful in their peaceful happiness, foretelling a rapturous future. (III~IV) Meanwhile, the brazen alarm bells scream frightfully in the night, with a discordant and desperate sound. In their clamor, these bells convey terror, horror, and anger. Finally, the iron bells are solemn and melancholy, while those in the church steeple are like ghouls who feel happiness. The king of the ghouls, who rings the bells, cheerfully keeps time with the moaning and groaning bells.

40. "The Eagle" By Alfred, Lord Tennyson (1809~1892)

갈고리 모양의 손으로 험준한 바위를 움켜쥐고,
고독한 대지에서 태양을 향한 채,
짙푸른 세상에 둘러싸여, 그는 서 있다.

주름진 바다가 그 아래로 기어가고,
그는 산야에 서서 지켜보고 있다가
벼락처럼 떨어진다.

41. "Delight In Disorder" by Robert Herrick (1591~1674)

의상(衣裳)의 멋진 무질서는
옷에 활기를 불지른다.
어깨 너머로 절묘히 혼란스레
내던져진 스카프;
여기저기서 진홍빛 스터머커를
매혹시키는 나부끼는 레이스;
소홀히 한 커프, 그리고 그 곁에
아무렇게나 흐르는 리본;
폭풍 치는 페티코트의
매혹적 물결, 눈길을 끄는,
매듭에서 내가 야성적 세련미를 발견하는
아무렇게나 맨 구두끈이;
기교가 모든 부분에서 너무나도 완벽할 때보다
나를 훨씬 더 매혹시키나니.

42. "She Dwelt Among The Untrodden Ways" by William Wordsworth (1770~1850)

그녀는 인적 없는 곳에서 살았지
다브 강 샘솟는 곳 옆에,
찬미할 이 하나 없고
사랑해 줄 이 없는 한 처녀가
사람들 눈에서 반쯤 가리어진
이끼 낀 바위 가의 한 송이 제비꽃!
—별처럼 아름다웠지, 혼자서
하늘에서 빛날 때.

그녀는 아는 이 없이 살아, 아무도 알 수 없었지
루시가 언제 죽었는지를
하지만 그녀가 묻히고, 그리고, 아,
온 세상 얼마나 달라졌는지!

43. "My Papa's Waltz" by Theodore Roethke (1908~1963)

당신 숨결에 묻어 있는 위스키 향은
어린 아이에겐 아찔했지요.
하지만 나는 죽어라 하고 매달렸지요.
그렇게 왈츠를 추는 것은 쉽지 않았어요.

우리는 찬장 그릇들이
주방 선반에서 미끄러 떨어질 때까지 쿵쾅거렸지요.
엄마는 찡그린 얼굴을
펴지 못했어요.

내 손목을 잡고 있는 손은
손 마디가 닳아 상처가 나있었죠.
당신이 발 디딤을 틀릴 때마다
나의 오른쪽 귀에는 허리띠 버클이 스쳐갔어요.

당신은 내 머리를 두드려 박자를 맞추었지요.
먼지가 잔뜩 묻은 손바닥으로.
그리고 왈츠를 추며 침대로 데려갔지요.
여전히 당신의 셔츠에 매달려 있는 저를요.

44. "Aunt Jennifer's Tigers" by Adrienne Rich (1929~2012)

제니퍼 숙모의 호랑이들이 자수막을 가로질러 뛰어다닌다,
 녹색 세상의 밝은 황옥 주민들이.
 그들은 나무 아래의 남성들을 두려워하지 않는다,
 그들은 빛나는 기사도 같은 확실함을 갖고 걷는다.

모직물을 통해 퍼득이는 제니퍼 숙모의 손가락들이
 상아 바늘을 뽑기가 어렵다는 것을 발견한다.
 삼촌의 결혼 반지의 육중한 무게는
 제니퍼 숙모의 손 위에 무겁게 앉아 있다.
숙모가 죽으면, 그녀의 공포에 질린 손들이
 그녀를 지배한 시련들로 여전히 둘러싸여 있을 것이다.
 그녀가 만든 자수막 속의 호랑이들이
 자신감 있게 두려움 없이 계속 뛰어다닐 것이다.

45. "Traveling Through The Dark" by William Stafford (1914~1993)

어둠속을 돌아다니다 사슴을 발견했네
윌슨 강 길 가에 죽어있는
보통은 협곡으로 굴려버리는 것이 최선이지:
그 길은 좁고; 차가 갑자기 방향을 틀면 더 많이 죽는다네.

미등 빛 옆에서 나는 차에서 휘청거리며 떨어져
그 무더기 옆에 섰다, 암사슴이네, 최근에 죽은;
이미 뻣뻣해져 있었고, 거의 차가웠다.
나는 그 사슴을 끌었다; 그 사슴은 배가 컸다.

그 사슴의 옆구리를 만지다 이유를 찾아냈다—
옆구리가 따뜻했다; 사슴은 거기서 찡그리고 누워 기다리고 있었는데,
살아있다, 여전히, 태어날 수 없는데.
산길 옆에서 나는 주저하였네.

앞으로 향한 차의 주차등을 아래로 향하게 하고;
계속 엔진이 부릉 소리를 내는 자동차 후드 밑에서
나는 빨갛게 변하는 따듯한 배기가스의 빛 속에 서서;
우리 무리 주변으로 야생동물들이 듣고 있는 소리가 났네.

나는 우리 모두를 위해 골똘히 생각했지—내가 갑자기 방향을 튼 것—,
그리고는 그 사슴을 길가 넘어 강으로 밀어버렸네.

VOCA
- canyon n. 협곡
- swerve v. 특히 자동차가 갑자기 방향을 바꾸다[틀다]
- tail light n. (자동차·자전거·기차의) 미등(尾燈)
- glare n. (불쾌하게) 환한 빛[눈부심], 노려봄
- purr v. (계속해서 낮게) 부웅부웅[부르릉] 하는 소리를 내다[내며 가다]

46. "When In Disgrace With Fortune And Men's Eyes (Sonnet 29)" by William Shakespeare (1564~1616)

운명에 버림받고 세상 사람들로부터 사랑을 받지 못한 채
나 홀로 나의 버림받은 처지를 한탄할 때,
부질없는 아우성으로 귀먹은 하늘을 괴롭히고
내 자신을 돌아보며 나의 운명을 저주할 때,
희망으로 풍요로운 사람 같이 되기를 바라며
친구들이 많은, 그런 사람 같기를 갈망할 때,
이 사람의 기술을 탐내고 저 사람의 역량을 부러워하며
내가 가장 즐기는 것에도 만족을 느끼지 못할 때,
그러나 이러한 생각들 속에 내 자신을 거의 경멸하다가도
우연히 당신을 생각하면 그 때 나의 처지는
새벽녘에 음울한 대지를 박차고 솟아오르는 종달새 같아
하늘 문가에서 찬양의 노래를 부르노라.
당신의 감미로운 사랑 떠올리면 너무도 풍요로워져
나는 내 자신의 처지를 왕과도 바꾸지 않으련다.

48. "The Sick Rose" by William Blake (1757~1827)

오 장미여! 병들었구나.
밤에 날아다니는
보이지 않는 벌레가
거센 폭풍우가 휘몰아 칠 때
진홍빛 기쁨 가득한
침대를 찾아와서
그의 어둡고도 은밀한 사랑이
너의 생명을 파괴하는구나.

49. "Volcanoes be in Sicily" by Emily Dickinson (1830~1886)

화산은 시실리에 있지
그리고 남아메리카에
내가 보는 지형으로는—
여기 가까이에 화산들이 있어
언제든 용암석 하나 밟아 가리
내가 올라가고 싶으면—
나는 분화구를 감상하리
집에서 베수비오 산을.

VOCA
volcano n. 화산
geography n.지리학, (한 지역의)지리, (사회적) 지형도
lava n. 용암, (식어서 굳은) 용암

crater n. 분화구
Vesuvius n. Mount ~ 베수비오 산 [(이탈리아 나폴리만(灣)에 면한 활화산)]

50. "Uphill" by Christina Rossetii (1830~1894)

길은 계속 오르막길로 꼬불꼬불 올라가는가?
　　그렇다네, 끝까지 그런 길이네.
여행은 하루 종일 걸리는가?
　　아침부터 밤까지라네, 친구.

그래도 밤엔 쉴 곳이 있겠지?
　　어둠이 천천히 다가올 때 집이 하나 나오지.
어두워서 찾지 못하거나 하지는 않겠지?
　　여관을 꼭 찾을 거네.

밤엔 다른 여행자들도 만나겠지?
　　먼저 떠난 사람들을 만날 걸세.
노크를 할까, 아니면 사람이 보이면 그때 부를까?
　　자네를 문 앞에 오래 세워 두지는 않을 걸세.

여행의 피로와 상처로부터 편안해질 수 있겠지?
   고생한 만큼의 대가가 있을 걸세.
나나 그곳에 가는 모든 사람을 위해 충분한 잠자리가 있을까?
   그렇다네, 여행하는 모든 사람을 위해 준비되어 있다네.

51. "Dreams of Suicide" by William Meredith (1919~2007)

I

내가 위험한 엽총에 손을 뻗은 것은 당신을 무장 해제시키는 것이
아니라, 금속 막대를 느껴보기 위함이네,
보송보송한 꿈의 세포막으로 된 털이 나 있는.
그 유니콘보다 더 확실하게
당신은 신비한 짐승.

II

아니면 나는 오븐 냄새를 맡네. 모든 네 발로
나는 토템 동물을 흉내 내고 있지만
그녀는 나의 토템이 아니며 내 종족의
토템이 아니며, 이것은 내 마술 오븐이 아니네.

III

내가 당신의 발목을 꽉 붙잡는다 해도,
당신은 철봉 난간에서 위로 날아 오르네.
당신의 아버지가 이 날개들을 만들었지,
자신의 날개를 만든 후에, 그리고 지금은 저 높은 곳에서
그가 당신에게 말하네, *날아 내려가*, 목소리로
나의 아버지는 말할 걸세, *걸어가라, 애야.*

VOCA **shotgun** n. 산탄총. 엽총   **disarm** v. 무장 해제시키다

52. "The courage that my mother had" by Edna St. Vincent Millay (1892~1950)

내 어머니가 가진 용기는
어머니가 가져가 여전히 가지고 계시네:
뉴질랜드에서 채석한 바위;
지금은 화강암 언덕의 화강암.

내 어머니가 꽂으셨던 금 브로치는
나보고 꽂으라고 남겨두셨네;
이보다 더 소중한 것은 없네:
그러나, 내가 안 쓰고 놔둘 수 있는 것이네.

오, 만약 대신에 어머니가 나에게

무덤으로 가져가신 것을 주셨더라면! —
바위 같은 용기, 어머니에게는
더는 필요 없고, 나에게는 필요하니.

VOCA quarry v. 〈돌을〉 쪼아 내다, 채석하다   granite n. 화강암

---

53. "Do not go gentle into that good night" by Dylan Thomas (1914~1953)

그 좋은 밤으로 순순히 가지 마세요.
노령은 낮의 끝에 불타고 분노해야 합니다.
분노하세요, 빛이 죽어가는 것에 분노하세요.

비록 현자들은 결국은 어둠이 옳음을 알지만,
그들의 말이 어떤 번개도 갈라지게 하지 못했기에 그들은
그 좋은 밤으로 순순히 가지 않습니다.

선한 사람들은, 마지막 물결 옆에 섰을 때, 푸른 만속에서
그들의 연약한 행동들이 얼마나 빛나게 춤추었을 것인가를 울부짖으며,
분노합니다, 빛이 죽어가는 것에 분노합니다.

난폭한 사람들은, 날아가는 태양을 붙잡고 노래했으나,
자신들이 그게 제 길을 가는 것을 슬퍼했음을 너무 늦게 깨달은 사람들은,
그 좋은 밤으로 순순히 가지 않습니다.

죽음에 임박한 사람들은, 죽음에 직면하여, 어두워지는 시력으로
눈이 멀어도 혜성처럼 불타고 즐거울 수 있음을 알기에,
분노합니다, 빛이 죽어가는 것에 분노합니다.

그리고 당신, 나의 아버지여, 그 슬픈 높은 곳에서,
당신의 치열한 눈물로 지금 나를 저주하고 축복해주기를 기도합니다.
그 좋은 밤으로 순순히 가지 마세요.
분노하세요, 빛이 죽어가는 것에 분노하세요.

54. "Summer" by Christina Rossetti (1830~1894)

겨울은 냉정하네
봄은 그러기도 하고 아니기도 한데,
가을은 이리 저리로 부는
바람개비;
나에게 있어서 여름날들은
모든 잎사귀가 나무에 붙어있을 때;

울새가 거지가 안 되고,
그리고 굴뚝새는 신부가 되고,
그리고 종달새는 노래하며, 노래하며, 노래하며, 내려오는
넓은 보리밭 위로,
그리고 백합위에 내려 타고,
그리고 줄에 매달린 거미도
이쪽에서 저쪽으로 흔들거리는,

그리고 짙은 남빛의 딱정벌레가 일을 하고,
그리고 각다귀가 무리지어 날아가며,
그리고 털 복숭이 애벌레가 재촉하며
낭비할 시간이 없다고 하고,
그리고 나방이 살찌고 번성하며,
그리고 무당벌레가 찾아온다.

푸른 사과가 빨게 지기 전에는,
푸른 견과류가 갈색이 되기 전에는,
왜, 시골에서의 하루는
도시에서의 한 달과 같은지;
하루하고 한 해를
먼지 쌓이고, 퀴퀴하고, 맨 뒤로 쳐지는 방식으로 보내는 것과 같다
다른 곳에서의 며칠이.

VOCA
- **robin** n. (유럽산) 울새(몸은 갈색에 가슴 부분은 빨간색이며 몸집이 작다.)
- **jenny wren** n. 굴뚝새
- **lark** n. 종달새, 종다리
- **gnat** n. 각다귀
- **caterpillar** n. 애벌레
- **musty** a. 퀴퀴한 냄새가 나는

---

55. "The Windhover" by Gerard Manley Hopkins (1844~1889)

오늘 아침 홀연히 눈에 띈
아침의 총아요, 햇빛 왕국의 태자요, 색동옷 여명을 앞세워 납신 새의 왕,
요동치는 대기를 길들여 타고 앉아 저 높은 곳에서 늠름한 모습으로
물결치는 날개를 고삐삼아 조종하며
황홀한 모습으로 선회하더니
다음 순간, 멋지게 원을 그리는 스케이트처럼
재빠르게 쭈욱 쭈욱 원을 그리고는
날쌔게 자신의 몸을 던져
활공으로 강풍을 물리쳤었네.
새를 보고—일개 짐승의 그 훌륭히 해 내는 솜씨를 보고—

내 가슴이 분발하였네.
야성적인 그 아름다움, 그 용맹, 그 감투
오, 그 늠름함, 그 자신감, 그 기세여, 자, 내 가슴에서
어우러져 승화하라! 그리하여, 오, 나의 기사여!
내 가슴 속에 숨어 있는 그대와 같은 속성이
자기희생의 불길로 승화할 때
더 아름답고 더 위력 있다는 찬미 천번 만번 들으리.
당연히 그러하리: 녹슨 쟁기도 흙 속에서 소박한 밭갈이로 스스로를 희생할 때
빛을 발하고, 푸르스름하게 죽어가는 잿덩이도 스스로를 던져 갈라질 때
속에서 붉은 빛을 발하기에.

56. "Meeting at Night" by Robert Browning (1812~1889)

잿빛 바다, 길고 검은 육지,
나즉이 커다란 노란 반달,
그리고 잠에서 놀란 듯 깨어나
투정부리며 퍼져가는 잔잔한 파문이 이네,
후미진 해안에 뱃머리 밀어 넣고
물 먹은 모래위에 속력을 멈출 때.

바다 내음 풍기는 훈훈한 해변 일 마일,
들판 셋을 건너 나타나는 농가,
창문 두드리는 소리, 날쌔게 예리하게 성냥 긋는 소리,
파란 불꽃,
반갑고 두려움에
맞닿은 두 가슴의 고동보다 낮은 목소리.

57. "Parting at Morning" by Robert Browning (1812~1889)

모롱이 돌아서며 바다가 내닫고
봉우리 위엔 태양이 넘다본다.
태양의 황금 길은 곧기만 하고
사나이 기다리는 세상일은 재촉이 성화같다(straight).

58. "How Do I Love Thee?" by Elizabeth Barrett Browning (1806~1861)

내가 얼마나 그대를 사랑하느냐고요? 내 사랑의 방법들을 얘기해보지요.
저는 존재와 이상적인 아름다움의 보이지 않는 끝에서
내 영혼이 닿을 수 있는 그 깊이와 넓이와 높이만큼 그대를 사랑합니다.
매일 밤이나 낮이나 가장 조용한 시간에도 절실히 그대를 사랑합니다.
저는 당신을 자유롭게 사랑합니다, 권리를 위해 투장하는 사람처럼.
저는 당신을 순수하게 사랑합니다, 칭찬받으면 달라지는 사람처럼.
나는 당신을 사랑합니다, 오랜 슬픔과 어린 시절의 믿음의 열정으로.
나는 당신을 사랑합니다, 이승에서 내가 잃은 사람을 잃어버릴 것 같은 애틋함으로.
나는 당신을 사랑합니다, 모든 삶속에서 숨결과, 웃음과, 눈물로.
그리고 신이 허락하신다면, 죽어서도 그대만을 더욱더 사랑할 것입니다.

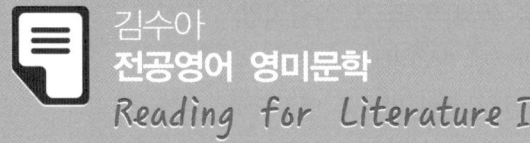

김수아
전공영어 영미문학
Reading for Literature I

PART 03

Reading for Practice

- **Chapter 01** Poems in the Text
- **Chapter 02** Poems in the Exam
- **Chapter 03** Poems in the Mock-Exam by Task

Poems in the Text

1. Formative Test

01 Read the poem and follow the directions. **4points**

> I met a traveller from an antique land
> Who said: "Two vast and trunkless legs of stone
> Stand in the desert … Near them, on the sand,
> Half sunk, a shattered visage lies, whose frown,
> And wrinkled lip, and sneer of cold command,
> Tell that its sculptor well those passions read
> Which yet survive, stamped on these lifeless things,
> The hand that mocked them, and the heart that fed:
> And on the pedestal these words appear:
> 'My name is Ozymandias, king of kings:
> Look on my works, ye Mighty, and despair!'
> Nothing beside remains. Round the decay
> Of that colossal wreck, boundless and bare
> The lone and level sands stretch far away."

Situational irony occurs when the situation itself contradicts readers' expectation. Locate situational irony in the poem and explain how it is related to the theme.

Answer:

02 Read the poem and follow the directions. 2points

Do not weep, maiden, for war is kind.
Because your lover threw wild hands toward the sky
And the affrighted steed ran on alone,
Do not weep.
War is kind.

    Hoarse, booming drums of the regiment
    Little souls who thirst for fight,
    These men were born to drill and die
    The unexplained glory flies above them
    Great is the battle-god, great, and his kingdom —
    A field where a thousand corpses lie.

Do not weep, babe, for war is kind.
Because your father tumbled in the yellow trenches,
Raged at his breast, gulped and died,
Do not weep.
War is kind.

    Swift, blazing flag of the regiment
    Eagle with crest of red and gold,
    These men were born to drill and die
    Point for them the virtue of slaughter
    Make plain to them the excellence of killing
    And a field where a thousand corpses lie.

Mother whose heart hung humble as a button
On the bright splendid shroud of your son,
Do not weep.
War is kind.

2-1 **Verbal irony** is created when words say one thing but mean another. Complete the commentary below by describing the theme of the poem with ONE word from the above poem. If necessary, you can change the word form.

> This poem is definitely all about war, which is very _____; it takes lovers from their maidens, fathers from their children, sons from their mothers. It causes nothing but death, heartbreak, loss, in short all kinds of bad stuff. And even though wars are no good, they keep on happening, largely because there are always people, like the guy in the second and fourth stanza, who are all to willing to send soldiers to their deaths.

Answer:

2-2 Locate verbal irony with your reason in relation to the theme.

Answer:

03 Read the poem and follow the directions. 4points

> When my mother died I was very young,
> And my father sold me while yet my tongue
> Could scarcely cry 'Weep! weep! weep! weep!'
> So your chimneys I sweep, and in soot I sleep.
>
> There's little Tom Dacre, who cried when his head,
> That curled like a lamb's back, was shaved; so I said,
> 'Hush, Tom! never mind it, for, when your head's bare,
> You know that the soot cannot spoil your white hair.'
>
> And so he was quiet, and that very night,
> As Tom was a-sleeping, he had such a sight! —
> That thousands of sweepers, Dick, Joe, Ned, and Jack,
> Were all of them locked up in coffins of black.
>
> And by came an angel, who had a bright key,
> And he opened the coffins, and let them all free;
> Then down a green plain, leaping, laughing, they run,
> And wash in a river, and shine in the sun.
>
> Then naked and white, all their bags left behind,
> They rise upon clouds, and sport in the wind;
> And the Angel told Tom, if he'd be a good boy,
> He'd have God for his father, and never want joy.
>
> And so Tom awoke, and we rose in the dark,
> And got with our bags and our brushes to work.
> Though the morning was cold, Tom was happy and warm:
> So, if all do their duty, they need not fear harm.

Dramatic irony occurs when a speaker believes one thing and readers realize something else. Identify the speaker in the poem and explain what has been happening to the speaker. Then locate dramatic irony in the poem with your reason.

Answer:

04 Read the poem and follow the directions. 4points

> A ringing tire iron
>   dropped on the pavement
> Whang of a saw
> brusht on limbs
> the taste
> of rust

Imagery evokes physical sensations with words and phrases used specifically to help the reader to imagine each of the senses: smell(olfactory), touch (tactile), sight(visual), hearing(aural/auditory), and taste(gustatory). Identify imagery used in the above poem and explain them in relation to the theme.

Answer:

05 Read the poem and follow the directions. **2points**

> Whose woods these are I think I know.
> His house is in the village, though;
> He will not see me stopping here
> To watch his woods fill up with snow.
>
> My little horse must think it queer
> To stop without a farmhouse near
> Between the woods and frozen lake
> The darkest evening of the year.
>
> He gives his harness bells a shake
> To ask if there is some mistake.
> The only other sound's the sweep
> Of easy wind and downy flake.
>
> The woods are lovely, dark and deep,
> But I have promises to keep,
> And miles to go before I sleep,
> And miles to go before I sleep.

Complete the commentary by filling in the blank (1) and (2) with ONE word for each from the above poem. If necessary, you can change the word form.

> This poem is a lonely poem, for our speaker finds himself far away from any other human being. So the wood offers perfect quiet and solitude with (1)_____ image, which helps make things even lonelier. He kind of digs this aloneness and is glad that no one is there to watch him. In addition, the world of the woods exists side by side with the realization that there is also another world, a world of people and social obligations, as the word (2)"_____" stands for. The poet is put in mind of the "promises" he has to keep, of the miles he still must travel. We are not told, however, that the call of social responsibility proves stronger than the attraction of the woods, which are "lovely" as well as "dark and deep."

Answer:

06 Read the poem and follow the directions. 4points

> Shall I compare thee to a summer's day?
> Thou art more lovely and more temperate.
> Rough winds do shake the darling buds of May,
> And summer's lease hath all too short a date.
> Sometime too hot the eye of heaven shines,
> And often is his gold complexion dimm'd;
> And every fair from fair sometime declines,
> By chance or nature's changing course untrimm'd;
> But thy eternal summer shall not fade
> Nor lose possession of that fair thou ow'st;
> Nor shall Death brag thou wander'st in his shade,
> When in eternal lines to time thou grow'st:
> So long as men can breathe or eyes can see,
> So long lives this, and this gives life to thee.

Figures of speech are expressions that use words to achieve effects beyond the power of ordinary language. Explain a figure of speech used in the poem in relation to the theme.

Answer:

07 Read the poem and follow the directions. `4points`

> I wandered lonely as a cloud
> That floats on high o'er vales and hills,
> When all at once I saw a crowd,
> A host, of golden daffodils;
> Beside the lake, beneath the trees,
> Fluttering and dancing in the breeze.
>
> Continuous as the stars that shine
> And twinkle on the milky way,
> They stretched in never-ending line
> Along the margin of a bay:
> Ten thousand saw I at a glance,
> Tossing their heads in sprightly dance.
>
> The waves beside them danced; but they
> Out-did the sparkling waves in glee:
> A poet could not but be gay,
> In such a jocund company:
> I gazed- and gazed- but little thought
> What wealth the show to me had brought:
>
> For oft, when on my couch I lie
> In vacant or in pensive mood,
> They flash upon that inward eye
> Which is the bliss of solitude;
> And then my heart with pleasure fills,
> And dances with the daffodils.

A simile is a comparison between two unlike items that uses *like* or *as*. Identify two similes used in the above poem and explain them in relation to the theme of the poem.

Answer:

08 Read the poem and follow the directions. 4points

> What happens to a dream deferred?
>
> Does it dry up
> like a raisin in the sun?
> Or fester like a sore —
> And then run?
> Does it stink like rotten meat?
> Or crust and sugar over —
> like a syrupy sweet?
>
> Maybe it just sags
> like a heavy load.
>
> Or does it explode?

A simile may be one of several related figures of speech that work together to convey a poem's meaning. Find a series of related similes in the poem and describe the theme of the poem.

Answer:

09 Read the poem and follow the directions. **4points**

> Constantly risking absurdity
> and death
> whenever he performs
> above the heads
> of his audience
> the poet like an acroexbat
> climbs on rime
> to a high wire of his own making
> and balancing on eyebeams
> above a sea of faces
> paces his way
> to the other side of the day
> performing entrechats
> and sleight-of-foot tricks
> and other high theatrics
> and all without mistaking
> any thing
> for what it may not be
> For he's the super realist
> who must perforce perceive
> taut truth
> before the taking of each stance or step
> in his supposed advance
> toward that still higher perch
> where Beauty stands and waits
> with gravity
> to start her death-defying leap
> And he
> a little charleychaplin man
> who may or may not catch
> her fair eternal form
> spreadeagled in the empty air
> of existence

Describe the theme of the poem and explain how **the extended simile**, comparing a poet to "an acrobat"(Line 6) throughout the poem, is related to the theme.

Answer:

10 Read the poem and follow the directions. `4points`

> Tell me not, Sweet, I am unkind
>   That from the nunnery
> Of <u>thy chaste breast and quiet mind</u>,
>   To war and arms I fly.
>
> True, a new mistress now I chase,
>   The first foe in the field;
> And with a stronger faith embrace
>   <u>A sword, a horse, a shield</u>.
>
> Yet this inconstancy is such
>   As you too shall adore;
> I could not love thee, Dear, so much,
>   Loved I not Honor more.

Metonymy is the substitution of the name of one thing for the name of another thing that most readers associate with the first. A specific kind of metonymy, **synecdoche**, is the substitution of a part for the whole or the whole for a part. Identify a figure of speeches that each underlined part employs. Then, explain how they are related to the theme of the poem.

Answer:

11 Read the poem and follow the directions. 13points

> I like to see it lap the Miles —
> And lick the Valleys up —
> And stop to feed itself at Tanks —
> And then — prodigious, step
>
> Around a pile of mountains —
> And, supercilious, peer
> In Shanties — by the sides of Roads —
> And then a Quarry pare
>
> To fit its Ribs
> And crawl between
> Complaining all the while
> In horrid — hooting stanza —
> Then chase itself down Hill —
>
> And neigh like Boanerges —
> Then — punctual as a star,
> Stop — docile and omnipotent
> At its own stable door —

Rhyme is the use of matching sounds in two or more words: "tight" and "might"; "born" and "horn"; "sleep" and "deep". The conventional way to describe a poem's rhyme scheme is to chart rhyming sounds that appear at that ends of lines.

(1) Identify the rhyme scheme of the above poem only for the 1st and 2nd stanza.

(2) Identify the rhyme scheme of the poems in *Poems to Read*: 2, 3, 8, 13, 17, 23, 24, 27, 28, 34, 38, 40.

12 Read the poem and follow the directions. 4points

> He clasps the crag with crooked hands;
> Close to the sun in lonely lands,
> Ringed with the azure world, he stands.
>
> The wrinkled sea beneath him crawls:
> He watches from his mountain walls,
> And like a thunderbolt he falls.

Alliteration is the repetition of consonant sounds in consecutive or neighboring words, usually at the beginning of words to enhance sound in a poem. Identify alliteration in the above poem and describe the theme of the poem.

13 Read the poem and follow the directions. 4points

> When in disgrace with fortune and men's eyes,
> I all alone beweep my outcast state,
> And trouble deaf heaven with my bootless cries,
> And look upon myself and curse my fate,
> wishing me like to one more rich in hope,
> Featured like him, like him with friends possessed,
> Desiring this man's art, and that man's scope,
> With what I most enjoy contented least;
> Yet in these thoughts myself almost despising,
> Haply I think on thee—and then my state,
> Like to the lark at break of day arising
> From sullen earth sings hymns at heaven's gate;
>
> For thy sweet love remembered such wealth brings,
> That then I scorn to change my state with kings.

The **sonnet is a** fourteen-line poem with a distinctive rhyme scheme and metrical pattern. The English or **Shakespearean sonnet**, which consists of fourteen lines divided into three quatrains and a concluding couplet, is written in iambic pentameter and follows the rhyme scheme *abab cdcd efef gg*. The **Petrarchan sonnet**, popularized in the fourteenth century by the Italian poet Francesco Petrarch, also consists of fourteen lines of iambic pentameter, but these lines are divided into an eight-line unit called an **octave** and a six-line unit (composed of two tercets) called a **sestet**. The rhyme scheme of the octave is *abba abba;* the rhyme scheme of the sestet is *cde cde*.

Identify the type of sonnet by explaining the rhyme scheme of the above poem. Then describe the theme of the poem.

14 Read the poem and follow the directions. 4points

> She dwelt among the untrodden ways
>   Beside the springs of Dove,
> Maid whom there were none to praise
>   And very few to love:
>
> A violet by a mossy stone
>   Half hidden from the eye!
> —Fair as a star, when only one
>   Is shining in the sky.
>
> She lived unknown, and few could know
>   When Lucy ceased to be;
> But she is in her grave, and, oh,
>   The difference to me!

Poetic rhythm, the repetition of stresses and pauses, is largely created by **meter**, the recurrence of regular units of stressed and unstressed syllables, and the basic unit of meter is a **foot** — a group of syllables with a fixed pattern of stressed and unstressed syllables.

The name for a **metrical pattern** of a line of verse identifies the name of the foot used and the number of feet the line contains. For example, the most common foot in English poetry is the **iamb**, most often occurring in lines of three (trimeter), four(tetrameter) or five feet(pentameter).

Identify the metrical pattern of the above poem. Then find a figure of speech and explain it in relation to the theme of the poem.

15 Read the poem and follow the directions. 4points

> O Rose, thou art sick!
> The invisible worm
> That flies in the night,
> In the howling storm,
>
> Has found out thy bed
> Of crimson joy:
> And his dark secret love
> Does thy life destroy

Identify TWO symbols employed in the above poem and write what each symbol stands for. Then, describe the theme of the poem.

16 Read the poem and follow the directions. 4points

> Volcanoes be in Sicily
> And South America
> I judge from my Geography -
> Volcanos nearer here
> A Lava step at any time
> Am I inclined to climb -
> A Crater I may contemplate
> Vesuvius at Home.

A **symbol** is an idea or image that suggests something else and transcends its literal, or denotative, meaning in a complex way. A symbol enables the poet to enrich a poem by giving it additional layers of meaning often recognized by its prominence or repetition.

Identify a symbol in the above poem and explain it in relation to the theme.

Answer keys for Chapter 01 Poems in the Text

1. **Situational irony** lies in the contrast between the "colossal wreck" and the boastful inscription on the pedestal of the monument: "Look on my works, ye Mighty, and despair!" It conveys the theme, transience, in that Ozymandias is a monument to the vanity of those who mistakenly think they can withstand the ravages of time.

2. (1) unkind
   (2) The speaker uses **verbal irony** in "War is kind" to express the warfare inhuman and impersonal. Though the speaker says war is kind in consoling tone to people who lost their loved ones in war, what he really means is the opposite idea, war is unkind.

3. The speaker, a little boy, forced into chimney sweeping, tells about his friend Tom and his dream, where many sweepers were locked in black coffins and an angel set them free. Awaking from that dream, Tom keeps doing his work happily believing his safety. Dramatic irony lies in the last line, where the speaker believes that the children do not fear harm while they do their duty, chimney sweeping, which is contradictory to the readers' realization that their work is quite hazardous.

4. **Aural, visual, and gustatory images** are used in the poem, which build up to the theme, **decaying** of the Iron Age. The sounds of a tire iron and a saw create a harsh chord evoking **uneasiness**; their being 'dropped' and 'brushed' describes **declining** of the mundane era visually; in gustatory sense, 'rust' stimulates rotten taste representing **deterioration** of the Iron Age into the rusty one.

5. (1) snowy
   (2) village

6. In the poem, the speaker compares a loved one to a summer's day to make the point that the loved one will remain forever within the poem unlike the fleeting summer. This suggests his confidence in his own talent and reputation and about the power of language than about the loved one's beauty.

7. **A simile** is employed in the first line by comparing "I" to "a cloud," implying that he is passively drifting like the cloud as a part of nature. Another simile in line 7 compares daffodils to "the stars," which stand for twinkling vitality that never-ends. These imply the speaker's happiness within nature full of life and vitality despite his solitude.

8. In the poem **a series of similes** are used in "like a raisin in the sun," "like a sore," "like rotten meat," "like a syrupy sweet," and "like a heavy load." These related similes suggest the depth of the problem of ignored dream the speaker is wondering about.

9. The speaker describes the tricky nature of finding truth in poetry. In the extended comparison of a poet and an acrobat, swinging recklessly on a trapeze and balancing carefully, the speaker suggests that the nature of the poet's pursuit of artistic truth is both exciting and unpredictably dangerous as a circus.

10. In the first underlined part, **synecdoche** is employed by using "breast" and "mind" to stand for all the loved one's physical and intellectual attributes, which expresses the love for a woman as part of the theme. In the second part, as **metonymy**, three items of "a sword, a horse, a shield" represent the war to contribute to the theme of the love for honor and sacrifice for the beloved.

11. (1) (ABCB) - the classic rhyme scheme for ballads)
    (2) 2 - (ABAB)[ballad]   3 - (ABCB) [ballad]
        8 - (ABABB)   9 - (AABB)
        13 - (AABB)   17 - (ABAB) [ballad]
        23 - ABAB BCBC CDCD EE [Spencerian sonnet]

24 - (AABA): aaba bbcb ccdc dddd
27 - ABAB CDCD EFEF GG [English sonnet]
28 - (ABABCC)   34 - (ABAB)
38 - (ABCB)   40 - (AAA)

12. **Alliteration** appears through out the poem with the use of hard "[k]" sounds in the words "clasps," "crag," "crooked," and "close," and also with "lonely lands" for "[l]" sounds and "wrinkled" and "watches" for "[w]" sounds. These repetition of sounds flows smoothly from beginning to end to describe powerful strength and falling skill of the eagle in the poem.

13. The poem is an **English sonnet** with its **rhyme scheme**: *abab* (eyes-state-cries-fate), *cdcd* (hope-possessed-scope-least), *efef* (despising-state-arising- gate), *gg* (brings-kings). It mainly describes the speake's desperate isolation and recovery through love that brings "wealth" in him to overcome.

14. The **metrical pattern** of the poem is iambic tetrameter in the first and third lines of each stanza; iambic trimeter in the second and fourth (ballad stanza). A simile is employed in "Fair as a star," comparing the maid to a star. This suggests her beauty and value that the speaker has discovered and his spiritual love that can not be realized because of her death.

15. 'Rose' is a **symbol** of happiness and joy with its 'crimson joy' while 'the invisible worm' symbolizes violence that destroys them. The speaker illustrates how destructive violence is. Even if it is from love as 'dark secret love' suggests, any violence is harmful like a worm to a rose.

16. Volcanoes are used as a **symbol** representing the speaker's awesome creative power and its destructiveness. This contributes to the theme, the speaker's attraction to power and danger of her own talent, by describing volcanoes as something to be feared as well as contemplated.

Chapter 02 Poems in the Exam

1. Poems in the Teacher Certification Exam

기입형

01 Read the poem and follow the directions. **2points** (17-A-5)

> The flower that smiles today
> Tomorrow dies;
> All that we wish to stay,
> Tempts and then flies.
> What is this world' delight?
> Lightning that mocks the night,
> Brief even as bright.
>
> Virtue, how frail it is!
> Friendship how rare!
> Love, how it sells poor bliss
> For proud despair!
> But we, though soon they fall,
> Survive their joy and all
> Which ours we call.
>
> Whilst skies are blue and bright,
> Whilst flowers are gay,
> Whilst eyes that change ere night
> Make glad the day,
> Whilst yet the calm hours creep,
> Dream thou — and from thy sleep
> Then wake to weep.

Complete the statement by filling in the blank with the ONE most appropriate word from the poem.

> One theme in the poem is that all good things in life come to an end, and as a result, we are left with the feeling of _____.

02 Read the poem and follow the directions. 2points (16-A-2)

> Some time when the river is ice ask me
> mistakes I have made. Ask me whether
> what I have done is my life. Others
> have come in their slow way into
> my thought, and some have tried to help
> or to hurt — ask me what difference
> their strongest love or hate has made.
>
> I will listen to what you say.
> You and I can turn and look
> at the silent river and wait. We know
> the current is there, hidden; and there
> are comings and goings from miles away
> that hold the stillness exactly before us.
> What the river says, that is what I say.

Complete the commentary by filling in the blank with ONE word from the poem.

> **Commentary**
> Out there will be the world confronting us both; we will both know we are surrounded by mystery, tremendous things that do not reveal themselves to us. That river, that world — and our lives — all share the depth and _____ of much more significance than our talk, or intentions. There is a steadiness and somehow a solace in knowing that what is around us so greatly surpasses our human concerns.

03 Read the poem and follow the directions.

> I look into my glass,
> And view my wasting skin,
> And say, "Would God it came to pass
> My heart had shrunk as thin!"
>
> For then, I, undistrest
> By hearts grown cold to me,
> Could lonely wait my endless rest
> With equanimity.
>
> But Time, to make me grieve,
> Part steals, lets part abide;
> And shakes this fragile frame at eve
> With throbbings of noontide.

Complete the statement by filling in the blank with ONE word from the poem.

> The speaker's distress will come to _____ when bodily and emotional deterioration go hand in hand.

01 Read the poem and follow the directions.

> Up into the cherry tree
> Who should climb but little me?
> I held the trunk with both my hands
>
> And looked abroad on foreign lands.
> I saw the next door garden lie,
> Adorned with flowers before my eye,
> And many pleasant places more
> That I had never seen before.
>
> I saw the dimpling river pass
> And be the sky's blue looking-glass;
> The dusty roads go up and down
> With people tramping in to town.
>
> If I could find a higher tree
> Farther and farther I should see,
> To where <u>the grown-up river</u> slips
> Into the sea among the ships,
>
> To where the roads on either hand
> Lead onward into fairy land,
> Where all the children dine at five,
> And all the playthings come alive.

Complete the commentary below by filling in the blank with the ONE most appropriate word from the poem. Then, explain what the underlined part means.

Commentary

Metaphor can in one way be defined as a figure of speech in which a word or phrase is applied to an object or action that it does not literally denote in order to imply a resemblance. According to this definition, the word "_____" in the poem is a metaphor for the river, the sight of which the speaker enjoys.

02 **Read the poem and follow the directions.** 4points (20-B-7)

In summer's mellow midnight,
A cloudless moon shone through
Our open parlor window
And rosetrees wet with dew.

I sat in silent musing,
The soft wind waved my hair:
It told me Heaven was glorious,
And sleeping Earth was fair.

I needed not its breathing
To bring such thoughts to me,
But still it whispered lowly,
"How dark the woods will be!

"The thick leaves in my murmur
Are rustling like a dream,
And all their myriad voices
Instinct* with spirit seem."

I said, "Go, gentle singer,
Thy wooing voice is kind,
But do not think its music
Has power to reach my mind.

"Play with the scented flower,
The young tree's supple bough,
And leave my human feelings
In their own course to flow."

The wanderer would not leave me;
Its kiss grew warmer still—

"O come," it sighed so sweetly,
"I'll win thee 'gainst thy will.

"Have we not been from childhood friends?
Have I not loved thee long?
As long as thou hast loved the night
<u>Whose silence wakes my song.</u>
"And when thy heart is laid at rest
Beneath the church-yard stone
I shall have time enough to mourn
And thou to be alone."

* Infused

Complete the commentary below by filling in each blank with the ONE most appropriate word from the poem, respectively. Then, explain what the underlined part in the poem means.

Commentary

Personification gives the attributes of a human being to an animal, an object, or a concept. In the poem, the "wind" is personified as a(n) "_____" and a(n) "_____." This use of personification offers clues to understanding the speaker's relationship with nature.

03 Read the poem and follow the directions. (4points)   (19-A-10)

Promise me no promises,
So will I not promise you;
Keep we both our liberties,
Never false and never true:
Let us hold the die uncast,
Free to come as free to go;
For I cannot know your past,
And of mine what can you know?

You, so warm, may once have been
Warmer towards another one;
I, so cold, may once have seen
Sunlight, once have felt the sun:
Who shall show us if it was
Thus indeed in time of old?
Fades the image from the glass
And the fortune is not told.

If you promised, you might grieve
For lost liberty again;
If I promised, I believe
<u>I should fret to break the chain</u>:
Let us be the friends we were,
Nothing more but nothing less;
Many thrive on frugal fare
Who would perish of excess

Complete the commentary below by filling in the blank with the ONE most appropriate word from the poem. Then, explain what the underlined part means. Do NOT copy more than TWO consecutive words from the poem.

Commentary

In the poem the speaker tells the man, "Promise me no promises." She is unwilling to be committed to the man, suggesting that they should remain as _____.

04 Read the poem and follow the directions. (18-A-11)

Rite of Passage

As the guests arrive at my son's party
they gather in the living room—
short men, men in first grade
with smooth jaws and chins.
Hands in pockets, they stand around
jostling, jockeying for place, small fights
breaking out and calming. One says to another
How old are you? Six. I'm seven. So?
They eye each other, seeing themselves
tiny in the other's pupils. They clear their
throats a lot, a room of small bankers,
they fold their arms and frown. *I could beat you
up,* a seven says to a six,
the dark cake, round and heavy as a
turret, behind them on the table. My son,
freckles like specks of nutmeg* on his cheeks,
chest narrow as the balsa* keel of a
model boat, long hands
cool and thin as the day they guided him
out of me, speaks up as a host
for the sake of the group.
We could easily kill a two-year-old,
he says in his clear voice. The other
men agree, they clear their throats
like Generals, they relax and get down to
playing war, celebrating my son's life.

• nutmeg: a powdered brown spice
• balsa: a tropical American tree or the wood from this tree

Considering the title of the poem, explain why the speaker describes the guests as "short men" (line 3), not little boys. Then, complete the commentary below with the TWO most appropriate consecutive words from the poem.

> The birthday cake shaped like "a turret" juxtaposes playfulness and violence because a birthday cake evokes enjoyment, whereas the word "turret" reminds us of a military weapon. In a related way, the activity of _____ can be interpreted to symbolize the same contradictory elements.

05 Read the poem and follow the directions. 5points   (14-B-서2)

> Say not the struggle naught availeth,
> The labour and the wounds are vain,
> The enemy faints not, nor faileth,
> And as things have been they remain.
>
> If hopes were dupes, fears may be liars;
> It may be, in yon smoke conceal'd,
> Your comrades chase e'en now the fliers,
> And, but for you, possess the field.
>
> For while the tired waves, vainly breaking,
> Seem here no painful inch to gain,
> Far back, through creeks and inlets making,
> Comes silent, flooding in, the main.
>
> And not by eastern windows only,
> When daylight comes, comes in the light;
> In front the sun climbs slow, how slowly!
> But westward, look, the land is bright!
>
> • yon: over there
> • fliers: runaway soldiers
> • the main: the sea

Describe the theme of the poem and explain how the metaphor, "the main" (Line 12), is related to the theme.

Answer keys for Chapter 02   Poems in the Teacher Certification Exam

기입형

1. dispair

2. stillness

3. rest

서술형

1. First, the word is 'looking-glass.' Second, the underlined part represents the speaker's wish to grow up. To explain, reaching farther places is what grown-ups can do as climbing a higher tree could provide farther view. In this view, the child speaker describes the river as a grown-up because it flows farther away all the way to where the river meets the sea.

2. The words are 'singer' and 'wanderer,' respectively. The underlined part means the silence of night magnifying the sound of wind. To explain, when the speaker is immersed in silence of night to muse alone, this deep silence allows her to hear the wind blowing as if the silence of night wakes up the wind to sing a song.

3. The word is 'friends.' The underlined part means the speaker's concern about the committed relationship. To explain, the speaker believes that she would distress herself to break the relationship with the man once they are committed to each other, which asserts to the man as a reason why she wants to remain free from each other.

4. The speaker describes the guests as "short men" to represent that they undergo a rite of passage, significant experience to become adults. To be specific, the children show violence to prove their masculinity like adults as a way of celebrating their lives. The words are 'playing war.'

5. The speaker insists the faith on consistent struggle for the goal. To be specific, the speaker asserts that we have to uphold hope in spite of any adversity we face right now. For this theme, he or she uses "the main" metaphorically to describe the goal, success. In the poem, "the main" floods in eventually even if there seemed no painful inch to gain for long, as your goal will be achieved so.

Poems in the Mock-Exam by Task

📝 1. Theme

1-1 Read the poem and follow the directions. **2points**

> When in disgrace with fortune and men's eyes,
> I all alone beweep my outcast state,
> And trouble deaf heav'n with my bootless cries,
> And look upon myself and curse my fate,
> Wishing me like to one more rich in hope,
> Featured like him, like him with friends possessed,
> Desiring this man's art, and that man's scope,
> With what I most enjoy contented least;
> Yet in these thoughts myself almost despising,
> Haply I think on thee, and then my state,
> Like to the lark at break of day arising
> From sullen earth, sings hymns at heaven's gate;
>   For thy sweet love rememb'red such wealth brings,
>   That then I scorn to change my state with kings.

Complete the commentary by filling in the blank with the ONE most appropriate word from the poem.

Commentary

The speaker feels _____ but, after some inner reflection, he suddenly remembers a loved one and it's enough to lift him out of his depression and give him a new outlook on life.

1-2 Read the poem and follow the directions. 2points

> The Frost performs its secret ministry,
> Unhelped by any wind. The owlet's cry
> Came loud — and hark, again! loud as before.
> The inmates of my cottage, all at rest,
> Have left me to that solitude, which suits
> Abstruser musings: save that at my side
> My cradled infant slumbers peacefully.
> 'Tis calm indeed! so calm, that it disturbs
> And vexes meditation with its strange
> And extreme silentness. Sea, hill, and wood,
> This populous village! Sea, and hill, and wood,
> With all the numberless goings-on of life,
> Inaudible as dreams!

Complete the commentary below by filling in the blank with the ONE most appropriate word from the passage.

> The speaker meditates on the intense _____ of the night, which starts to seem kind of disturbing. He imagines the secret goings-on that must be happening in Nature and in the town.

1-3 Read the poem and fill in the blank with the ONE most appropriate word from the passage. 2points

> Youth is not a time of life; it is a state of mind; it is not a matter of rosy cheeks, red lips and supple knees; it is a matter of the will, a quality of the imagination, a vigor of the emotions; it is the freshness of the deep springs of life.
>
> Youth means a temperamental predominance of courage over timidity of the appetite, for adventure over the love of ease. This often exists in a man of sixty more than a boy of twenty. Nobody grows old merely by a number of years. We grow old by deserting our ideals.
>
> Years may wrinkle the skin, but to give up enthusiasm wrinkles the soul. Worry, fear, self-distrust bows the heart and turns the spirit back to dust.
>
> Whether sixty or sixteen, there is in every human being's heart the lure of wonder, the unfailing child-like appetite of what's next, and the joy of the game of living. In the center of your heart and my heart there is a wireless station; so long as it receives messages of beauty, hope, cheer, courage and power from men and from the infinite, so long are you young.
>
> When the aerials are down, and your spirit is covered with snows of cynicism and the ice of pessimism, then you are grown old, even at twenty, but as long as your aerials are up, to catch the waves of optimism, there is hope you may die _____ at eighty.

1-4 Read the essay and follow the directions. 2points

> A little learning is a dangerous thing;
> Drink deep, or taste not the Pierian spring:
> There shallow draughts intoxicate the brain,
> And drinking largely sobers us again.
> Fired at first sight with what the Muse imparts,
> In fearless youth we tempt the heights of arts,
> While from the bounded level of our mind
> Short views we take, nor see the lengths behind:
> But more advanced, behold with strange surprise
> New distant scenes of endless science rise!
>
> So pleased at first the towering Alps we try,
> Mount over the vales, and seem to tred the sky,
> The eternal snows appear already past,
> And the first clouds and mountains seem the last;
> But, those attained, we tremble to survey
> The growing labours of the lengthened way,
> The increasing prospect tires our wandering eyes,
> Hills peep over hills, and Alps on Alps arise!
>
> • Pierian spring: In Greek mythology, the Pierian Spring of Macedonia was sacred to the Muses.

Complete the statement by filling in the blank with the ONE most appropriate word from the poem. Change the word form if necessary.

> A little knowledge will only mislead us to the illusion that we know more than in fact we do. Remedy for this problem lies in continuing to _____ .

1–5 Read the poem and follow the directions. 2points

Mirror

I am silver and exact. I have no preconceptions.
Whatever I see I swallow immediately
Just as it is, unmisted by love or dislike.
I am not cruel, only truthful —
The eye of a little god, four-cornered.
Most of the time I meditate on the opposite wall.
It is pink, with speckles. I have looked at it so long
I think it is part of my heart. But it flickers.
Faces and darkness separate us over and over.

Now I am a lake. A woman bends over me,
Searching my reaches for what she really is.
Then she turns to those liars, the candles or the moon.
I see her back, and reflect it faithfully.
She rewards me with tears and an agitation of hands.
I am important to her. She comes and goes.
Each morning it is her face that replaces the darkness.
In me she has drowned a young girl, and in me an old woman
Rises toward her day after day, like a terrible fish.

Complete the commentary below by filling in each blank with the ONE most appropriate word from the poem.

The speaker transforms from a mirror into a/an ____①____, who takes the same pride in that it can exactly ____②____ as the mirror does, be useful in showing the drowning of youth and rising of old age more vividly than the mirror could.

1-6 Read the passage and follow the directions. **4points**

> Twirling your blue skirts, travelling the sward
> Under the towers of your seminary,
> Go listen to your teachers old and contrary
> Without believing a word.
>
> Tie the white fillets then about your hair
> And think no more of what will come to pass
> Than bluebirds that go walking on the grass
> And chattering on the air.
>
> Practice your beauty, blue girls, before it fail;
> And I will cry with my loud lips and publish
> Beauty which all our power shall never establish,
> It is so frail.
>
> For I could tell you a story which is true;
> I know a woman with a terrible tongue,
> Blear eyes fallen from blue,
> All her perfections tarnished — yet it is not long
> Since she was lovelier than any of you.

Summarize the speaker's THREE commands to 'blue girls' from the first stanza to the third stanza and explain why he is giving these commands. Do not copy more than THREE consecutive words from the poem.

1-7 Read the passage and follow the directions. `4points`

> When I was one-and-twenty
> I heard a wise man say,
> "Give crowns and pounds and guineas
> But not your heart away;
> Give pearls away and rubies
> But keep your fancy free."
> But I was one-and-twenty,
> No use to talk to me.
>
> When I was one-and-twenty
> I heard him say again,
> "The heart out of the bosom
> Was never given in vain;
> 'Tis paid with sighs a plenty
> And sold for endless rue."
> And I am two-and-twenty,
> And oh, 'tis true, 'tis true.

The following is a reader's commentary on the poem. Complete it by filling in each blank with about 10 words.

Commentary

Maybe the journey from 21 to 22 is life-changing enough for the speaker. At first, the speaker gets some advice from an older, wiser person: _____(1)_____. Like any young person, he promptly ignores the advice. At this time, he's 21. Now he's 22. And as it turns out, _____(2)_____: love hurts.

2. Figures of Speech

2-1 Read the passage and follow the directions. *2points*

> That time of year thou mayst in me behold,
> When yellow leaves, or none, or few, do hang
> Upon those boughs which shake against the cold,
> Bare ruined choirs, where late the sweet birds sang.
> In me thou seest the twilight of such day,
> As after sunset fadeth in the west,
> Which by and by black night doth take away,
> Death's second self, that seals up all in rest.
> In me thou seest the glowing of such fire,
> That on the ashes of his youth doth lie,
> As the death-bed whereon it must expire,
> Consumed with that which it was nourished by.
>   This thou perceiv'st, which makes thy love more strong,
>   To love that well which thou must leave ere long.

Complete the statement by filling in the blank with the ONE most appropriate word from the poem. You can change the word form if necessary.

> The speaker seems definitely haunted by his own mortality, and loads the poem down with metaphors related such as ashes, nighttime, and cold. This all sounds very depressing. However, we get the solace in the closing lines, which tell us that _____ helps people love and cherish each other more while they are still on earth.

2-2 Read the passage and follow the directions. 2points

My father worked with a horse-plough,
His shoulders globed like a full sail strung
Between the shafts and the furrow.
The horse strained at his clicking tongue.

An expert. He would set the wing
And fit the bright steel-pointed sock.
The sod rolled over without breaking.
At the headrig, with a single pluck

Of reins, the sweating team turned round
And back into the land. His eye
Narrowed and angled at the ground,
Mapping the furrow exactly.

I stumbled in his hob-nailed wake,
Fell sometimes on the polished sod;
Sometimes he rode me on his back
Dipping and rising to his plod.

I wanted to grow up and plough,
To close one eye, stiffen my arm.
All I ever did was follow
In his broad shadow round the farm.

I was a nuisance, tripping, falling,
Yapping always. But today
It is my father who keeps stumbling
Behind me, and will not go away.

• wing, sock: parts of a plough
• shafts: the long pieces of wood between which a horse is hitched to the plow
• headrig: head harness

Complete the commentary by filling in the blank ① with the ONE most appropriate word from the poem and the blank ② with the TWO most appropriate consecutive words from the poem. Write your answers in the correct order.

Commentary

Literally the speaker stumbled around the chunks of sod and struggled to ___①___ his dad. Figuratively he failed in trying to ___②___ to be just like his father.

2-3 Read the poem and follow the directions. 4points

I

I walk through the long schoolroom questioning;
A kind old nun in a white hood replies;
The children learn to cipher and to sing,
To study reading-books and history,
To cut and sew, be neat in everything
In the best modern way—the children's eyes
In momentary wonder stare upon
A sixty-year-old smiling public man.

II

I dream of a Ledaean body, bent
Above a sinking fire, a tale that she
Told of a harsh reproof, or trivial event
That changed some childish day to tragedy—
Told, and it seemed that our two natures blent
Into a sphere from youthful sympathy,
Or else, to alter Plato's parable,
Into the yolk and white of the one shell.

Describe literally what has been happening to the speaker. Then, explain the metaphorical meanings of the underlined part.

2-4 Read the poem and follow the directions. 4points

She walks in beauty, like the night
Of cloudless climes and starry skies;
And all that's best of dark and bright
Meet in her aspect and her eyes:
Thus mellowed to that tender light
Which heaven to gaudy day denies.

One shade the more, one ray the less,
Had half impaired the nameless grace
Which waves in every raven tress,
Or softly lightens o'er her face;
Where thoughts serenely sweet express
How pure, how dear their dwelling place.

And on that cheek, and o'er that brow,
So soft, so calm, yet eloquent,
The smiles that win, the tints that glow,
But tell of days in goodness spent,
A mind at peace with all below,
A heart whose love is innocent!

• tress: a woman's tresses are her long flowing hair.

Complete the statement by filling in the blank ① with the ONE most appropriate word from the poem. Then fill in the blank ② by identifying the literary device used in the first line of the above poem and by explaining its purpose.

Commentary

The speaker explores the many different kinds of ___①___ that one woman possesses. He praises her soft features and raven tresses. He then praises her eloquent and apparent intelligence. The speaker also plays with the themes of light and dark. He introduces the theme of darkness in the first line, where ___②___. He then describes the interplay of light and dark within her emphasizing the balance of these elements. Were these elements out of balance, the speaker claims, she would be just half as beautiful, but would still possess the "nameless grace" that inspired the poem.

2-5 Read the poem and follow the directions. 4points

As a teenager I would drive Father's
Chevrolet cross-county given me

Reluctantly: "Always keep the tank
Half full, boy, half full, ya hear?"

The fuel gauge dipping, dipping
Toward Empty, hitting Empty, then
—thrilling!—'way below Empty,
myself driving cross-country

mile after mile, faster and faster,
all night long, this crazy kid driving

the earth's rolling surface,
against all laws. Defying chemistry,

rules, and time, riding on nothing
but fumes, pushing luck harder

than anyone pushed before, the wind
screaming past like the Furies

I stranded myself only once, a white
night with no gas station open, ninety miles

from nowhere. Panicked for awhile
at standstill, myself stalled.

At dawn the car and I both refilled. But,
Father, I am running on empty still.

Explain literally what has been happening to the speaker of the poem. Then, complete the commentary below with the ONE most appropriate word from the poem. Change the word form if necessary.

> While the older perspective, that of the father, is focused toward safety, the younger perspective, that of the teenager, is focused toward risk taking. He is "running on empty still" for the _____ of his life. He's taking advantage of his youth and going for it.

2-6 Read the poem and follow the directions. 2points

You may write me down in history
With your bitter, twisted lies,
You may tread me in the very dirt
But still, like dust, I'll rise.

Just like moons and like suns,   5
With the certainty of tides,
Just like hopes springing high,
Still I'll rise.

Did you want to see me broken?
Bowed head and lowered eyes?   10
Shoulders falling down like teardrops.
Weakened by my soulful cries.

Out of the huts of history's shame
I rise
Up from a past that's rooted in pain   15
I rise
I'm a black ocean, leaping and wide,
Welling and swelling I bear in the tide.
Leaving behind nights of terror and fear
I rise   20
Into a daybreak that's wondrously clear
I rise
Bringing the gifts that my ancestors gave,
I am the dream of the slave.
I rise   25
I rise
I rise.

Explain why the speaker is described as "a black ocean" (line 17). Then, complete the commentary by filling in the blank with the ONE most appropriate word from the poem.

Commentary

This poem is about the humiliation that blacks have felt as a result of racism and oppression over the past centuries, calling them to stand up for themselves with pride and dignity. The speaker's refusal to give in to the untruth of _____ and the commitment to succeed in spite of all of such false beliefs that others have brings a powerful message.

2-7 Read the poem and follow the directions. 4points

> O my Luve is like a red, red rose
> That's newly sprung in June;
> O my Luve is like the melody
> That's sweetly played in tune.
>
> As fair art thou, my bonnie lass,
> So deep in luve am I;
> <u>And I will luve thee still, my dear,
> Till a' the seas gang dry.</u>
>
> Till a' the seas gang dry, my dear,
> And the rocks melt with the sun;
> And I will luve thee still, my dear,
> While the sands of life shall run.
>
> And fare thee weel, my only luve,
> And fare thee weel awhile!
> And I will come again, my luve
> Though it were ten thousand mile.
>
> • luve: love
> • art: are
> • thou, thee: you
> • a': all
> • gang: go
> • weel: well

Describe the theme of the poem and explain how the underlined part is related to the theme.

3. Imagery, Symbol, Tone, Sound

3-1 Read the poem and follow the directions. *2points*

> The people I love the best
> jump into work head first
> without dallying in the shallows
> and swim off with sure strokes almost out of sight.
> They seem to become natives of that element,
> the black sleek heads of seals
> bouncing like half-submerged balls.
>
> I love people who harness themselves, an ox to a heavy cart,
> who pull like water buffalo, with massive patience,
> who strain in the mud and the muck to move things forward,
> who do what has to be done, again and again.
>
> I want to be with people who submerge
> in the task, who go into the fields to harvest
> and work in a row and pass the bags along,
> who are not parlor generals and field deserters
> but move in a common rhythm
> when the food must come in or the fire be put out.

Complete the commentary by filling in the blank ① with the TWO most appropriate consecutive words from the poem and the blank ② with the ONE most appropriate word from the poem.

> **Commentary**
>
> What is the importance of the imagery, such as metaphor and simile, in this poem? It is not simply a fancy way of illustrating what the poet might have said in abstract terms. The poet enacts through its imagery the very statement that people should work hard industriously with self-fulfillment. For this theme, the poet gives the interesting imagery such as (①) where people that dived head first into icy, deep water not worrying but enjoying the stinging cold is envisioned. Likewise, the imagery of a(an) (②) conveys strength, perseverance, and commitment.

type	imagery
simile	①
metaphor	②

3-2 Read the essay and follow the directions. 2points

> Daughters of Time, the hypocritic Days,
> Muffled and dumb like barefoot *dervishes,
> And marching single in an endless file,
> Bring diadems and fagots in their hands.
> To each they offer gifts after his will,
> Bread, kingdom, stars, and sky that holds them all.
> I, in my pleached garden, watched the pomp,
> Forgot my morning wishes, hastily
> Took a few herbs and apples, and the Day
> Turned and departed silent. I, too late,
> Under her solemn fillet saw the scorn.
>
> *A dervish is a member of a Muslim religious group which has a very active and lively dance as part of its worship.

Complete the statement by filling in the blank with the ONE most appropriate word from the poem.

> One theme in the poem is that man is free to accomplish whatever his heart _____. But mankind is not aware of this freedom.

3-3 Read the poem and follow the directions. 2points

Before I got my eye put out —
I liked as well to see
As other creatures, that have eyes —
And know no other way —

But were it told to me, Today,
That I might have the Sky
For mine, I tell you that my Heart
Would split, for size of me —

The Meadows — mine —
The Mountains — mine —
All Forests — Stintless stars —
As much of noon, as I could take —
Between my finite eyes —

The Motions of the Dipping Birds —
The Morning's Amber Road —
For mine — to look at when I liked,
The news would strike me dead —

So safer — guess — with just my soul
Open the window pane
Where other creatures put their eyes —
Incautious — of the Sun —

Commentary below with the ONE most appropriate word from the poem.

> Tone reflects the writer's attitude toward a topic. It is the emotional message behind the writer's words. Tone is chiefly controlled by the words the writer chooses, words that color ideas, evoke desired emotions, and imply judgments.
>
> The tone of the poem keeps on changing throughout. Starting in slow and mellow tone, the poem ends with an astonishing tone, since the speaker has come to realise now that the only possible means to approach the divine truth is through her very _____ .

3-4 Read the passage and follow the directions. 4points

> Nature's first green is gold,
> Her hardest hue to hold.
> Her early leaf's a flower;
> But only so an hour.
> Then leaf subsides to leaf.
> So Eden sank to grief,
> So dawn goes down to day.
> <u>Nothing gold can stay</u>.

Explain what the underlined part means. Then, complete the commentary below by filling in each blank with the ONE most appropriate word from the passage.

> In an important sense the imagery is the poem. Through its imagery the poem starts by talking about the colors of spring, saying that nature is first gold, then green. Leaves, the poem says, start out as flower buds. But these golden flowers don't stick around for long — they turn green and become leaves. According to our speaker, this natural process is related to the fall of _____①_____, as well as the change of _____②_____.

3-5 Read the poem and follow the directions. 4points

Men at forty
Learn to close softly
The doors to rooms they will not be
Coming back to.

At rest on a stair landing,
They feel it
Moving beneath them now like the deck of a ship,
Though the swell is gentle.

And deep in mirrors
They rediscover
The face of the boy as he practices trying
His father's tie there in secret

And the face of that father,
Still warm with the mystery of lather.
They are more fathers than sons themselves now.
Something is filling them, something

That is like the twilight sound
Of the crickets, immense,
Filling the woods at the foot of the slope
Behind their mortgaged houses.

Explain the meaning of the underlined words. Then, complete the commentary below with the ONE most appropriate word from the poem.

Men at forty close the doors "softly", not with a boisterously youthful slam of the door. In a related way, the _____ landing of a stair moving beneath them "like the deck of a ship" can be interpreted to symbolize the middle-stage of one's life voyage.

3-6 Read the poem and follow the directions. 4points

> We wear the mask that grins and lies,
> It hides our cheeks and shades our eyes,—
> This debt we pay to human guile;
> With torn and bleeding hearts we smile
> And mouth with myriad subtleties,
>
> Why should the world be over-wise,
> In counting all our tears and sighs?
> Nay, let them only see us, while
>   We wear the mask.
>
> We smile, but oh great Christ, our cries
> To thee from tortured souls arise.
> We sing, but oh the clay is vile
> Beneath our feet, and long the mile,
> But <u>let the world dream otherwise</u>,
>   We wear the mask!

Explain what the underlined words mean. Then complete the commentary by filling in each blank with the ONE most appropriate word from the poem. Write your answers in the correct order.

> There's some symbolism in the poem that's getting at the essence of our humanity and the way we express (or don't express) our true feelings. "____①____" often indicate how we're feeling (think of blushing) and "____②____" are thought to be the windows to our soul. So if both of these are hidden, then we know we're not showing how we really feel.

3-7 Read the passage and follow the directions. 4points

> Nothing is so beautiful as spring —
> When <u>weeds, in wheels</u>, shoot long and lovely and lush;
> Thrush's eggs look little low heavens, and thrush
> Through the echoing timber does so rinse and wring
> The ear, it strikes like lightnings to hear him sing;
> The glassy peartree leaves and blooms, they brush
> The descending blue; that blue is all in a rush
> With richness; the racing lambs too have fair their fling.
>
> What is all this juice and all this joy?
> A strain of the earth's sweet being in the beginning
> In Eden garden. — Have, get, before it cloy,
>
> Before it cloud, Christ, lord, and sour with sinning,
> Innocent mind and Mayday in girl and boy,
> Most, O maid's child, thy choice and worthy the winning

The speaker of the above poem presents the radiance of the spring season. Name the literary device that produces a sound effect in the underlined part and explain its purpose. Then, complete the statement by filling in the blank with the ONE most appropriate word from the poem. If necessary, you can change the form.

> In the poem, the speaker gets explicit about his concerns. He thinks it would be great if we didn't have to leave the _____ of spring and youth.

Answer keys for Chapter 01   Poems in the Mock-Exam by Task

1. Theme

1-1. alone

Expressions & Vocabulary

sullen a. 음침한, 침울한   **hymn** n. 찬송가, 찬가

Sua TOKS!

Task

theme (17-A-5)(16-A-2)

Poetry – *Sonnet 29* by William Shakespeare

Organization-Keywords

When in disgrace with **fortune** and men's eyes,
운명에 버림받고 세상 사람들로부터 사랑을 받지 못한 채

I **all** <u>alone</u> beweep my **outcast state**,
나 홀로 나의 버림받은 처지를 한탄할 때,

And trouble deaf heav'n with my bootless cries,
부질없는 아우성으로 귀먹은 하늘을 괴롭히고

And look upon myself and curse my fate,
내 자신을 돌아보며 나의 운명을 저주할 때,

Wishing me like to one more rich in hope,
희망으로 풍요로운 사람 같이 되기를 바라며

Featured like him, like him with friends possessed,
친구들이 많은, 그런 사람 같기를 갈망할 때,

Desiring this man's art, and that man's scope,
이 사람의 기술을 탐내고 저 사람의 역량을 부러워하며

With what I most enjoy contented least;
내가 가장 즐기는 것에도 만족을 느끼지 못할 때,

Yet in these thoughts myself almost despising,
그러나 이러한 생각들 속에 내 자신을 거의 경멸하다가도

Haply I **think on thee**, and then my state,
우연히 당신을 생각하면 그 때 나의 처지는
Like to the lark at break of day arising
새벽녘에 음울한 대지를 박차고 솟아오르는 종달새 같아
From sullen earth, sings hymns at heaven's gate;
하늘 문가에서 찬양의 노래를 부르노라.
  For thy sweet love rememb'red such wealth brings,
  당신의 감미로운 사랑 떠올리면 너무도 풍요로워져
  That then I scorn to change my state with kings.
  나는 내 자신의 처지를 왕과도 바꾸지 않으런다.

[Theme of Isolation]

For the first 8 lines of the sonnet, our speaker insists that he's got zero **friends** and that God has been completely ignoring him. There's evidence that our speaker is physically **isolated** as well — the sonnet makes it clear that he's been separated from someone who loves him. In the end, the speaker finds comfort in his memory of the person's love. In the end, we get the sense that loved ones can be with us in spirit, if not physically present in our lives.

[Commentary]

The speaker feels friendless and alone, but, after some inner reflection, he suddenly remembers the **"sweet love"** of some unnamed mystery person and it's enough to lift him out of his depression and give him a new outlook on life. Not only that, but this friendship is so powerful that it functions as the speaker's spiritual salvation. That's a pretty big testament to the power of friendship.

1-2. silentness

Expressions & Vocabulary

hark　v. (옛글투) (명령문으로만 쓰여) 잘 들어라
cottage　n. (특히 시골에 있는) 작은 집
abstruse　a. 난해한
musing　n. 사색; 사색한 것을 말하기
slumber　v. (문예체) 잠을 자다, n. 잠, 수면

vex　v. 성가시게[짜증나게] 하다
silentness　n. 조용함, 소리가 없음
populous　a. (격식) 인구가 많은
goings-on　n. (비격식) (이상한·놀라운·부정직한) 행위[일]
suit　v. (특히 옷색상 등이) 어울리다

Sua TOKS!

Task

theme (17-A-5) (15-A-6)

Poetry – *Frost at Midnight* by Samuel Taylor Coleridge

Organization-Keywords

The Frost performs its **secret** ministry,
서리가 은밀한 봉직(奉職)을 수행하고 있다
Unhelped by any wind. The owlet's cry
바람의 도움도 없이. 새끼 올빼미의 울음소리가
Came **loud** — and hark, again! **loud** as before.
요란하게 들려왔다 — 그런데 다시 들어보라! 전처럼 요란한 소리를.
The inmates of my cottage, all at **rest**,
내 오두막집 동숙자들은 모두 잠들어
Have left me to that **solitude**, which suits
한층 더 심원한 묵상에 알맞은 저 고독에
Abstruser **musings**: save that at my side
나를 남겨놓았다. 내 곁에서
My cradled infant slumbers peacefully.
요람에 든 내 아기가 평온하게 선잠 들어 있는 것 빼고는.
'Tis **calm indeed! so calm**, that it disturbs
정말 고요하구나! 너무 고요해서 그 기이한
And vexes **meditation** with its strange
극도의 정적으로 명상을 어지럽히고
And **extreme silentness**. Sea, hill, and wood,
괴롭히는구나. 바람, 언덕, 그리고 숲,
This populous village! Sea, and hill, and wood,

이 사람 많은 마을! 바다, 그리고 언덕, 그리고 숲,
With all the numberless goings-on of life,
꿈처럼 귀에 들리지 않는 무수한
Inaudible as dreams!
세상사들!

The speaker meditates on the **intense** _____ of the night, which starts to seem kind of disturbing. He imagines the secret goings-on that must be happening in Nature and in the town.

[Theme of Man and the Natural World]

In "Frost at Midnight," Coleridge views **Nature as a source of wisdom for humanity.** What he wasn't able to find in his boring classroom, he thinks his son will be able to find in Nature. **Humans have made everything in the city, but God has made everything in Nature**, which, in Coleridge's view, makes it **a superior source of instruction and knowledge.** Even if something in Nature seems unpleasant or weird or mildly creepy or hostile to life — like the frost, arguably — it is still testifying to God's creative power. Since God has "all things in himself," says Coleridge, **people should be able to find evidence of God in all things.**

[Commentary]

As the poem begins, frost starts creeping through the midnight. Coleridge — writing from his own point of view and starring as his own speaker — stays up alone, hosting a pajama party of one. All the people living in Coleridge's cottage are asleep, and his baby son slumbers in a cradle next to where Coleridge is thinking. **He meditates on the intense stillness and silence of the night, which starts to seem kind of disturbing. He imagines the secret goings-on that must be happening in Nature and in the town.**

[Analysis]

In freezing the earth and creating icicles, the Frost performs a kind of **"ministry"** because it (the frost) is the agent (or "minister") of a higher power: God. (This is how Coleridge views everything in Nature — **all natural processes testify to the power of God.**) Also, the frost's ministry is "secret" because it's hidden by the night.

Dreams aren't audible because, well, they're in someone's head. Everything that's going on at night is just as secret, just as hidden (except for the crying owl, and Coleridge's breathing baby).

1-3. young

Expressions & Vocabulary

temperamental a. 신경질적인, 괴팍한, 질적인
timidity n. 겁 많음, 수줍음
lure n. 유혹, 매력
aerial n. 안테나

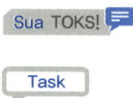

Theme, interpretation (08서-7)

Poetry – *Youth* by Samuel Ullman

[Meaning of Youth]

Youth is not a time of life; it is <u>a state of mind</u>; it is not a matter of rosy cheeks, red lips and supple knees; it is a matter of **the will**, a quality of **the imagination**, a vigor of **the emotions**; it is **the freshness** of the deep springs of life.

[Conditions of Growing Old(1)]

Youth means a temperamental predominance of courage over timidity of the appetite, for adventure over the love of ease. This often exists in a man of sixty more than a boy of twenty. Nobody **grows old** merely by a number of years. <u>**We grow old by deserting our ideals**</u>.

[Conditions of Growing Old(2)]

Years may **wrinkle** the skin, but to give up enthusiasm **wrinkles the soul**. Worry, fear, self-distrust **bows** the heart and **turns the spirit back** to dust.

[Conditions for Maintaining Youth]

Whether sixty or sixteen, there is **in every human being's heart** the lure of wonder, the unfailing child-like appetite of what's next, and the joy of the game of living. <u>**In the center of your heart**</u> and my heart there is a wireless station; so long as it receives messages of **beauty, hope, cheer, courage and power** from men and from the infinite, **so long are you young**.

[Conditions for Maintaining Youth]

When the aerials are down, and your spirit is covered with snows of cynicism and the ice of **pessimism**, then **you are grown old, even at twenty, but** as long as your aerials are up, to catch the waves of **optimism**, there is hope <u>you may **die young** at eighty</u>.

[Translation]

청춘은 인생의 한 시기가 아니라 마음의 한 상태이다. 청춘은 장밋빛 뺨과 앵두 같은 입술과 나긋나긋한 무릎을 말하는 것이 아니라, 강철 같은 의지, 풍부한 상상력, 생기가 넘치는 태도를 말한다. 청춘은 인생의 깊은 샘에서 솟아나오는 신선함에 대한 갈망을 뜻한다.

청춘은 정신적인 나약함이 아니라 용기를, 안락함에 대한 사랑이 아니라 모험심을 의미한다. 이런 청춘의 모습을 이십대 청년보다 육십대 노인이 자주 보여준다. 늙음은 나이가 든다는 것을 뜻하는 게 아니다. 이상을 포기할 때 늙어가는 것이다.

세월이 피부를 쭈그러뜨릴지 모른다, 하지만 열정을 포기하면 영혼을 시들게 한다. 근심, 두려움, 자기 불신이 마음의 기를 꺾고, 정신을 무너뜨리게 만든다.

육십대든 이십대든, 모든 인간 마음에는 경이로움에 매료되려는 갈망이 있고, 다음은 무엇일까라는 아이 같은 호기심이 있으며, 삶에서 즐거움을 얻으려는 욕망이 있다. 당신 마음과 내 마음 한 가운데 무선 수신소 같은 게 있다. 당신 마음이 사람들과 신으로부터 미, 희망, 격려, 용기와 힘의 메시지를 받는 한, 당신은 청춘이리라.

마음의 귀를 닫아, 당신 정신이 눈과 같은 차가운 냉소와 얼음 같은 비관에 사로잡히면, 당신은 이십대일지라도 늙어간다. 하지만 당신 마음의 귀를 열어 낙관적인 정신을 유지한다면, <u>**당신은 팔십에도 젊게 죽으리라**</u>.

[Overview]

- Samuel Ullman was a former confederate soldier, businessman, a very religious man and a poet too. At the age of 78 he wrote his most popular and motivating poem "Youth" - **An optimistic Celebration of Youth**. He wrote: "**Nobody grows old by merely living a number of years; people grow old by deserting their ideals.**"
- **With a wave of optimism**, the poem became a favorite of General Douglas MacArthur who framed and hung Ullman's words in his offices in Manila and Tokyo.
- This Poem has motivated the Japanese after the World War II to come out of the ashes like a Phoenix and Build one of the best Economies.

1-4. learn

Expressions & Vocabulary

intoxicate v. 취하게 하다, 흥분시키다, 열중시키다, 중독시키다 (poison)

Sua TOKS!

Task

Theme, Interpretation (17-A-5)

Poetry – *An Essay on Criticism* by Alexander Pope

Organization–Keywords

① A little learning is a dangerous thing;
어설픈 학문 경지 위험천만이라.
② Drink deep, or taste not the Pierian spring:
피에루스 샘물이랑 마시려든 실컷 마시고 아니면 맛도 보지 마소.
There ① shallow draughts intoxicate the brain,
몇 모금만 마시면 머리가 몽롱하지만
And ② drinking largely sobers us again.
흠뻑 마시면 머리가 다시 맑아지오.
Fired at first sight with what the Muse imparts,
뮤즈가 주는 선물보고 첫눈에 불이 붙어
In fearless youth we tempt the heights of arts,
예술의 산곡대기를 넘보는도다.
While from the bounded level of our mind
우리의 식견이 좁은 탓에
Short views we take, nor see the lengths behind:
짧은 생각에 빠져있어 그 이상을 보지를 못하는지라.
But more advanced, behold with strange surprise
그러나 한걸음 더 나가보면 볼수록 경이롭게도
New distant scenes of endless science rise!
끝없는 학문풍경이 새록새록 펼쳐진다!
So pleased at first the towering Alps we try,
처음에는 재미있어 우뚝 솟은 알프스에 겁 없이 도전하여
Mount over the vales, and seem to tred the sky,
계곡만 오르고도 하늘을 밟는 기분,
The eternal snows appear already past,

끝없는 운산봉도 거뜬히 지난 기분,
And the first clouds and mountains seem the last;
처음 보는 구름산은 최후의 산만 같네.
But, those attained, we tremble to survey
그러나 첫 산들을 오르고서야
The growing labours of the lengthened way,
기다리는 고행만리에 볼수록 떨려오고,
The increasing prospect tires our wandering eyes,
뻗어간 전망 앞에 놀란 눈은 힘이 빠지네.
Hills peep over hills, and Alps on Alps arise!
산넘어 산이요, 알프스 넘어 알프스로다.

---

① **A little knowledge** will only mislead us to the illusion that we know more than in fact we do. Remedy for this problem lies in ② continuing to **learn**.

[Commentary]

- A little learning or knowledge (the "shallow draughts") will only befuddle ("intoxicate the brain"), misleading us into thinking we know more than in fact we do. Remedy for this problem lies in continuing to learn ("drinking largely" at the "Pierian spring," the spring sacred to the Muses and the source of the knowledge of art and science).
- A small amount of knowledge can mislead people into thinking that they are more expert than they really are.
- It is said that "a little learning is a dangerous thing". It means that 'superficial knowledge is worse than ignorance'.
- A person with little or no learning is very often seen to be vain, as he tries to show that he knows more than he does. He attempt is to pass for a scholar in polite society.
- We should try to understand its true essence of the proverb.
- No knowledge, whether great or small, is bad. A man with little education is much better that an illiterate person. It is not the little knowledge but the pride (vanity or egoism) of learning that poses danger to a person.
- People who know only a little do not understand how little they know and are therefore prone to error.
- one can become falsely overconfident about his expertise in a certain subject if he possesses a small amount of knowledge about it.

1-5. ① lake ② reflect

Expressions & Vocabulary

flicker v. 깜박거리다
mist v. (유리 등에 김이 서려) 뿌옇게 되다
agitation n. 불안, 동요

speckle n. 작은 반점
reach n. (기관체제 등의) 상층부, 하층부 등

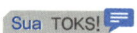

interpretation, metaphor (18-B-2)

Poetry – *Mirror* by Sylvia Plath

Mirror

I am silver and **exact**. I have **no preconceptions**.
Whatever I see I swallow immediately
Just as it is, **unmisted by love or dislike**.
I am not cruel, only truthful—
The eye of a little god, four-cornered.
Most of the time I meditate on the opposite wall.
It is pink, with speckles. I have looked at it so long
I think it is part of my heart. But it flickers.
Faces and darkness separate us over and over.

Now I am a lake. A woman bends over me,
Searching my reaches for **what she really is.**
Then she turns to **those liars,** the candles or the moon.
I see her back, and **reflect it faithfully.**
She rewards me with tears and an agitation of hands.
I am important to her. She comes and goes.
Each morning it is her face that replaces the darkness.
In me she has drowned a young girl, and in me an old woman
Rises toward her day after day, **like a terrible fish.**

The speaker transforms from a mirror into a/an ① _____, who takes the same pride in that it can exactly ② _____ as the mirror does, be useful in showing the drowning of youth and rising of old age more vividly than the mirror could.

[Translation]

거울

나는 은빛이며 정확하다. 나는 선입견이 없다.
무엇을 보든지 나는 즉시 삼켜 버린다.
있는 그대로, 사랑이나 증오로 흐려지지 않는다.
나는 잔인하지 않다. 단지 솔직할 뿐이다.
네 귀퉁이를 갖고 있는 작은 신의 눈이다.
대부분의 시간 동안 나는 반대쪽 벽을 보며 명상한다.
그 벽은 작은 얼룩이 있는 분홍빛이다. 너무 오랫동안 봐 왔기 때문에
마치 내 심장의 일부 같다. 그러나 그것은 깜박인다.
얼굴과 어둠이 우리를 자꾸 갈라놓는다.

이제 나는 호수다. 한 여인이 내 위로 몸을 숙이고,
자신의 진정한 모습을 찾으려 내 한계까지 들여다본다.
그런 다음 저 거짓말쟁이들, 촛불이나 달에게로 고개를 돌린다.
나는 그녀의 등을 본다. 그리고 그것을 충실하게 반영한다.
그녀는 눈물과 안절부절못하는 손짓으로 나에게 보상해 준다.
나는 그녀에게 중요하다. 그녀는 왔다가 간다.
매일 아침 어둠을 대신하는 것은 그녀의 얼굴이다.
그녀는 내 속에서 젊은 소녀를 익사 시켰고, 내 속에서 늙은 여인이
매일 아침 그녀를 향해 솟아오른다. 끔찍한 물고기처럼.   0

> 화자는 거울에서 ① _____ (으)로 변하는데 자신이 거울이 하는 것처럼 정확하게 ② _____ 할 수 있다는 것에 똑같이 자부심을 가지고 있으며, 이것은 젊음이 익사하고 노년이 떠오르는 것을 거울이 하는 것보다 더 생생하게 보여주는 데 유용하다.

[Commentary]

The transformation from a mirror into a lake is abrupt. In the second stanza, we'll see the lake, who takes the same pride in its exact reflections as the mirror does, be useful in showing the drowning of youth and rising of old age more vividly than the mirror could. After all, it wouldn't be as thorough of a metaphor if the young girl drowned in her bathroom mirror. And it'd be pretty laughable if a terrible fish started rising with the background of a pink speckled wall.

[Theme of Appearance]

A poem written from the point of view of a mirror is practically required to be, to some extent, about appearances. This mirror tells us repeatedly about how accurate and unbiased it is in showing appearances – which doesn't work out so well for the aging woman in the second stanza, who seems very concerned with the way that she looks. This poem explores the importance and transience of appearances.

1-6. First, the speaker admonishes blue girls to listen to their "old and contrary" teachers without believing anything they hear. Second, he urges them to concentrate on their appearance and to show no more concern for the future. Third, he implores the girls to practice their beauty. The reason for his commands is the transitory nature of beauty. To explain, he believes the woman's beauty is tarnished as the woman he remembers.

Expressions & Vocabulary

sward n. 풀밭, 초지, 잔디밭
filet n. (그물눈 모양의) 레이스

blear a. 〈눈이〉 (눈물이나 염증으로) 흐린, 침침한, 헌; [시어] 희미한(dim)

Sua TOKS!

Task

Theme, interpretation (12-2차-2)
Poetry − *Blue girls* by John Crowe Ransom

Organization

1. Summarizing the speaker's THREE commands to 'blue girls' from the first stanza to the third stanza **2points**
   − First, ~ . Second/Next, ~ . Third/Lastly, ~ .
2. Explaining why he is giving these commands. Do not copy more than THREE consecutive words from the poem. **2points**
   − The reason for his commands is NP. To explain/That is/To be specific, ~ .

Keywords

Twirling your blue skirts, travelling the sward
Under the towers of your seminary,
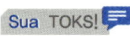 Go listen to your teachers old and contrary
Without believing a word.

 Tie the white fillets then about your hair
And think no more of what will come to pass
Than bluebirds that go walking on the grass
And chattering on the air.

③ **Practice your beauty, blue girls, before it fail;**
And I will cry with my loud lips and publish
Beauty which all our power shall never establish,
It is so frail.

For I could tell you a story which is true;
I know a woman with a terrible tongue,
Blear eyes fallen from blue,
All her perfections tarnished — yet it is not long
Since she was lovelier than any of you.

[Translation]

너의 푸른 치마를 흔들며, 너의 학교의 탑 아래
잔디밭을 거니는 푸른 소녀,
늙고 모순된 선생들의 말을 들으러 가라,
한 마디도 믿지는 말라.

하얀 리본으로 머리를 묶고,
미래는 생각지 마라,
풀밭 위에 걸어 다니며
하늘에서 재잘거리는 파랑새 마냥.

푸른 소녀야, 미가 사라지기 전에 너의 미를 즐겨라,
나는 내 큰 입술로 외치며, 우리가 온 힘을 다해도
미란 붙잡을 수 없다는 것을 알리노라,
미가 너무 덧없기에.

실화를 하나 말해주리라.
입이 거친 한 여인을 알고 있지.
푸른 눈이 흐릿해졌고,
그녀의 모든 완벽함은 사라졌지,
하지만 얼마 전에 그녀는 어느 누구보다도 사랑스러웠지.

[Theme of carpe diem]

John Crowe Ransom's "Blue Girls," **a four-stanza lyric in iambic meter**, explores the traditional theme of **the transitory nature of beauty**. Yet Ransom's poem varies significantly from this tradition in that the speaker is not a young man who has a personal goal of seduction or pleasure in mind. Rather, **he is an elderly man who, despite his urging the young girls to enjoy the moment**, seemingly has only a casual relationship with them and is interested in them not as individuals but as **representatives of youth and beauty.**

[Analysis]

In the first stanza, the speaker (generally assumed to be **an elderly man**, perhaps even a teacher at the seminary) watches a group of young women walking across the grounds of a private school and in a gently ironic tone mentally admonishes them to listen to their "old and contrary" teachers without believing anything they hear.

Stanza 2 continues with another command that the speaker clearly expects the girls to heed even though he apparently never actually voices it. He urges them to concentrate on their **appearance** and to show no more concern for the future than bluebirds fluttering on the grass or through the air.

In the third stanza the tone becomes more serious and impassioned as the speaker implores the girls to **practice their beauty**. He also introduces for the first time a reason for his commands: **the transitory nature of beauty**. His focus then shifts from the girls to himself as he pledges **what he will do if the girls obey his wishes**. He, as speaker — as poet — will **proclaim loudly, write about, and celebrate beauty.**

In the concluding stanza the speaker offers a specific example of beauty's frailty by referring to a women he knows and perhaps lives with. Age has rapidly destroyed her beauty, but her loveliness once surpassed that of any of the young women he has been admiring.

Although the speaker is generally assumed to be an elderly male, the poem does not limit itself to that interpretation. The speaker could instead be a female, even the woman with the "terrible tongue." Such a reading makes the conclusion even more poignant as the lost beauty is experienced personally, not merely observed.

1-7. (1) don't bank too much on love (more answers: love is a game that only fools play/ falling in love may be foolish)

(2) the advice he got was pretty good

Expressions & Vocabulary

rue n. 후회

Sua TOKS!

Task

Theme, interpretation (05서-12)
Poetry – *When I was One-and-Twenty* by A.E. Housman

Organization-Keywords

When I was one-and-twenty
내가 스물하고도 하나였을 때
I heard a wise man say,
한 현명한 사람이
"Give crowns and pounds and guineas
"동화와 은화와 금화를 주되,
But not your heart away;
네 마음을 주지 마라,
Give pearls away and rubies
보석과 루비는 주되,
But keep your fancy free."
너의 상상력은 자유롭게 가져라"라고 한 말을 들었다.
But I was one-and-twenty,
하지만 나는 스물하고도 하나였고,
No use to talk to me.
나에게 말해도 소용없었다.

When I was one-and-twenty
내가 스물하고도 하나였을 때,

I heard him say again,

난 그가 다시

"The heart out of the bosom

"가슴으로부터 우러나오는 마음은

Was never given in vain;

결코 헛되이 주어지지 않는 법이다.

'Tis paid with sighs a plenty

많은 탄식으로 갚아야하고,

And sold for endless rue."

끝없는 후회로 팔아야한다"고 한말을 들었다.

And I am two-and-twenty,

그리고 나는 스물하고도 둘이었고,

And oh, 'tis true, 'tis true.

그리고 오, 그것은 진실이었다, 진실이었다.

[Theme of Foolishness and Folly]

(As you grow older you get wiser.) We've said it before, but we'll say it again: any time you start a piece of literature with a reference to a wise man, chances are that the wise man will be ignored and some really stupid mistake is coming around the corner. "When I was One-and-Twenty" is no exception. Unless, of course, you happen to disagree with the "wise man" when he says that **love is a game that only fools play. After all, falling in love may be foolish** — but, as this poem demonstrates, falling away from love might be just as ridiculous.

[Summary]

When the speaker announces his age in the first line of this poem – maybe the journey from 21 to 22 is **life-changing** enough for him. At first, the speaker gets some advice from an older, wiser person: (1) **don't bank too much on love.** Like any young person, **he promptly ignores the advice.** At this time, he's 21. Now he's 22. And **as it turns out,** (2) **the advice he got was pretty good: love hurts.**

2. Figures of Speech

2-1. death

Expressions & Vocabulary

behold v. (옛글투 또는 문예체) (바라)보다

whereon adv. [부사] [의문사] 무엇의 위에 (on what), 누구에게

ere (옛글투 또는 문예체) …의 전에(before)

Sua TOKS!

Task

Theme, metaphor (17-A-5)
Poetry – *Sonnet 73: That Time of year thou mayst in me behold* by William Shakespeare

Organization-Keywords

< 1st quatrain >

That time of year thou mayst in me behold,
당신은 나에게서 이런 계절을 볼 것입니다.
When yellow leaves, or none, or few, do hang
노란 잎이 없거나 몇 개만 붙어 있는 (계절을요.)
Upon those boughs which shake against **the cold**,
추위에 떨고 있는 저 가지 위에서
① **Bare ruined** choirs, where late the sweet birds sang.
예전엔 아름다운 새들이 노래했지만 지금은 텅 비어 합창단은 폐허가 된 것을요.

< 2nd quatrain >

In me thou seest the twilight of such day,
당신은 나에게서 그런 날의 석양을 볼 것입니다.
As after sunset fadeth in the west,
해가 서쪽으로 졌기 때문에
Which by and by **black night** doth take away,
조금씩 어두운 밤이 앗아가는 (날의 석양이요.)
① **Death's second self**, that seals up all in rest.
모든 것을 휴식 속에 감추는 죽음의 또 다른 자아(모습).

< 3rd quatrain >

In me thou seest the glowing of such fire,
당신은 나에게서 그런 불이 타오르는 것을 볼 것입니다.
That on **the ashes** of his youth doth lie,
그 젊은 날이 타버린 재 위에 (타오르는 불이요.)
As the ① death-bed whereon it must expire,
소멸되고 말 그 죽음의 자리는
① **Consumed** with that which it was nourished by.
양분을 주고 성장시켰던 것에 의해 소멸되었기 때문에.

< Couplet >

This thou perceiv'st, which makes thy love more strong,
이것을 그대가 이해를 한다면, 그대의 사랑은 더욱 강해질 것입니다.
② To love that well which thou must leave ere long.
당신이 곧 잃을 것을 사랑하도록 말입니다.

The speaker seems definitely haunted by his own ① mortality, and loads the poem down with **metaphors** related such as **ashes, nighttime, and cold**. This all sounds very depressing. However, we get the solace in the closing lines, which tell us that ① _____ helps people love and ② cherish each other more while they are still on earth.

2-2. ① follow ② grow up

Expressions & Vocabulary

shaft n. 수직 통로, 수갱
furrow n. 이랑
wing, sock n. 쟁기의 부분
headrig n. head harness

pluck n. 잡아당김, 뽑기
stumble v. 발이 걸리다, 발을 헛디디다
plod v. -dd- (특히 지쳐서) 터벅터벅 걷다

Sua TOKS!

Task

metaphor, theme (16-A-2)(12-2차-2)
Poetry – *Follower* by Seamus Heaney

Organization-Keywords

My father worked with a horse-plough,
His shoulders globed like a full sail strung
Between the shafts and the furrow.
The horse strained at his clicking tongue.

An expert. He would set the wing
And fit the bright steel-pointed sock.
The sod rolled over without breaking.
At the headrig, with a single pluck

Of reins, the sweating team turned round
And back into the land. His eye
Narrowed and angled at the ground,
Mapping the furrow exactly.
I stumbled in his hob-nailed wake,
Fell sometimes on the polished sod;
Sometimes he rode me on his back
Dipping and rising to his plod.

I wanted to grow up and plough,
To close one eye, stiffen my arm.
All I ever did was follow
In his broad shadow round the farm.

I was a nuisance, tripping, falling,
Yapping always. **But today**
It is my father who keeps **stumbling**
Behind me, and will not go away.

[Translation]

내 아버지는 말 쟁기로 일하셨고,
그의 어깨는 굴대와 이랑 사이에 매단
천처럼 굽어 있다.
말들은 소리를 내는 그의 혀에 긴장하였다.
전문가. 그는 쟁기의 날개를 고쳐 잡고,
밝은 강철 부분을 맞춘다.
흙은 깨어지지 않고 굴렀다.
머리 마구에, 고삐를 한번 당기자,

땀 흘리는 한 조의 말이 둥글게 돌아 다시 땅으로
들어왔다. 그의 눈은
좁아졌고, 땅에 맞추어졌고,
이랑을 정확하게 헤아렸다.

나는 구두징이 박힌 길을 따르다 발부리가 걸려,
운이 나는 흙 위에 때때로 넘어졌다.
때로는 그는 나를 그의 등 위에 태우고,
그의 쟁기질에 오르락 내리락 하게 하였다.
나는 자라면서 쟁기질하기를 원하였다,
한 눈을 감고서, 내 팔을 강화시키기를 원하였다.
내가 여태 한 일은 농장 주변에
그의 넓은 그림자 속에 따르는 일이었다.

난 골칫거리였다, 언제나 걸려, 넘어지고,
투덜대었다. 그러나 오늘
내 아버지가 내 뒤에서 계속 발부리가 걸려,
멀리 떨어지려고 하지 않았다.

[Summary]

The poem opens with the speaker's father plowing in the fields. He seems pretty darn good at it, too. He leads his powerful horses through the field with grace, and Heaney describes the taxing nature of the work. The young speaker follows his father as he works, but he's nowhere near as comfortable with the task. He's clumsy, and often **stumbles and falls trying to keep up with the father-horse duo**. The speaker talks about how he looked up to his dad, and wanted to grow up to plow too, but how he was never skilled enough to make it happen, which seems like kind of a bummer until we realize that the speaker turns out perfectly alright. At the end of the poem, we're sped up to **the present day, where, in a complete turn of events, the elderly father is now following the grown-up son, just as the son used to follow in his father's wake while he was plowing the fields**. It's a complete one-eighty, and shows that, although the speaker was kind of a dud when it came to farming, that he turned out to be his own person and now his father actually looks to him for guidance.

[Theme of Family]

The fact that the son admires his father so much only reinforces the power of **the father-son relationship** in "Follower"—they're nothing alike in terms of skill set, and yet the son is so completely fixated on the father as a role model, and the father is at least able to tolerate the bumbling son. Their family bond goes way beyond the camaraderie of shared interests. They're bound by blood, a fact that's driven home by the poem's ending as the two switch roles in each other's lives. The family that takes turns annoying each other together stays together.

[Theme of Admiration]

Oh, papa—this little dude really and truly looks up to his dad. Told through his eyes, his father is the most magnificent plowman to have ever walked the face of the earth, and man, does he want to be like him. The speaker of "Follower" is like a little puppy dog, **following him** around while he works, stumbling and chatting (probably a complete distraction for his hard-working dad). He simply wants to be around him. The son's admiring eye takes in with impressive detail his father's expert moves in the field. Though the son shows no signs of the skillfulness his dad has, that doesn't stop him from wanting to **follow** in his footsteps.

[Commentary]

This is a good example of the boy literally following his dad around, and figuratively trying to keep up with him. Literally we can see him bumbling around the chunks of sod and struggling to keep up. But we can also see that he "stumbles" in trying to <u>grow up</u> to be just like his father. He's never the crazy skilled farmer that his dad is, and never will be. He'll always be stumbling in that regard.

2-3. The poem describes the speaker's visit to a school. At the sight of children, he is reminded of a girl, his beloved, and recalls a particular day when she had told him how trivial incidents and reproof from the teacher would make her unhappy and he expressed sympathy. The underlined part emphasizes his complete sympathy with her by comparing it to an egg as if there two selves seemed to blend into one like the yolk and white of an egg.

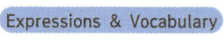

cipher n. (글로 쓰인) 암호, 이름 첫 글자들   **yolk** n. (달걀 등의) 노른자(위)

interpretation, simile (12-2차-2)
Poetry – *Among School Children* by William Butler Yeats

1. **Describing literally what has been happening to the speaker.** 2points
    – In the poem, the speaker experiences/undergoes/(v)/ ~
    – The poem describes NP, where ~
2. **Explaining the metaphorical meanings of the underlined part.** 2points
    – The underlined part compares/likens (A) to (B) ~

I

I walk through the long schoolroom questioning;
A kind old nun in a white hood replies;
The children learn to cipher and to sing,
To study reading-books and history,
To cut and sew, be neat in everything
In the best modern way — the children's eyes
In momentary wonder stare upon
A sixty-year-old smiling public man.

II

I dream of a Ledaean body, bent
Above a sinking fire, **a tale that she**
Told of a harsh reproof, or trivial event
That changed some childish day to tragedy—
Told, and it seemed that **our two natures blent**
Into <u>a sphere from youthful sympathy,</u>
Or else, to alter Plato's parable,
Into <u>the yolk and white of the one shell.</u>

[Translation]

I

나는 긴 교실을 걸으며 질문을 한다,
흰 두건을 쓴 친절한 늙은 수녀가 대답한다.
아이들은 암송하고 노래하는 법,
독서와 역사를 공부하는 법,
자르고, 재봉하고, 모든 것에
가장 현대적으로 단정하기를 배운다.
아이들의 눈은 순간적으로 의아스러워
예순이 된 미소 짓는 공직자를 응시한다.

II

나는 꺼져가는 불 위에 몸을 굽힌 레다의 육신,
그녀가 들려준 거친 비판이나 어떤 어린시절을
비극으로 만든 사소한 일에 대한 이야기를 꿈꾼다.
그러자 우리 두 본성이 젊은 공감으로부터 하나의
구로 섞이는 것으로 여겨졌다,
달리 플라톤의 비유로 바꾸어 말한다면,
<u>한 알의 노른자와 흰자로 섞이는 것으로 여겨졌다.</u>

[Commentary]

The poem Among School Children was composed after the poet's visit to a convent school in Waterford Ireland in 1926. This poem moves from a direct consideration of the children to Yeats' early love, Maude Gonne, and then to a passionate philosophical conclusion in which all of Yeats's platonic thinking blends into an exalted hymn of raise to the glory and the puzzle of human existence.

As Yeats entered the school, he was received by an old nun who conducted him through different classes. The children in the classes looked with wonder at the sixty year old smiling public man (poet). At the sight of children, **he is reminded of Maude Gonne; his beloved as she must have been a student like the girls who stood before him at the time.** He recalls a particular day when she had told him how trivial incidents and reproof from the teacher would make her unhappy and turn the entire day into the cheerless void.

The poet had listened to her account and expressed sympathy, till he completely identified with her: it was **as if there two selves seemed to blend into one like the yolk and white of an egg.** At this point, there is an allusion of the myth that claims that man and woman were originally one, but since they forcefully separated, they always attempt to come together.

Synonyms

- 예상하다 (v)
    - expect — 예상[기대]하다
    - nticipate — 예기하다, 예상하다; 기대하다, 고대하다; 미리 걱정하다, 예상하다
    - predict — 예언하다, 예측하다, 예보하다
    - suppose — (이미 알고 있는 지식에 의거하여) 생각하다, 추정[추측]하다
    - assume — (사실일 것으로) 추정[상정]하다

- 결점 (n)
    - flaw — (사물의) 결함
    - defect — 결점, 결함; 단점, 약점; 흠
    - weakness — 약점, 결점
    - fault — 결점, 흠, 단점, 결함
    - blemish — 흠, 결점, (도덕상의) 오점
    - drawback — 결점, 문제점

- 초래하다 (v)
    - originate — 일으키다, 발생시키다, 유래하다
    - generate — 일으키다, 발생시키다, 초래하다

	raise	불러일으키다, 자아내다, 발생시키다
	cause	…을 야기하다[초래하다]
	create	야기하다, 초연하다
	provoke	불러일으키다, 자극하여 …시키다
	produce	(특히 필요한 기술을 들여) 만들어 내다[창조하다]
• 부족 (n)	shortage	부족
	deficiency	부족, 결핍
	want	결핍, 부족; 결점
	lack	부족, 결핍, 결여
	scarcity	부족, 결핍
	insufficiency	불충분, 부족; 부적임
• 만연한 (a)	widespread	광범위한, 널리 퍼진
	prevalent	(특정 시기·장소에) 일반적인
	extensive	넓은, 광대한
	common	공통의, 공동의, 공유의; 단결한, 일치된
	general	일반의, 총체적인, 전반적인
	current	현행의, 통용하는, 유통되고 있는, 현재 유행하는, 사회의 공통적인
	universal	보편적인, 전반적인; 일반적인; 전칭의
	usual	흔히 하는[있는], 평상시의, 보통의
• 증가하다 (v)	expand	확장하다, 확대하다; 전개시키다; 전개하다 (n. expansion)
	enlarge	확장하다; 넓히다 (n. enlargement)
	broaden	넓어지다, 퍼지다
	swell	부풀다, 붓다, 팽창하다; 부어오르다; 부풀다
	increase	(양·수·가치 등이) 증가하다, 인상되다, 증가[인상]시키다
	raise	늘리다, 높이다; 지르다
	grow	성장하다, 크다, 발육하다; 자라다; 자라다 (n. growth)
	spread	퍼지다, 유포되다, 만연하다
	escalate	단계적으로 확대[증가/악화]되다[시키다] (n. escalation)

2-4. The word for the blank ① is 'beauty.' The blank ② can be filled as follows: 'simile' is employed as the literary device while likening/comparing the woman to a clear and cloudless night for the purpose of praising her beauty. ('simile' is employed as the literary device for the purpose of praising her beauty by likening/comparing the woman to a clear and cloudless night.)

Expressions & Vocabulary

gaudy   a. (색깔이) 야한[천박한]

mellow   v. (사람이[을] 특히 연륜이 쌓여) 부드러워지다 [부드럽게 만들다]

Sua TOKS!

Task

theme, simile (16-A-2)(08서-20)(09-39)(10-2차-4)(10-2차-4)(13-37)(13-40)(12-40)
Poetry - *She Walks in Beauty* by George Gordon, Lord Byron

Organization

1. Completing the statement by filling in the blank ① with the ONE most appropriate word.   **1points**
   - The word for the blank ① is '_____.'
2. Identifying the literary device used in the first line of the above poem.   **1points**
   - '_____' is used/employed as the literary device
3. Explaining its purpose.   **2points**
   - for the purpose of (theme) / to describe ~ (theme)
   - by likening/comparing (원관념) to (보조관념)

Keywords

She walks in beauty, like the night	걷고 있는 그녀는
Of cloudless climes and starry skies;	구름 한점 없이 별이 빛나는 밤하늘처럼 아름답네.
And all that's best of dark and bright	가장 아름다운 빛과 그림자가
Meet in her aspect and her eyes:	그녀의 모습과 눈 속에서 어울려
Thus mellowed to that tender light	저토록 은은한 빛으로 무르익으니
Which heaven to gaudy day denies.	번쩍거리는 낮 하늘에선 저런 아름다움 못 보네.

One shade the more, one ray the less,	그림자 한 줄기를 더 했어도, 빛 한줄기를 더 했어도
Had half impaired **the nameless grace**	저 우아함은 반감 되었으리
Which waves in every raven tress,	검은 머리카락마다 물결치는,
Or softly lightens o'er **her face**;	또는 그녀 얼굴에 은은히 빛나는.
Where **thoughts serenely sweet** express	얼굴에 깃든 고요하고 고운 사상은
How pure, how dear their dwelling place.	순수하고 귀한 보금자릴 자랑하네.
And on that cheek, and o'er that brow,	눈언저리에 어리고, 뺨에 서리어
So soft, so calm, yet eloquent,	너무도 부드럽고 고요하게, 그러나 웅변으로 말해주네,
The smiles that win, the tints that glow,	사람의 마음을 사로잡는 미소와, 발그레 빛나는 홍조는
But tell of days in goodness spent,	선하게 살아온 세월을,
A mind at peace with all below,	지상의 모든 것과 화목했던 정신을,
A heart whose love is innocent!	순진무구한 사랑이 담긴 가슴을!

[Summary]

An unnamed speaker describes a woman of remarkable beauty. In the first lines, he compares her to a clear, cloudless night full of sparkling **stars**. He praises her beauty, in which "all that's best of dark and bright/ meet." To him, she's beautiful both in the light of day and in the tender light of night.

The speaker admires the balance of darkness and light in the woman, proclaiming that "one shade the more, one ray the less" would have marred her beauty. Instead, this perfect balance accentuates the "nameless grace" of her "raven" colored hair and her soft features.

The speaker notes how calm the woman is and how eloquently she expresses herself. She smiles happily, with a glow that speaks to her inherent goodness and beauty. She seems perfectly at peace and loves with a kind of innocence and simplicity that inspires the speaker to write this poem in her honor.

> [Themes]
>
> In "She Walks in Beauty," Lord Byron explores **the many different kinds of beauty that one woman possesses**. The speaker notices her **physical beauty** first and **praises** the beauty of her soft features and raven tresses. He then **praises** her inner beaauty, citing her eloquent speech and her apparent intelligence. **Her inner beauty enhances her outer beauty**, making her perfect in the speaker's eyes.
>
> Byron also plays with **the themes of light and dark.** He introduces the theme of darkness in the first line, **where he likens the woman to a clear and cloudless night.** He then describes the interplay of light and dark within her and how the balance of these elements contributes to her beauty. Were these elements out of balance, Byron claims, she would be just half as beautiful, but would still possess the "nameless grace" that inspired the poem.

Synonyms

- **알리다** (v)
  - notify ~ sb (of sth) | ~ sth to sb (공식적으로) 알리다[통고/통지하다]
  - inform ~ sb (of/about sth) (특히 공식적으로) 알리다[통지하다]
  - advise ~ (sb) (against sth/against doing sth) 조언하다, 충고하다, 권고하다
  - tell ~ sb (sth) | ~ sth to sb 사람이 (말·글로) 알리다[전하다], 말하다
  - give information, communicate to, tip someone off

- **인정하다** (v)
  - acknowledge (사실로) 인정하다, (권위나 자격을) 인정하다
  - accept (기꺼이) 받아들이다
  - admit (사실임을 마지못해) 인정하다, (범행·잘못 등을) 자백하다[인정하다]
  - grant (특히 공식적·법적으로) 승인[허락]하다
  - concede (특히 마지못해) 내주다[허락하다]

- **초래하다** (v)
  - originate 일으키다, 발생시키다, 유래하다
  - generate 일으키다, 발생시키다, 초래하다
  - raise 불러일으키다, 자아내다, 발생시키다
  - cause …을 야기하다[초래하다]
  - create 야기하다, 초연하다
  - provoke 불러일으키다, 자극하여 …시키다

	produce	(특히 필요한 기술을 들여) 만들어 내다[창조하다]
• 촉진하다 (v)	promote	증진[촉진]하다, 진척시키다, 진행시키다, 활성화시키다
	boost	후원하다, 밀어주다; …의 경기를 부양하다, 선전하다 《up》
	enhance	(좋은 점·가치·지위를) 높이다[향상시키다]
	improve	개선되다, 나아지다, 개선/향상시키다
	increase	늘다, 늘리다, 늘어나다, 증가하다
	strengthen	강하게 하다, 튼튼하게 하다, 증강하다, 강화하다, 증원하다
	reinforce	강화하다, …의 힘을 북돋우다, 보충하다
	encourage	~ sb (in sth) 격려[고무]하다
• 다양한 (a)	diverse	다양한
	various	여러 가지의, 각양각색의, 다양한, 다양한 특징을 지닌
	varied	다양한, 다채로운
	miscellaneous	잡다한, 갖가지의
	several	몇몇의, 수개의, 몇 개의, 몇 명의, 몇 번의
	varying	바뀌는, 변화하는; 가지각색의
• 다른 (a)	different	다른, 차이가 나는
	contrasting	대조적인, 대비[대조]를 이루는
	distinctive	독특한
	distinguishing	특징적인, 다른 것과 구별되는, 특색 있는
	disparate	서로 전혀 다른, 이질적인
	dissimilar	~ (from/to sb/sth) 같지 않은, 다른

2-5. Literally the father tells his son to always keep the car's gas tank half full, but the speaker ignores his advice and drives until the gas tank is almost empty in defiance. Eventually the car runs out of gas and he is stranded for the night. Next day, the car is refilled and he still keeps his way of behavior. The word is 'thrill.'

Expressions & Vocabulary

run on empty (《종종 진행형으로》) 자력(資力)[방책]이 다하다, 힘을 잃다, 역부족이다
cross-country a. (특히 간선 도로를 이용하지 않고) 국토를 횡단하는
defy (defying) v. (권위·법률·규칙 등에) 반항하다
fume n. [종종 pl.] (유해·불쾌한) 연기, 김, 증기, 연무, 훈김, 열기, (술 등의) 독기(毒氣)

Furies n. (그리스·로마신화) pl. [the ~] 세 자매의 복수의 여신 (《머리카락은 뱀이고 날개를 닮》)
strand v. 좌초시키다
push[press] one's luck 운을 너무 믿고 덤비다
thrill v. 황홀감, 흥분, 설렘, 전율

Sua TOKS!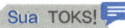

Task

interpretation, metaphor (12-2차-2) (18-A-11)

Poetry – *Running on Empty* by Robert Phillips

Organization

1. Explaining literally what has been happening to the speaker of the poem. **2points**
   – (Literally describe the event happening in the poem.)
2. Completing the commentary below with the ONE most appropriate word from the poem. Change the word form if necessary. **2points**
   – The word is '_____.'

Keywords

As a teenager I would **drive Father's Chevrolet** cross-county given me	십대인 나는 아버지의 쉐보레를 타고 전국을 달리곤 했지
Reluctantly: "Always keep the tank Half full, boy, half full, ya hear?	"항상 기름을 반은 채워 놔야해, "애야, 반은, 알아들었지?" 주저하며 그렇게 주신 차로

The fuel gauge dipping, dipping
Toward Empty, hitting Empty, then
— **thrilling**! — 'way below Empty,
myself driving cross-country
mile after mile, faster and faster,
all night long, **this crazy kid driving**

the earth's rolling surface,
against all laws. Defying chemistry,

rules, and time, riding on nothing
but fumes, pushing luck harder

than anyone pushed before, the wind
screaming past like the Furies

I stranded myself only once, a white
night with no gas station open, ninety miles

from nowhere. Panicked for awhile
at standstill, myself **stalled**.

At dawn **the car and I both refilled**. But,

Father, I am running on **empty** still.

연료계는 떨어지고, 떨어지고,
완전히 비도록, 완전히 비면, 그러면
— 흥분되네! — 훨씬 더 빈 상태로,
나는 국토를 횡단해 달리네
한 마일, 한 마일, 더 빠르게 더 빠르게,
종일 밤을, 이런 아이적 광란적인 질주는

지구의 둥근 지면을,
법을 어기며 달리네. 반응과 규칙과, 시간에

반항하며 연기만을 타고,
그 이전 누구보다도 더 강하게 자신의 운을

믿고 덤비는데, 바람은 복수의 여신처럼
소리 지르며 지나가네

나는 처음으로 혼자 길 잃은 신세로,
90마일 주변으로는 열려있는 주유소 하나 없어 하얀 밤을 지세고

잠시 넋을 잃고
가만히 서서, 내가 시동이 꺼져버렸네.

새벽에 자동차나 나나 둘 다 채워졌네. 그러나,
아버지, 나는 여전히 빈 채로 질주를 합니다.

While the older perspective, that of the father, is focused toward safety, the younger perspective, that of the teenager, is focused toward risk taking. He is "running on empty still" for the _____ of his life. He's taking advantage of his youth and going for it.

아버지의 시각처럼 나이든 사람들의 시각은 안전에 초점을 두고 있는 반면, 십대의 시각처럼 젊은이의 시각은 위험을 감수하는 것을 향해 꽂혀있다. 그는 인생의 _____을 위해 "여전히 빈 채로 질주를 한다."

[Commentary]

- "Running on Empty" is **a narrative**. The narrator creates **the character of a teenager**. Most people can relate to **the theme of being on their own for the first time**, whether it be something they have experienced or something they will experience.
- The poem contains colloquial diction. Phillip uses words such as **"empty" and "stalled" as metaphors to compare the teenager's life to the Chevy**. He repeats "mile" and "faster" to intensify the risk he is taking.
- "…a white night with no gas station open, ninety miles from nowhere" creates the image that the teenager is truly alone. This is a consequence of his new independence.
- Phillips creates an optimistic tone as the reader gains his new independence. Toward the end it shifts to reflective, but regains optimism in the last stanza.
- **Opposing Viewpoints:** The younger perspective, that of the teenager, is focused toward risk taking. He is "running on empty still" for the thrill of his new found independence. He's taking advantage of his youth and going for it [life]. The older perspective, that of the father, is focused toward safety. He tells his son to "Always keep the tank half full, boy, half full, ya hear?" He could have made this mistake as a teenager and now understands the consequences. The father also wants his son to take care of his Chevrolet, which he "reluctantly" gave him, by keeping it fueled for the health of the engine.

2-6. The speaker is described as "a black ocean" to represent the speaker's self-determination of struggles with hope for success in hardships. In the poem, the speaker is expected to rise just like "a black ocean," which certainly waves up in the tide by leaping and swelling and leave behind fears of nights. The word is 'history.'

(The speaker is described as "a black ocean" to represent the speaker's self-determination of <u>continuing struggles</u> for the dream in <u>hardships</u>. In the poem, the speaker is expected to rise just as "a black ocean" certainly waves up in the tide by leaping and swelling and leaves behind fears of nights. The word is 'history.')

Expressions & Vocabulary

hut n. (간단하게 집이나 쉼터로 지은) 오두막[막사]
soulful adj. 감정이 풍부한, 혼이 담긴 (듯한)
well v. (액체가) 솟아 나오다[흐르다], 샘솟다

Sua TOKS!

Task

theme, metaphor (18-B-5)(14-B-서2)

Poetry – *Still I Rise* by Maya Angelou

1. Explaining why the speaker is described as "a black ocean" (line 17). **3points**
   - The speaker is described as "a black ocean" to represent ~
   - The speaker compares (A) to (B)   * (A)원관념 (B)보조관념
   - (A) is metaphorically described as (B)
   - (A) is likened/compared to (B)
   as in the poem ~ [description in the poem]

2. Filling in the blank with the ONE most appropriate word from the poem. **1points**
   - The word is '_____.'

Organization-Keywords

You may write me down in **history**   당신들이 모질고 왜곡된 거짓말로
With your bitter, **twisted lies**,   역사에 기록할지도 모른다.
You may tread me in the very dirt   나를 먼지 속에서 짓밟을지도 모르지만
But still, **like dust**, I'll rise.   여전히 나는, 먼지처럼, 일어날 것이다.

Just **like moons and like suns**,	5	달처럼 그리고 해처럼	5
With the certainty of tides,		반드시 밀물과 썰물이 있듯이	
Just **like hopes springing high**,		높이 솟아나는 희망처럼	
Still I'll rise.		여전히 나는 일어날 것이다.	
Did you want to see me broken?		내가 무너지는 것을 기대했는가?	
Bowed head and lowered eyes?	10	머리도 조아리고 눈도 내리깔고	10
Shoulders falling down like teardrops.		눈물처럼 어깨를 떨구면서	
Weakened by my soulful cries.		영혼의 절규로 약해져 있기를.	
Out of the huts of history's shame		역사의 부끄러움 헛간에서 나와	
I rise		나는 일어난다.	
Up from a past that's rooted in pain	15	고통에 뿌리박은 과거로부터 분연히	15
I rise		나는 일어난다.	
I'm **a black ocean**, leaping and wide,		나는 검은 대양, 넓게 뛰어오르네,	
Welling and swelling I bear in the tide.		솟구치고 출렁이는 물결을 품고.	
Leaving behind nights of terror and fear		공포와 두려움의 밤을 뒤로 하고 떠나면서	
I rise	20	나는 일어난다	20
Into a daybreak that's wondrously clear		멋진 맑은 새벽 속으로	
I rise		나는 일어난다	
Bringing the gifts that my ancestors gave,		내 선조들이 준 선물을 가지고,	
I am the dream and the hope of the slave.		나는 노예들의 꿈과 희망이다.	
I rise	25	나는 일어난다	25
I rise		나는 일어난다	
I rise.		나는 일어난다.	

[Theme of Hope and Dreams]

Maya Angelou's poem "Still I Rise" is about the humiliation that blacks have felt as a result of racism and oppression over the past centuries, calling them to stand up for themselves with pride and dignity. The speaker's refusal to give in to **the lies of history**, and succeed in spite of all of the false beliefs that others have, brings a powerful message.

The imagery in the poem makes it clear that this is a work **about the experiences blacks have suffered as a result of latent racism.** Whether it is the "huts of history's shame" or the "black ocean, leaping and wide," the audience of this speaker is clear. For those who look down on strong black women for not fitting in to expected racial and gender stereotypes, the speaker asks if her "sassiness" is a cause for concern, or if her "haughtiness" is offensive? Her point of view is that **she has a mission to bring "the gifts that [her] ancestors gave."** As a result, she is "the dream and the hope of the slave." All of those who have fallen victim to the ravages of racism have become part of a legacy that demands the best in terms of dignity from today's generation.

Synonyms

- 어려움 (n)

	difficulty	(주로 복수로) 어려움, 곤경, 장애
	hardship	돈, 식품 등의 부족에서 오는 어려움,
	failure	실패
	obstacle	장애, 방해, 지장이 되는 것, 장애물, 반대
	despair	절망
	hurdle	장애물, 허들, 곤란
	painful moments/events	힘든 순간/일들
	ordeal	시련, 고난; 괴로운 체험
	problem	다루거나 이해하기 힘든 문제
	trouble	불편, 폐, 분쟁, 근심, 근심거리
	issue	(걱정거리가 되는) 문제
	worry	걱정, 우려, 걱정거리, 걱정(되는 일)
	adversity, pressure, (a)repressed	

- 지속하다 (v)

	keep	<어떤 상태·동작을> 계속하다
	maintain	유지하다
	continue	쉬지 않고 계속되다
	retain	계속 유지하다, 간직하다
	sustain	견디다, 유지하다, 지속하다

- 노력, 수고 (n)

	struggle	고분, 분투, 수고, 애; 수고를 요하는 것의 의미인 경우,
	effort	수고, 애; 수고를 요하는 것
	labour	노동, 수고,
	exertion	노력, 진력, 분발, 행사, 격심한 활동
	cf. resist(resistant/resistance)	

2-7. The poem mainly describes the speaker's powerful, undying love. That is, he lets us know his love is so great to love her eternally. To illustrate this theme, the underlined part emphasizes the fact that he will love her forever or at least until long after their lives are over because the seas will probably never go dry.

Expressions & Vocabulary

lass n. 아가씨, 처녀   a bonnie(=bonny) lass n. 예쁜 소녀

Sua TOKS!

Task

theme, hyperbole (14-B-서2)

Poetry – *Oh, My love Is like a Red, Red Rose* by Robert Burns

---

[Literary Terms]

Hyperbole: Intentional exaggeration — saying more than is actually meant.

---

1. **Describing the theme of the poem** 2points
    - The theme (of the poem) is ~
    - The speaker (in the poem) exhorts/urges/suggests/insists ~
    - The poem (mainly) describes/depicts the importance/essense/power of ~
    - The poem is about ~
    - (+) That is/In other words/To explain, ~

2. **Explaining how the underlined part is** 2points
    - For the theme/To illustrate the theme, the underlined part emphasizes ~

3. **related to the theme**
    - as in the poem ~ [description in the poem]

Organization-Keywords

O my Luve is **like a red, red rose**	오, 내 사랑은 유월에 갓 핀 장미처럼
That's newly sprung in June;	붉고 붉어라.
O my Luve is **like the melody**	오, 내 사랑은 아름답게 연주되는 선율처럼
That's sweetly played in tune.	감미로워라.

As fair art thou, my bonnie lass,　　　　　내 사랑스런 소녀여, 그대 아름다움만큼
　　So deep in luve am I;　　　　　　　　나 그댈 깊이 사랑하노니
And I will luve thee still, my dear,　　　　바다가 다 마르도록
<u>　　Till a' the seas gang dry.</u>　　　　　　변함없이 그대를 사랑하리.

Till a' the seas gang dry, my dear,　　　내 사랑이여, 바다가 마르고
　　And the rocks melt with the sun;　　바위가 햇빛에 녹아내릴 때까지
And I will luve thee still, my dear,　　　　변함없이 그대를 사랑하리.
　　While the sands of life shall run.　　　생명의 모래가 흐르는 한은,

And fare thee weel, my only luve,　　　　그러니 하나뿐인 내 사랑이여,
　　And fare thee weel awhile!　　　　　안녕, 잠시 동안만 안녕!
And I will come again, my luve　　　　　천만리 먼 길이래도
　　Though it were ten thousand mile.　　내 다시금 찾아오리니!

[Summary]

　　The Poem, *A Red, Red Rose* by Robert Burns is about **the poet's beloved and her beauty**. The poem begins with a simile where he says that his beloved is like a red rose that newly blossomed in the month of June. He then calls her a melody which is sweetly played in tune. He says that **his beloved is so beautiful and he will love her till all the seas dry up**. He bids her farewell for a short period and promises that he will return.

[Theme of Love]

　　A Red, Red Rose is one of the most famous love poems in the English language, and it's pretty clear why—the entire poem is **an expression of the speaker's powerful, undying love**. Line after line, **he lets us know his love is lasting, for real, and awesomely awesome**. So awesome, in fact, that he would even walk ten thousand miles to see his bonnie lass again.

[Theme of Time]

　　A Red, Red Rose has time on its side. The lovers may be apart for a while, but that's no matter because **their love transcends time**. It can practically survive an apocalypse, for crying out loud. That is, **time is no object when it comes to great love**.

Synonyms

- 영원히 (adv)
forever	(英 또한 for ever) 영원히
eternally	영원히; 영원히 변치 않고
perpetually	영구히, 영속적으로
evermore	(문예체) 항상, 언제나
for good	영원히
in perpetuity	영구히, 영원히

3. Imagery, Symbol, Tone, Sound

3-1. ① half-submerged balls ② ox

Expressions & Vocabulary

head first 머리부터 먼저[거꾸로], 제대로 생각도 해 보지 않고 [성급하게]
dally v. 빈둥빈둥 지내다; 우물쭈물하다 《about, over》
sleek a. 매끄러운(smooth), 윤나는(glossy)
harness v. (동력원 등으로) 이용[활용]하다, ~ sth (to sth) (말 등의 동물에[을]) 마구를 채우다

ox n. 황소(특히 과거 일을 시키기 위해 거세한 수소)
strain v. ~ (sth) (to do sth) 안간힘을 쓰다
muck n. 외양간 거름, 퇴비, 비료; 쓰레기, 오물; 진흙, 진창
smear v. 〈기름 등을〉 바르다, 칠하다, 더럽히다
botch 서투르게 깁다, 망쳐 놓다 《up》

Sua TOKS!

Task

imagery, simile, metaphor (08서-20)
Poetry – *To Be of Use* by Marge Piercy

[Literary Terms]

Imagery : Words or phrases that **describe the sense**; Language that evokes a physical sensation produced by one or more of the five senses — sight, hearing, taste, touch, smell.

Metaphor : An imaginative **comparison** between two unlike items that do not use *like* or *as* — that is, when it says "a *is b*" rather than "a *is like b*" — it is a metaphor.)

Simile : A comparison between two unlike items that uses *like* or *as*.

Organization-Keywords

The people I love the best
내가 가장 사랑하는 사람들은
jump into work head first
제일 먼저 일로 뛰어들어
without dallying in the shallows
얕은데서 우물쭈물하지 않고
and **swim** off with sure strokes almost out of sight.
확실하게 치고 사라지며 수영해나간다.

They seem to become natives of that element,
반쯤 잠긴 공들처럼 출렁이는
the black sleek heads of seals
검고 매끈한 물개의 머리들,

bouncing like half-submerged balls.
이들은 이런 종류의 태생이 된 것 같다.
I love people who harness themselves, **an ox to a heavy cart,**
나는 스스로 무거운 수레를 맨 황소처럼 스스로를 활용하는 사람을 사랑한다.
who pull **like water buffalo,** with **massive patience,**
물소처럼 육중한 인내로 끌고,
who strain in the mud and the muck **to move things forward,**
앞으로 전진하기 위해 진흙과 진창에서 애를 쓰며,
who do what has to be done, **again and again.**
해야 할 것을 하고, 또 하는 사람.

I want to be with people who submerge
나는 자신을 업무에 잠기게 하는 사람들,
in the task, who go into the fields to harvest and work in a row and pass the bags along,
들판으로 가서 열 맞추어 담는 통을 옆으로 전달하며 수확하고,
who are not parlor generals and field deserters
집안에 앉아있는 장군과 탈영병이 아니라
but move in a common rhythm
음식이 들어오고 불이 꺼져야 할 때
when the food must come in or the fire be put out.
같이 리듬에 맞춰 움직이는 사람들이다.

[Commentary]

What is the importance of the imagery, such as metaphor and simile, in this poem? It is not simply a fancy way of illustrating what the poet might have said in abstract terms. The poet enacts through its imagery the very statement that people should work hard industriously with self-fulfillment. For this theme, the poet gives the interesting imagery such as (①) where people that dived **head first** into icy, deep water not worrying but **enjoying** the stinging cold is envisioned. Likewise, the imagery of a(an) (②) conveys **strength, perseverance, and commitment.**

type	imagery
simile	_____ ① _____
metaphor	_____ ② _____

[Theme]

1. The poet is inspired by the people who work hard. The poet gives examples of seals, water buffaloes, farmers and pitcher makers to paint a picture of an industrious person. In our world, 'manual labour' is unappreciated and people are in mad race for white collar job. The poet is trying to tell that we should appreciate their hard work.
2. It is only through hard work that we convert something that has no value (like mud) into something of a value and a purpose (like a pitcher or vase).
3. Along with hard work, cooperation among the workers is also important. It is through contribution of many that a bigger objective can be achieved.

[Imagery]

When the speaker references seals and their similitude to "half-submerged balls", I conjure an extraordinarily vivid mental image of those seals bobbing up and down, just as beach balls do. It is an effective piece of sensory writing, and also serves to relate how one can become "a native of that element". Seals are perfectly adapted for their element. They love to play in the water. They love to laze in the water. They love to do practically anything in the water. They are native of that element. Seals feel comfortable in aquatic environments. Biologically, they are superbly equipped to handle the different circumstances that water may pose. This is the same with hard working people. They feel comfortable in service situations. They can deal with other people effectively with love and charm. They only really feel at ease when they are working and moving and doing something as does the metaphor, "an ox to a heavy cart", which conveys strength, perseverance, and commitment.

3-2. wishes

Expressions & Vocabulary

hypocritic a. (synonym of. hypocritical) 위선의, 위선(자)적인
dervish n. 데르비시(극도의 금욕 생활을 서약하는 이슬람교 집단의 일원. 예배 때 빠른 춤을 춤)
muffle v. (소리를) 죽이다
diadem n. 왕관[머리띠]
fagot n. [야금] (가공용의) 쇠막대 다발; 지금(地金) 뭉치; ((일반적으로)) 다발, 묶음

pleach v. 〈나뭇가지 등을〉 엮다; 〈머리를〉 땋다
pomp n. (공식 행사·의식의) 장관
solemn a. 사람이 침통한; 근엄한
filet (←FILLET) n. (그물눈 모양의) 레이스

Sua TOKS!

Task

Theme, symbol (17-A-5)
Poetry – *Days* by Ralph Waldo Emerson

Organization-Keywords

Daughters of ① **Time**, the hypocritic ① **Days**,
시간의 딸들, 위선자 나날들이
Muffled and dumb like barefoot *dervishes,
맨발의 수도사처럼 몸을 감싸고 묵묵히
And marching single in an endless file,
일렬로 끝없이 줄지어 행진하여
Bring ② **diadems and fagots in their hands.**
저마다 손에 왕관과 섶단을 들고 온다.
To each they offer ② **gifts** after ③ **his will,**
저마다 제 뜻에 따라 선물을 주고받는다,
② **Bread, kingdom, stars, and sky that holds them all.**
빵, 왕국, 별들과, 그 모두를 품은 하늘을.
I, in my pleached garden, watched the pomp,
가지 얽힌 정원에서 그 화려한 행렬을 바라보느라,
Forgot ③ **my morning wishes,** hastily
나의 아침 소원을 깜빡 잊고 있다가, 다급히

Took ③-1) **a few herbs and apples**, and ① **the Day**
채소 몇 포기 사과 몇 개 땄을 뿐인데, 날이
Turned and departed silent. I, too late,
돌아서 조용히 떠나버렸다. 나는, 뒤늦게,
Under ① **her** solemn fillet saw the scorn.
그녀의 장엄한 머리띠 아래 서린 냉소를 보았다.

One theme in the poem is that man is ① ② free to accomplish ③ **whatever his heart wishes**. But mankind is not aware of ① ② **this freedom**.

[Commentary]

This short philosophical poem is notable for its compression, its symbolism, and its expression of Emerson's belief in taking practical advantage of all of one's opportunities. "Hypocritic Days," who are the "daughters of Time," come to us in single file, offering us whatever **gifts** we choose to take from them. In other words, we can do with Time whatever we wish, and we are free to take what we want from each day: "Bread, kingdoms, stars, and sky that holds them all." **Man, Emerson says, is free to accomplish whatever his heart desires. But mankind is not aware of this freedom.** The Day (symbolizing a lifetime) comes and offers the poet infinite **gifts**. The poet, forgetting his early desire for glorious achievements in his life, snatches a few insignificant gifts from Time. When the Day turns away with contempt, he realizes that he has passed up glorious opportunities.

3-3. soul

Expressions & Vocabulary

stintless a. 무제한의, 아낌없는
for size 크기[사이즈]를 정하기 위하여, 크기에 따라서
amber n. 호박색, 황색
meadow n. (특히 건초를 만들기 위한) 목초지

windowpane n. 창유리
incautious a. 부주의한, 경솔한
throughout adv. 내내, 전체가
mellow a. 색깔·소리가 부드럽고 풍부한, 그윽한

Sua TOKS!

Task

theme, tone (09-37)

Poetry – *Before I got my eye put out* by Emily Dickinson

Organization-Keywords

Before I got **my eye** put out —	이 눈 (아주) 불편해지기 전엔 —
I liked as well to **see**	나 또한 다른 존재들, 눈을 가진 그들처럼
As other creatures, that have **eyes** —	보는 것을 좋아했는데 —
And know no other way —	그리고 다른 방법은 몰랐네 —
But were it told to me, Today,	그러나 오늘 누가 내게
That **I** might have the Sky	하늘을 내 것일 수 있다고
For mine, I tell you that my Heart	한다면, 내 심장이
Would split, for size of me —	찢어질 것 같다고 말하리 —
The Meadows — **mine** —	초원들이 — 내 것 —
The Mountains — **mine** —	산들이 — 내 것 —
All Forests — **Stintless stars** —	모든 숲들을 — 무수한 별들을 —
As much of noon, as I could take —	낮까지, 내가 가질 수 있다면 —
Between **my finite eyes** —	내 한정된 두 눈에 —
The Motions of the Dipping Birds —	내리 나는 저 새들의 움직임들 —
The Morning's Amber Road —	아침 호박색길이 —
For mine — to **look at** when I liked,	내 것 — 내가 보고자 하면,
The news would strike me dead —	이 소식은 내가 감당하기엔 너무 엄청난 것이리라 —

So safer — guess — **with just my soul**
Open the window pane
Where **other creatures** put their **eyes** —
Incautious — of the Sun —

그러니 더 안전하게 — 그래 — 그냥 내 영혼으로
다른 존재들이 눈을 두고 —
부주의하게도 — 태양을 보는 —
유리창을 열고 보리라

Tone reflects the **writer's attitude** toward a topic. It is the **emotional message** behind the writer's words. Tone is chiefly **controlled by the words** the writer chooses, words that color **ideas**, evoke **desired emotions**, and imply **judgments.**

The tone of the poem keeps on changing throughout. Starting in slow and mellow tone, the poem ends with an astonishing tone, since the speaker has come to realise now that the only possible means to approach the divine truth is through her very _____.

[Theme]

Emily Dickinson's "Before I got my eye put out" revolves around a speaker whose eyes have been gouged out. In this poem, the speaker is partially blind (implied by the singular use of "eye") and **misses the power sight can offer.** Sight is the extended metaphor here as **with sight comes power and experience**, which she desires at first. However, there is a shift as **the speaker realizes the dangers of sight and decides that he/she prefers not to have sight restored to both eyes.** Dickinson's consistent use of dashes helps set the pace and establish the mood.

[Commentary]

The tone of the poem keeps on changing throughout. In the beginning two stanzas, she uses **slow and mellow tone** because of the fact that she has lost her sight. In the next two stanzas, **the tone is rising**, as she is seen as wondering about the infinite elements of nature. And subsequently, the poem ends with **an astonishing tone, since the speaker has come to realise now that the only possible means to approach the divine truth is through her very soul.**

[Analysis]

In the second stanza, she feels that her heart would burst with joy if she could "have the Sky". **This ownership suggests, again, that sight is powerful.** Here, her **delighted tone reveals that she feels positively towards having sight.**

The dashes in the third stanza confirms her tone. Before in the first two stanzas, there were few dashes except at the end of the sentences. These stanzas thus have a rather **slow and calm pace**, as if she's reminiscing about her lost sight and misses it. Also, the dashes in "—mine—" of the third stanza **cut the sentences short and makes it sound rushed**, as if the speaker is greedy, even **desperate, for "Meadows"** and **"Mountains"**. However, there is a shift when she **contrasts "finite eyes" with the "Stintless stars"**, which serves to show **that in reality, what sight offers is too much to take on for her two eyes.**

The fourth stanza suggests the same as the "news would strike me dead". "Dead" has a rather strong and harsh connotation, which reveals that **sight is overwhelming and getting her vision back is no longer what she wants. Instead, she'd rather play it safe by looking through "just [her] soul" instead of being blinded by too much light (or burned by the Sun).** The shift is evident because by the last stanza, she calls creatures the "other", to indicate that she is no longer one of those creatures who put their eyes recklessly on the window pane. **Her tone though is uncertain as she says "guess"**, but she still seems to lean more towards the idea that she doesn't need sight to experience the world.

3-4. The underlined part indicates that all the things in our lives that are so wonderful and so transient at the same time. The words for the blanks are ① Eden and ② dawn.

(Possible answers: the most beautiful things in life often have the least longevity/it is inevitable that something wonderful that has faded away incredibly fast.)

Expressions & Vocabulary

hue 빛깔, 색조   subside 가라앉다, 진정되다, 지다, 내려앉다, 침하되다

Sua TOKS!

Task

Theme, imagery, symbol (08서-20, 07-23)
Poetry – *Nothing Gold Can Stay* by Robert Frost, 1874~1963

Organization

1. **Explaining what the underlined part means** `2points`
   - The underlined part means/implies/indicates that ~
2. **Filling in each blank with the ONE most appropriate word from the passage**
   `2points`
   - The words for the blanks are ~ .
   -

Keywords

Nature's first green is **gold**,
자연의 첫 번째 푸르름은 황금빛,
Her hardest hue to hold.
간직하기에 가장 어려운 빛이다.
Her early leaf's a flower;
새로 돋아나는 어린잎은 꽃;
But only so an hour.
그러나 겨우 한 시간 남짓일 뿐.
Then leaf **subsides** to leaf.
그리고서 잎은 잎으로 진다.

So **Eden** **sank** **to** grief,
그처럼 에덴동산은 슬픔으로 가라앉고,
So **dawn** **goes** **down** **to** day.
그처럼 새벽녘은 낮으로 내려앉는다.
Nothing gold can stay.
황금빛은 오래 머물지 못한다.

> [Commentary]
> The most significant meaning we can take away from "Nothing Gold Can Stay" is that, well, nothing gold can stay. Let's face it: the most beautiful things in life often have the least longevity. **The poem uses the examples of spring blooms, the Garden of Eden,** and sunrise to get this point across, leaving us to think about **all the things in our lives that are so wonderful and so transient.** Whether it's the euphoria of winning a soccer game, or the youth of our minds and bodies, we've all **experienced something wonderful that has faded away incredibly fast.**

3-5. The underlined words mean time passing and aging. That is, the boys in the past who copied the adult's behavior as their fathers do now became adults of the same age as their fathers. The word for the blank is 'gentle.'

Expressions & Vocabulary

stair landing n. 계단참(계단 등의 도중에 설치되는 수평면 부분)

deck n. (배의) 갑판

lather n. 비누 거품

Sua TOKS!

Task

theme, symbol (18-A-11)

Poetry – *Men at Forty* by Donald Justice

Organization

1. Explaining the meaning of the underlined words. **2points**
   – The underlined words mean (NP). That is/To be specific/In other words, ~ .
   – The underlined words mean that ~ . That is/To be specific/In other words, ~ .

2. Completing the commentary below with the ONE most appropriate word from the poem. **2points**
   – The word (for the blank) is '_____.'

Keywords

Men at forty	남자들은 마흔이 되면
Learn to close softly	돌아오지 않을 문을
The doors to rooms they will not be	슬그머니 닫는
Coming back to.	법을 배운다.
At rest on **a stair landing**,	계단 위에서 쉴 때도
They feel it	그들 아래 계단이
Moving beneath them now **like the deck of a ship**,	
	배 갑판처럼 움직이는 것을 느낀다,
Though **the swell is gentle**.	비록 그 출렁임은 미세하지만.
And deep in mirrors	그리고 거울을 보면 그 안에서
They rediscover	아버지의 넥타이를 몰래 매보는

The face of the boy as he practices trying	소년의 얼굴을
His father's tie there in secret	다시 발견한다.
And **the face of that father**,	그리고 그 아버지의 얼굴은
Still warm with the mystery of lather.	비누거품의 신비함으로 하여 여전히 따사롭다.
They are more fathers than sons themselves <u>now</u>.	
	이제 그들은 아들이 아니라 아버지이다.
Something is filling them, something	무언가가 그들을 채우고 있다,
That is **like the twilight sound**	황혼녘 귀뚜라미 소리처럼
Of the crickets, immense,	저당 잡힌 그들의 저택
Filling the woods at the foot of the slope	뒤란 언덕기슭의 숲을 태우는
Behind their mortgaged houses.	심대한 무엇인가가.

Men at forty close the doors "softly", not with a boisterously youthful slam of the door. In a related way, the <u>gentle</u> landing of a stair moving beneath them "like the deck of a ship" can be interpreted to symbolize the middle-stage of one's life voyage.

40대 남자들은 젊은이들처럼 거칠게 문을 세게 닫지 않고 "부드럽게" 문을 닫는다. 비슷한 방식으로, "배의 갑판처럼" 그들 아래에서 <u>가볍게</u> 움직이는 계단참은 인생 여정에서 중간 단계를 상징한다고 해석할 수 있다.

[Commentary]

- **Mutability and loss** are recurrent themes in Justice's poetry, and "Men at Forty" is no exception. Doors closing, a stair landing in motion, a father's features becoming discernible in his son's face, and men being filled with something like the sound of crickets **all become intimations of mortality.**

- The poem's five declarative sentences affirm different facts about **the situation of men at forty, all of which have to do with a sense of time passing.** Rooms are one's past which adults learn to leave behind — not with a boisterously youthful slam of the door, but with a quiet, perhaps wistful, close. In the poem's second sentence the men feel the landing of a stair moving beneath them "like the deck of a ship." Again the image seems not literal but rather to be a way of referring to the impression one has in middle age of being carried along on a voyage.

3-6. The word for the blank ① is 'cheeks' and ② is 'eyes.' The underlined words mean that "the world" need not be aware of the true feelings of the sufferers. That is, the speaker suggests that the world should only be allowed to them when they hide the truth, their feelings, beyond merely dissembling for the sake of duplicity or dishonesty.

Expressions & Vocabulary

dissemble v. (진짜 감정·의도를) 숨기다, 가식적으로 꾸미다   **guile** n. 간교한 속임수

Sua TOKS!

Task

symbol, interpretation (16-A-9) (15-A-6)

Poetry – *We Wear The Mask* by Paul Lawrence Dunbar

Organization

1. Explaining what the underlined words mean. **2points**
   - The underlined words mean (NP). That is/To be specific/In other words, ~ .
   - The underlined words mean that ~ . That is/To be specific/In other words, ~ .

2. Completing the commentary by filling in each blank with the ONE most appropriate word from the poem. **2points**
   - The words are ①'_____' and ②'_____.'
   - The word for the blank ① is '_____,' and ② is '_____.'
   - The words for the blank ① and ② are '_____' and '_____,' respectively.

Keywords

We wear the mask that grins and lies,	우리는 조소하고 거짓말하는 가면을 씁니다.
It hides our cheeks and shades our eyes,—	우리의 얼굴과 눈을 감추는 가면을 씁니다.
This debt we pay to human guile;	인간의 교활함에 대해 치러야 할 이 빚
With torn and bleeding hearts we smile	찢기고 피 흘리는 가슴으로 우리는 미소를 짓습니다.
And mouth with myriad subtleties,	그리고 수많은 거짓으로 지껄여댑니다.
Why should the world be over-wise,	왜 세상은 우리의 모든 눈물과 한숨을 헤아리는 데만 그다지도 열심일까요?
In counting all our tears and sighs?	

Nay, let them only see us, while

    We wear the mask.

We smile, but oh great Christ, our cries
To thee from tortured souls arise.
We sing, but oh the clay is vile
Beneath our feet, and long the mile,
But let the world dream otherwise,

    We wear the mask!

아니, 세상 사람들이 그저 보게 내버려 두십시오

    우리가 가면을 쓰고 있는 것을.

오, 그리스도여, 우리는 미소 짓지만 당신을 향해 우리의 고통스러운 영혼은 애걸하고 노래합니다. 하지만 우리의 발밑에 길게 펼쳐진 진흙은 얼마나 미천합니까? 그러나 세상은 그대로 꿈꾸게 내버려 두십시오

    우리는 가면을 씁니다.

There's some symbolism in the poem that's getting at the essence of our humanity and the way we express (or don't express) our true feelings. "_____①_____" often indicate how we're feeling (think of blushing) and "_____②_____" are thought to be the windows to our soul. So if both of these are hidden, then we know we're not showing how we really feel.

이 시에서는 우리 인간성과 우리가 진짜 감정을 표현하는(또는 표현하지 않는) 방식의 본질을 이해하게 되는 상징성이 있다. "_____①_____"는 종종 우리가 어떻게 느끼는지를 (얼굴이 붉어지는 것을 생각할 때)알려주고, "_____②_____"은 우리 영혼의 창이라고 여긴다. 그래서 이 두 가지를 가리면, 우리가 정말로 어떻게 느끼는지를 안보여줄 수 있다고 우리는 알고 있다.

[Commentary]

- Sure the mask might look nice with all those smiles and grins, but it's certainly not helping matters in, 'We Wear the Mask.' The lies and deceit aren't just reserved for the outside world either. Those lies are also used by black Americans themselves when conversing with one another about the issues at hand. So, in this case no one is being honest and yet the pain that's felt is awfully real.

- In line 2 the people wearing them are "shad[ing] [their] eyes" (some figurative language here), which suggests they can't even "see" clearly and likewise can't be seen by others. There's some symbolism then in line 2 that's getting at the essence of our humanity and the way we express (or don't express) our true feelings. "Cheeks" often indicate how we're feeling (think of blushing) and "eyes" are thought to be the windows to our soul. So if both of these are "hidden." then we know we're not showing how we really feel.

[Symbol Analysis: Mask and Smile]

- Masks were often used as a symbol for deception, hypocrisy, and lies. Dunbar's poem is no different. The speaker refers to them, directly and indirectly, as the reason why black Americans and people in general are unable to speak honestly about their suffering. He's not talking about a real mask of course, but rather it's a symbolic one that represents the things people say and do that aren't honest. But Dunbar also reminds us that masks are sometimes a crucial part of self-preservation, bearing in mind the dangers that black Americans often faced if they chose the more honest route.

- It's more like the kind of smile a person has when (s)he is upset, but doesn't want to upset you, too. So that person may just grin and bear it and hide his true feelings. But that kind of smile isn't helping matters in Dunbar's poem. In fact, it's making things worse because that smile is hiding the full extent of the emotional conflict he's referring to.

3-7. First, the literary device employed in the underlined part is 'alliteration.' The repetition of the common sound /w/ in natural ("weeds") and man-made ("wheels") world represents a subtle sense of harmony between man and nature. Second, the word for the blank is 'innocence.'

Expressions & Vocabulary

luch a. (식물·정원 등이) 무성한, 우거진
thrush n. 개똥지빠귀
wring v. ~ sth (out) (빨래를) 짜다
cloy v. (쾌락이나 단맛이) 물리다, 질리다
sour v. [동사] 안 좋아지다, 틀어지다; 안 좋아지게[틀어지게] 만들다

Sua TOKS!

Task

Theme, alliteration (13-2차-2 참조 유형)
Poetry – *Spring* by Gerard Manley Hopkins

> **[Literary Terms]**
>
> **alliteration**: Repetition of consonant sounds in consecutive or neighboring words.

Organization

1. **Name the literary device that produces a sound effect** `1points`
   – The literary device is '_____.'
2. **Explaining its purpose** `2points`
   – ~ is employed in the poem to represent/emphasize ~ .
   – ~ represent/emphasize ~ .
3. **Completing the statement by filling in the blank** `1points`
   – The word for the blank is '_____.'

Keywords

Nothing is so **beautiful** as spring –

When ① **weeds, in wheels,** shoot long and lovely and lush;

② **Thrush's eggs** look little low heavens, and ③ **thrush**

Through the echoing timber does so rinse and wring

The ear, it strikes like lightnings to hear him sing;

④ **The glassy peartree leaves and blooms**, they brush

The descending **blue**; that blue is all in a rush

With **richness**; the racing lambs too have fair their fling.

What is all this **juice** and all this **joy**?

A strain of **the earth's sweet** being in the beginning

In Eden garden. — Have, get, before it cloy,

Before it cloud, Christ, lord, and sour with sinning,

Innocent mind and Mayday in girl and boy,

Most, O maid's child, thy choice and worthy the winning

[Translation]

봄만큼 아름다운 것은 없다 —
수레바퀴 속의 잡초가 길게 사랑스럽고 무성하게 자라나고
지빠귀의 알이 나즈막한 작은 천국같이 보이고
지빠귀가 반향하는 숲을 통해서 귀를 헹궈주어
그의 노래 소리 들으면 **천둥소리처럼 들리고**
거울같이 매끈한 배나무 잎들과 꽃들이
내려앉은 하늘을 쓸어 **푸르름이 일시에 풍요로워지고**
마음껏 뛰어노는 어린양들이 **힘차게 내닫는.**

이 모든 **활기와 즐거움**은 무엇인가?
에덴 동산의 시초에 존재했던 **지상의 아름다움의**
한가닥 줄기라오, 그것이 망쳐지기 전에,

그리스도여, 주님이여, 마음이 흐려지고 죄를 지어 상하기 전에
오월제를 즐기는 **소년 소녀들의 순결한 마음을**
오! 그리스도여, 그들을 선택하시오, 선택할 가치가 분명히 있소.

[Theme of Man and the Natural World]

- Hopkins singles out spring for description and praise, since he feels that it is the time of year that brings mankind closest to **the harmony of man and nature** (and God) that existed in the biblical Garden of Eden. We get the feeling that praising nature in its various earthly aspects is, for our speaker, also a way of praising God, the creator. Without nature, it seems, he could not get so close to God.
- The speaker brings natural ("weeds") and man-made ("wheels") imagery together to set up a subtle sense of **harmony between man and nature.**

[Summary]

Hopkin's poem focuses on **the radiance of the spring season,** calling on specific examples of how beautiful and fresh the world is, such as weeds, eggs in birds' nests, bird song, lambs, blue skies, and lush greenery. The world feels clean and bright to the speaker, and his appreciation for its loveliness makes him compare it the Garden of Eden. Reflecting on the sorry end of the Garden of Eden, the speaker uses the last lines of the poem to ask God to protect the **innocence** of spring and youth.

Synonyms

- **손상하다** (v)

harm	해치다, 상하게 하다, 훼손하다
damage	손해를 입히다, 못쓰게 만들다
hurt	다치게 하다; 아프게 하다
spoil	망치다, 상하게 하다, 못 쓰게 만들다; 썩히다
stain	더럽히다, 얼룩지게 하다
taint	더럽히다, 오염시키다
tarnish	흐리게 하다, 녹슬게 하다, 변색시키다
mar	-rr- (좋은 것을) 손상시키다[망치다]
scar	흉터를 남기다
ruin	파멸시키다, 황폐케 하다, 못쓰게 만들다
impair	감하다, 덜다, 약하게 하다, 손상시키다, 해치다, 나쁘게 하다
deform	추하게 하다; 볼품없게 하다, 불구로 만들다; 변형시키다

- **위협하다** (v)

threaten	협박[위협]하다
intimidate	협박하다; 위협하여 …을 시키다

	menace	위협하다, 으르다, 협박하다
	pressurize	…에 압력을 가하다
	endanger	위험에 빠뜨리다, 위태롭게 하다
	imperil	위태롭게 하다, 위험하게 하다
	jeopardize	태롭게 하다, 위험에 빠뜨리다
• 위험 (n)	danger	위험한 것, 위협
	risk	위험; 모험, 도박
	hazard	위험, 위난; 모험; 위험 요소, 해악, 해독, 장해물
	menace	협박, 위협, 공갈; 위험한 것
	peril	위험, 위난, 위태; 모험; 위험한 것
• 다루다/대처하다 (v)	tackle	부딪치다, 다루다; 부지런히 시작하다
	deal with	…을 다루다, 상대하다
	cope with	…에 대처하다; …에 대항하다
	face	정면으로 대하다, 대항하다; 용감하게 맞서다
	challenge	전하다; 걸다, 신청하다; …에게 대답을 요구하다
	encounter	부닥치다
	stand up to	맞서다

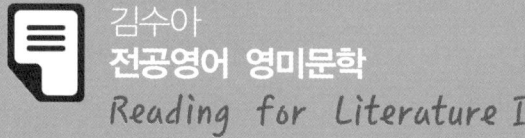

김수아
전공영어 영미문학
Reading for Literature I

PART 04

Literary Terms

Chapter 01 Literary Terms

Literary Terms

01. Allegory

Allegory is a form of narrative that conveys a message or doctrine by using people, places, or things to stand for abstract ideas.

02. Alliteration

Repetition of consonant sounds in consecutive or neighboring words.

03. Allusion

An allusion is a brief reference to a person, place, or event (fictional or actual) that readers are expected to recognize. Like symbols and allegories, allusions enrich a work by introducing associations from another context.

04. Apostrophe

A poem's speaker addresses an absent person or thing — for example, a historical or literary figure or even an inanimate object or an abstract concept.

05. Asides

Comments to the audience in plays that other characters do not hear.

06. Assonance

Repetition of vowel sounds at the ends of words.

07. Blank verse

Unrhymed poetry with each line written in a set pattern of five stressed and five unstressed syllables called iambic pentameter.

08. Carpe diem theme

The belief that life is brief, so we must seize the day.

09. Connotation

Emotional associations that define your response. What a word suggests.

10. Consonance

Repetition of consonant sounds at the ends of words.

11. Couplet

A two-line stanza with rhyming lines of similar length and meter is called a couplet.

12. Denotations

What a word signifies without emotional associations, judgements, or opinions.

13. Dramatic Irony

Dramatic irony occurs when a narrator (or character) perceives less than readers do — when the main character see less than readers do.

14. Extended simile or metaphor

A single simile or metaphor is developed throughout a poem.

15. Figures of speech

Expressions that use words to achieve effects beyond the power of ordinary language.

16. Flashbacks

A flashback moves out of sequence to examine an event or situation that occurred before the time in which the story's action takes place. Flashbacks in dramas depict events that occurred before the play's main action. Dialogue can also summarize events that occurred earlier, thereby overcoming the limitations set by the chronological action on stage.

17. Foot

A group of syllables with a fixed pattern of stressed and unstressed syllables.

18. Foreshadowing

Dialogues in dramas can foreshadow, or look ahead to, future action. In many cases, seemingly unimportant comments have significance that becomes clear as the play develops.

19. Formal diction

It is characterized by a learned vocabulary and grammatically correct forms. In general, formal diction does not include colloquialisms, such as contractions and shortened word forms (*phone* for *telephone*).

20. Heroic Couplet

Heroic couplet, first used by Chaucer and especially popular throughout the eighteenth century, consists of two rhymed lines of iambic pentameter, with a weak pause after the first line and a strong pause after the second.

21. Hyperbole

Intentional exaggeration—saying more than is actually meant.

22. Imagery

Words or phrases that describe the sense; Language that evokes a physical sensation produced by one or more of the five senses—sight, hearing, taste, touch, smell.

23. Informal diction

It is the language closest to everyday conversation. It includes colloquialisms

— contractions, shortened word forms, and the like — and may also include slang, regional expressions, and even nonstandard words.

24. Irony

A contradiction or discrepancy between two different levels of meaning.

25. Metaphor

An imaginative comparison between two unlike items that do not use *like* or *as* — that is, when it says "a *is* b" rather than "a *is like* b" — it is a metaphor.)

26. Meter

The recurrence of regular units of stressed and unstressed syllables. A stress (or accent) occurs when one syllable is emphasized more than another, unstressed, syllable.

27. Metonymy

The substitution of the name of one thing for the name of another thing that most readers associate with the first — for example, using hired gun to mean "paid assassin" or suits to mean "business executives."

28. Monologue

An extended speech by one character.

29. Onomatopoeia

It occurs when the sound of a word echoes its meaning, as it does in common words such as *bang, crash,* and *hiss.*

30. Open form

An open form poem may make occasional use of rhyme and meter but has no easily identifiable pattern or design: no conventional stanzaic divisions, no consistent metrical pattern or line length, no repeated rhyme scheme.

31. Oxymoron

An oxymoron puts together two seemingly contradictory words or phrases that actually end up making a whole lot of sense. For example, in "The jumbo shrimp she brought to the party was terribly good," "terribly good" means 'very good,' not 'terrible.'

32. Oxymoron

A form of paradox where two contradictory terms are combined in one phrase. Examples: cold fire, honest thief

33. Paradox

A statement that appears to be absurd, untrue, or contradictory, but may actually be true. Example: From "Death, Be Not Proud, Though Some Have Called Thee"
"One short sleep past, we wake eternally, And death shall be no more; death, thou shalt die." (John Donne)

34. Personification

A special kind of comparison, closely related to metaphor, that gives life or human characteristics to inanimate objects or abstract ideas.

35. Petrarchan sonnet

The Petrarchan sonnet, popularized in the fourteenth century by the Italian poet Francesco Petrarch, also consists of fourteen lines of iambic pentameter, but these lines are divided into an eight-line unit called an octave and a six-line unit (composed of two tercets) called a sestet. The rhyme scheme of the octave is *abba abba;* the rhyme scheme of the sestet is *cde cde.*

36. Plot

Plot is more than "what happens"; it is how what happens is revealed, the way in which a story's events are arranged. Plot is shaped by causal connections—historical, social, and personal—by the interaction between characters, and by the juxtaposition of events.

37. Shakespearean sonnet

The English or Shakespearean sonnet, which consists of fourteen lines divided into three quatrains and a concluding couplet, is written in **iambic pentameter** and follows the rhyme scheme *abab cdcd efef gg*.

38. Simile

A comparison between two unlike items that uses *like* or *as*.

39. Situational Irony

Situational irony occurs when what happens is at odds with what readers are led to expect — when the situation itself contradicts readers' expectations.

40. Soliloquies

A monologue revealing a character's thoughts and feelings, directed at the audience and presumed not to be heard by other characters.

41. Spencerian sonnet

A sonnet form composed of three quatrains and a couplet in **iambic pentameter** with the rhyme scheme *abab bcbc cdcd ee*.

42. Stage directions

Notes that comment on the scenery, the movements of the performers, the lighting, and the placement of props in dramas.

43. Stanza

A group of two or more lines with the same metrical pattern — and often with a regular rhyme scheme as well — separated by blank space from other such groups of lines. Stanzas in poetry are like paragraphs in prose: they group related ideas into units.

44. Symbol

A symbol is an idea or image that suggests something else and transcends its literal, or denotative, meaning in a complex way. Symbol is using an object or action that means something more than its literal meaning. A symbol enables the poet to enrich a poem by giving it additional layers of meaning often recognized by its prominence or repetition.

45. Synecdoche

A specific kind of metonymy. The substitution of a part for the whole. For example, using bread — as in "Give us this day our daily bread" — to mean "food".

Or the substitution of the whole for a part. For example, saying "You can take the boy out of Brooklyn, but you can't take Brooklyn [meaning its distinctive traits] out of the boy".

46. Tone

The tone of a poem conveys the speaker's attitude toward his or her subject or audience. Tone in novels and dramas reveals a character's mood or attitude. Tone can be flat or emotional, bitter or accepting, affectionate or aloof, anxious or calm.

47. Understatement

The opposite to hyperbole — saying less than it meant.

48. Verbal Irony

A contradiction between what a narrator (or speaker or character) says and what he or she means. Verbal irony occurs when the narrator says one thing but actually means another. When verbal irony is particularly biting, it is called **sarcasm**.

김수아 영미문학

ISBN 979-11-90700-82-5

- 발행일 · 2020年 12月 11日 초판 1쇄
- 발행인 · 이용중
- 저 자 · 김수아
- 발행처 · 도서출판 배움
- 주 소 · 서울시 영등포구 영등포로 400 신성빌딩 2층 (신길동)
- 주문 및 배본처 · Tel : 02) 813-5334   Fax : 02) 814-5334

저자와의
협의하에
인지생략

본서의 無斷轉載·複製를 禁함. 본서의 무단 전재·복제행위는 저작권법 제136조에 의거 5년 이하의 징역 또는 5,000만 원 이하의 벌금에 처하거나 이를 병과할 수 있습니다. 파본은 구입처에서 교환하시기 바랍니다.

정가 24,000 원